GREEK GOLD

GREEK

JEWELLERY OF THE

GOLD

DYFRI
WILLIAMS
AND
JACK
OGDEN

CLASSICAL WORLD

PUBLISHED FOR THE

TRUSTEES OF THE BRITISH MUSEUM

BY BRITISH MUSEUM PRESS

© 1994 The Trustees of the British Museum
Published by British Museum Press
A division of British Museum Publications Ltd
46 Bloomsbury Street, London WC1B 3QQ

British Library Cataloguing in Publication Data
A catalogue record for this book is available from the British Library

ISBN 0-7141-2202-5 (cased)
ISBN 0-7141-2205-X (paper)

Designed by Harry Green
Typeset in Linotron Bembo by Rowland Phototypesetting Ltd
Colour origination by Colourscan, Singapore
Printed and bound in Italy by
Arnoldo Mondadori Editore, Verona

HALF-TITLE PAGE Gold pediment-shaped brooch,
said to come from Patras, 340–320 BC (no. 24).

TITLE PAGE Gold strap diadem with a central
Herakles knot (detail). From Chersonesos,
300–280 BC (no. 131).

Contents

Preface

Greek Gold brings together for the very first time nearly two hundred of the finest pieces of Greek jewellery of the Classical period from all parts of the Mediterranean world. Such an international project, which combines the treasures of The State Hermitage in St Petersburg, The Metropolitan Museum of Art in New York and The British Museum, has been achieved thanks to the close and enthusiastic collaboration between three of the world's greatest museums, which are working together for the first time on a joint exhibition.

No single museum could ever present, solely from its own resources, such a revealing vision of the genius of ancient Greek jewellers at the peak of their craft. The collections of our three museums complement each other perfectly, spanning the whole of the ancient world: the Hermitage provides the extravagant pieces specially made for the wealthy peoples of the Crimea and excavated from the huge burial mounds of that region, while the British Museum and the Metropolitan Museum offer material not only from the cities of ancient Greece, but also from the rich Greek colonies in southern Italy, the Greek cities of Asia Minor, Cyprus and the rest of the eastern Mediterranean.

We welcome the opportunity to display this splendid material to the public of our three nations, an event that has been facilitated by the inspired and generous sponsorship of Cartier.

Dr R.G.W. Anderson, Director of the British Museum
Philippe de Montebello, Director of the Metropolitan Museum of Art
Professor M. Piotrovsky, Director of the State Hermitage

TO THE MEMORY OF REYNOLD HIGGINS

Acknowledgements

The authors would like to record their warm and sincere thanks to the Director and Staff of the Hermitage Museum in St Petersburg and the Metropolitan Museum of Art in New York, for without them this catalogue would not have been possible. In the Hermitage, special mention should be made of Dr Yuri Kalashnik and Dr Liubov Nekrassova, who were unfailingly patient and extremely helpful, as well as the Keeper of the Department, Dr Sophia Boriskovskaya, who was always supportive. In New York, Dr Joan Mertens kindly checked the New York entries and co-ordinated the New York photography and conservation, while the Curator-in-Charge, Dr Carlos Picón, made light work of any problem.

All the catalogue entries are the joint work of the authors; except where indicated, the introductory essays are by Dyfri Williams.

The photographs of all the Hermitage and British Museum pieces were taken by Ivor Kerslake and Nick Nicholls of the British Museum's Photographic Service: they have worked exceptionally hard under difficult conditions and have always remained the friendliest of colleagues. The Metropolitan's photographs were all taken by Oi-Cheong Lee, photographer of the Metropolitan Museum, who uncomplainingly gave up a vacation to meet the deadline. We are also very grateful to Barbara Bridgers, Manager of the Photographic Studio at the Metropolitan Museum, for her kind co-operation. The results produced by all the photographers are stunning. The maps are by Susan Bird.

For the conservation work done on the pieces from the Metropolitan Museum of Art and the British Museum the authors are particularly grateful to Richard E. Stone and Abigail Haberland of the Metropolitan and Marilyn Hockey of the British Museum. In addition, Dr Nigel Meeks of the British Museum's Department of Scientific Research very kindly made some SEM photographs of selected pieces from the British Museum to help illustrate technological details: they also give the reader some idea of what one sees when one looks down a microscope, an essential tool in working with ancient jewellery.

Finally, we should like to thank Teresa Francis of British Museum Press for all her hard work and seemingly boundless patience. It is a much better book because of her: the faults that remain are all the authors'.

The dedication of our work to Reynold Higgins is made with deep gratitude for his friendship and inspiration. He was truly the father of British studies in ancient jewellery. He was excited at the prospect of this exhibition: we only wish that he had lived to see it.

Introduction

Gold has caused passions to flare ever since it was first discovered. Its appeal is both visual and tactile; its magic is its virtual indestructibility. These qualities, together with its rarity, meant that it was ideal for transformation into jewellery, and gold jewellery has been worn by both men and women since time immemorial. There is, however, much more to the study of jewellery than any such initial emotional reaction. Like any category of art, jewellery represents a marriage of raw materials, individual skills and ingenuity with the social or religious traditions that dictated its forms. To understand ancient jewellery we must combine stylistic, structural and material-based research, and to understand its significance we must set it in its social and historical context.

This catalogue aims to present as fully as possible some of the finest Classical Greek jewellery to have been preserved, with a detailed description of each piece and its context, as far as this is known. Comparable pieces are also briefly discussed. Each section of the catalogue begins with a short introduction to one particular region of production and its history. This introductory essay, however, will examine wider aspects of Classical Greek jewellery, including the technology of ancient jewellery and what we can discover of the jewellers themselves; the functions of Greek jewellery and how it was worn; its iconography and its relationship to sculpture and drawing.

The Nature of the Evidence

Most Greek jewellery preserved in museums today is of gold. However, this is unlikely to give a true picture of jewellery in the Classical period: not only was there undoubtedly much more gold jewellery in existence in antiquity, but both silver and bronze jewellery were probably even more common by reason of their relative inexpensiveness. This catalogue includes a small amount of silver jewellery, but only one bronze earring (Fig. 1). Although bronze jewellery is not mentioned in the inventories of the treasuries of Greek temples, numerous finds have been made in sanctuaries as well as in domestic contexts and it is most likely that this was the material most commonly used for jewellery in the Greek world. It could be combined with more expensive materials, especially gold, to give extra strength and weight, and some bronze earrings, like that in Fig. 1, were made with silver hoops, perhaps to reduce discomfort.

Organic materials, such as ivory, bone and amber, were also frequently employed, as well as semi-precious stones, such as cornelian, garnet and emerald. Rock crystal and glass were used as protective covers or in their own right (Fig. 2). Finally, fired clay – that is, terracotta – usually gilded (Fig. 3), was also pressed into service: to judge from what

FIGURE 1 Bronze earring with silver hoop, about 400 BC (British Museum GR 1846.2-17.183; said to be from Same on Kephallenia).

FIGURE 2 Glass acorn-shaped pendant from a necklace, about 350 BC (British Museum GR 1857.12-20.43; from the Mausoleum at Halikarnassos).

FIGURE 3 Gilded terracotta earring pendants, 330–300 BC: *above*, a boat-shaped pendant with an Eros on either end (British Museum *BMCJ* 2164; from Cyrenaica); *left*, Nike (British Museum *BMCJ* 2154; from Cyrenaica); *right*, siren (British Museum *BMCJ* 2153; said to be from Crete).

remains, this may often have been made specially for the tomb, although a group has been found in a sanctuary, that of Demeter at Knossos.

We can gain some picture of the missing body of material, whether gold, silver or bronze, by looking at representations of jewellery in other arts and crafts, such as vase-painting (Figs 4 and 33), sculpture, bronzes (Fig. 31), terracottas (Fig. 32) and coins (Fig. 30). There are references, too, in ancient literature and in the inscriptions recording the treasures of various Greek sanctuaries. This written evidence is not always very precise, but even the legendary story of Eriphyle's necklace tells us something of the function of jewellery. The necklace was said to have been specially made by Hephaistos, the divine smith, for Harmonia, the daughter of Ares and Aphrodite, on her marriage to Kadmos, king of Thebes. Harmonia later gave it to Polyneikes and he used it to bribe Eriphyle into persuading her husband, Amphiaraos, to join the doomed

FIGURE 4 Detail from an Athenian red-figured *pelike* of about 360–350 BC, showing women washing and putting on their jewellery (reverse of Fig. 43): here a woman puts on an earring (Hermitage Kek 8; from the Kekuvatsky kurgan, see pp. 164–5).

expedition against Thebes. Ancient sources record Eriphyle's necklace as being preserved in at least three sanctuaries throughout the Greek world: Delphi, Delos and the sanctuary of Aphrodite and Adonis at Amathus on Cyprus.

BIBLIOGRAPHY: On terracotta jewellery see I. Blanck, *Antike Welt*, 7 (1976), pp. 19–27. For the example from Knossos see J.N. Coldstream, *Knossos. The Sanctuary of Demeter* (London 1973), nos 322–31.

The Materials

Greece is not naturally rich in gold, and so the quantity of gold jewellery produced in Greece itself at any period generally reflects foreign trade and influence. There had been gold mines of some importance on the Greek island of Siphnos, but they were flooded by the sea in the late sixth century BC. Thasos, too, produced some gold during the early Iron Age, but the deposits were not extensive and were probably of minimal importance by the Classical period. To the north, the streams surrounding what Euripides called 'the gold-soiled mountain mass of Pangaion' in Thrace were probably providing gold by the seventh century BC and were probably still able to supply enough for the prolific coinage issues of the reign of Philip II (359–336 BC). Nevertheless, by the time of Alexander the Great there may have been little gold to be mined in Greece itself or even in Lydia to the east.

Around the Mediterranean gold was to be found in Egypt, in the Eastern Desert and Nubia, and in Spain. It was also known in antiquity in the Caucasus at the eastern end of the Black Sea, especially at Colchis (modern Vani), where the legend of Jason and the Golden Fleece originated. The richness of the Scythian tombs to the north of the Crimea, however, points to substantial gold sources to the east, probably northern Kazakhstan and the Altai Mountains at the end of a caravan route. Again knowledge of this was converted into myth: Herodotos wrote of strange tales of gold deposits guarded by griffins (Fig. 4a), while Pliny recorded a version in which the griffins dug up the gold. In Greek art barbarians, normally identified as one-eyed Arimasps, are often shown fighting griffins for the gold that they guarded (Fig. 49, p. 159). Furthermore, the symbol of the chief city of the Bosporan kingdom, Pantikapaion, was a griffin (Fig. 44, p. 122).

It is hardly coincidence that the route of Alexander's conquests after 331 BC passed through all the main gold-supplying regions of the former Persian empire. In the literature of the Early Classical period, such as Aeschylus' *The Persians*, produced in Athens a few years after the battle of Salamis, we find clear evidence that the Greeks saw the East as having fabulous sources of gold, ranging from the 'great golden Pactolos' of Lydia to the placers of India. Even so, although gold may have been

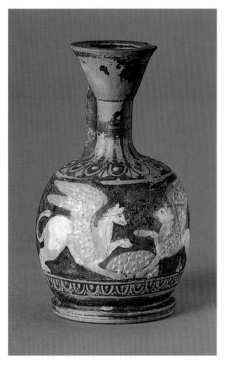

FIGURE 4a Athenian red-figured squat *lekythos* of about 380 BC showing a pair of griffins guarding a heap of gold (British Museum GR 1894.12-2.4; said to be from Eretria).

more readily available after the Persian wars, it was not abundant, and probably only became common in Greece towards the end of the fourth century BC. The jewellers themselves must often have obtained the gold direct from their customers, sometimes as coins or scrap, or purchased the gold with money advanced to them by their customers. Only rarely would a goldsmith have the capital to amass a stock of precious metal.

Silver was more abundant in Greece than gold. The exploitation of silver on Siphnos, and also at Laurion in Attica, dates back to the Early Bronze Age, and the Laurion mines were particularly productive during the fifth century. Further north, in Macedonia and Illyria, silver was also exploited from an early period. Asia Minor was another very important source for the ancient Near East.

At least some of the precious-metal trade, both domestic and international, was in private hands. In the mid-fifth century Sophocles, in his play *Antigone*, tells of the profit to be made trading in Lydian electrum and Indian gold, and a fourth-century lead plaque from Dodona (now in the Ioaninna Museum) preserves an enquiry to the oracle of Zeus by one Tinodamas regarding the profits from his silver mine.

The actual recovery of gold from the earth is relatively simple. Gold is found in nature not as a complex metallic ore but in almost ready-to-use metallic form, either in veins in rocks or as dust or nuggets in what are or were once river beds. The gold from river beds, termed alluvial gold, is the easiest to recover, and the evidence is that the Greeks largely relied on this type, at least in Greece itself. The removal of gold from rock veins requires the laborious breaking up and grinding of the rock. Most methods of separating the gold from the accompanying sand, gravel or ground-up rock rely on some type of washing with water to flush away all but the heavy gold. Grinders, washing tables and other gold-working paraphernalia have been found at various gold-mining areas in the ancient world, and a good description of the process has survived in the writings of Diodorus Siculus, quoting Agatharchides. Sheeps' fleeces are often used in gold-washing, since the gold readily adheres to the greasy wool, and this process might well lie behind the legend of Jason and his voyage to Colchis to win the Golden Fleece.

Gold as found is rarely, if ever, totally pure and usually contains some silver, a bit of copper and often traces of various other metals including iron, tin and members of the platinum family. The gold can be employed as found or it can be refined (that is, have the accompanying silver and copper removed); alternatively, both native gold and refined gold can be debased by the addition of extra silver or copper, perhaps for economic or fraudulent reasons. Refining gold dates back to the Bronze Age, but was probably uncommon before the sixth century BC when the blossoming coinage industry began to demand standardisation.

The purity of the gold used for the jewellery in this catalogue varies considerably, with silver contents ranging from over 25 per cent down to under 2 per cent. To some extent the composition of the gold seems to reflect the time and place of manufacture, and sometimes it is related to the type of object being produced. High-quality workmanship is by no means always matched by high-purity gold, and perhaps only when we have a far greater number of analyses of accurately provenanced and dated objects will we be in a position to understand the factors at work. The earlier goldwork tends to have a palish, almost lemony colour which points to a purity of only around 75 per cent – a feature also seen in almost all the sixth- to fifth-century BC goldwork from Sindos in Macedonia, as well as in much Scythian and Etruscan goldwork of similar date. Certainly it would appear that gold was generally used 'as mined', at least well into the fifth century

The various trace elements, such as tin and platinum, present in the gold should, in theory, help to connect objects with particular mines, but gold has always been traded, looted and recycled and we can hardly expect to find a large selection of Classical Greek gold objects all made from the uncontaminated, unrefined or unalloyed gold from a single mine. Members of the platinum family of metals are of particular interest. Ancient gold, including some Greek gold, often contains minute but visible inclusions which have proved to be natural alloy grains of various platinum-like metals, typically osmium, iridium and ruthenium. As goldsmiths in more recent times have noted, these minute but very hard metal inclusions cause problems when making thin gold sheet and fine wires, so it may not be coincidence that such inclusions are often present in the more massive objects of the Classical period, such as the signet rings, but are almost non-existent in the delicate sheet gold and filigree objects. This might reflect the deliberate use of gold from different sources, or perhaps the goldsmiths could somehow remove the specks when necessary. Such inclusions are clearly seen in most of the solid gold rings in the catalogue (Fig. 5); rare examples of sheet-gold objects with such inclusions include nos 84, 95 and 183. The arrangement and orientation of these inclusions in goldwork can provide information about the processes of manufacture.

Silver jewellery is most typical of northern Greece and Illyria. Much the same repertoire of techniques could be used for silver as for gold, although sheet gauges tend to be slightly thicker and, if anything, the properties of the metal mean that fine work in silver requires greater care than in gold. Silver jewellery of superb workmanship has been found in later sixth- and fifth-century BC burials at Sindos, and an unusual bracelet, said to be from Akarnania, is included here (no. 27).

A readily noticeable feature of the Greek goldwork of the Classical

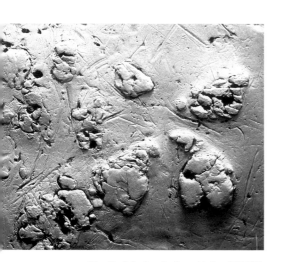

FIGURE 5 Detail of the bezel of a gold ring (*BMCR* 51; not in catalogue), showing a cluster of platinum-group metal inclusions. They average about 0.1 mm across.

period is the general absence of gemstones. Polychromy was not lacking – much of the goldwork was originally enamelled – but stones were seldom used. This must reflect local taste as much as lack of supply, since the areas that supplied gold also produced an attractive array of coloured gemstones. Countries such as Egypt and Persia had long used bright-coloured stones set in gold. In this apparent scorn for gemstones, Greece is more like its contemporaries in Europe than the Middle East. The fashion for coloured gems in Greek jewellery is generally linked with Alexander the Great's opening up of trade with the east. However, even early Hellenistic goldwork is still largely devoid of inset stones, and the flamboyant use of garnets, emeralds and pearls is more characteristic of the later third or even second century BC onwards. A rare example of an early Hellenistic emerald-set ring (no. 34) and a garnet where the

FIGURE 6 Filigree enamel on the collars of the Herakles-knot diadem from Melos (no. 18). The blue and green enamel is still largely preserved and the pattern is delineated with spiral-beaded wire.

crystal faces have been lightly polished to give a faceted appearance (no. 35) are included here.

The use of enamel, which is essentially just coloured glass fused in place, was widespread in the Classical period. It was employed by Mycenaean goldsmiths and then far more generally in the Near Eastern and Mediterranean worlds from the early first millennium BC. Enamel can be seen in many of the objects in this catalogue and was probably originally present in many more. Enamel of the mid- to late first millennium BC is most typically 'filigree enamel', that is enamel bordered by fine wires. In Classical Greek and Hellenistic goldwork these wires are normally spiral-beaded (see below) and no doubt their irregularity helped the adhesion of the enamel (Fig. 6). Colour could also be introduced in filigree enamel in the form of pigments, and examples of blue, green, black and white may be found here. The production of red enamel on gold was tricky, and red cinnabar pigment was sometimes used instead. It can be seen, for example, on nos 69, 89 and 170. Other applied pigments, not mixed with glass, were also sometimes used, such as the green backing to the earrings from Kul Oba (no. 88), while the blue material (generally assumed to be an enamel) that fills the rosettes on the gold *larnax* from the so-called tomb of Philip II at Vergina might repay further examination. Such pigments were possibly preferred to enamel when larger areas were to be filled and relative differences in degrees of contraction on cooling were more likely to be a problem.

Reddish colorations can also be caused by certain burial environments and it is possible that over the years some cinnabar and other intentional colours have been cleaned off gold jewellery by well-intentioned conservators. The lion-head terminals of a pair of bracelets in New York with very fragile blue glass hoops were recently noticed to have traces of intentional red cinnabar in the ears and the mouths of the lions. [J.O.]

BIBLIOGRAPHY: J.T. Bent, 'On the gold and silver mines of Siphnos', *JHS* 6 (1885), pp. 195–8; O. Davies, 'Ancient mines in Southern Macedonia', *Journal of the Royal Anthropological Institute* 62 (1932), pp. 145–6; Hoffmann and Davidson, pp. 19–21; Higgins *GRJ*[2], pp. 7–10; Ogden *JAW*, pp. 11–19. See also R. Fuchs *et al.*, *Gold und Vergoldung bei Plinius dem Älteren* (Tübingen 1993). Published analyses of Classical and Hellenistic gold are few and far between, but see Hoffmann and Davidson, pp. 21–2 and 49, and Ogden, forthcoming. On enamel: Higgins *GRJ*[2], pp. 24–6. New York bracelets (57.11.8–9): Pfrommer, pl. 17, 4.

The Techniques of the Greek Goldsmith

Classical Greek gold jewellery is usually built up from numerous separate components and is thus, in constructional terms, more reminiscent of architecture or woodwork than sculpture. The Greek goldsmiths and silversmiths worked with a minimal repertoire of tools, relying on time and skill to produce their wares. Gold jewellery was usually formed from hammered-out sheet. The sheet was cut into the required pieces with a small chisel and, if necessary, shaped with tools ranging from wooden sticks to bronze punches and dies. Simple sheet work includes the leaves on wreaths. A regular lattice-like decoration, giving a cross-corrugated effect, is sometimes to be seen around the edge of disc earrings (Fig. 7). This unusual effect was to reappear in Roman times on ring and bracelet hoops.

Among the most difficult of hammered objects, in spite of their simple form, are the gold signet rings. Some, particularly the earliest, are constructed from separately made and soldered bezel and hoop, but most typically they are made from a single piece of gold or silver by precise

FIGURE 7 Detail of the cross-corrugated border strip from one of the earring studs from Kyme (no. 51).

hammering. Apart from these solid rings, three-dimensional forms were most often constructed from two or more pieces of shaped gold sheet soldered together. A good example of this is the griffin-head in Fig. 8, where the central vertical seam is clearly visible.

A series of identical sheet-gold forms could be almost mass-produced by using dies or formers, a number of which have survived from the ancient Greek world. The gold could be pushed into an intaglio die made in wood, stone or metal (Fig. 10a). The metal could be worked

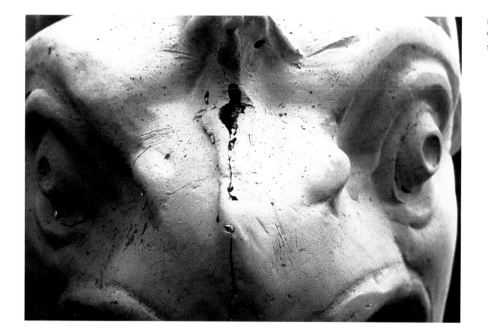

FIGURE 8 Face of the griffin from one of the Cypriot ear spirals (no. 165), showing the vertical solder seam.

FIGURE 9 Eros holding a cockerel, from the top of the Cypriot diadem pendant (no. 170). The sharp detail reveals the use of a metal die.

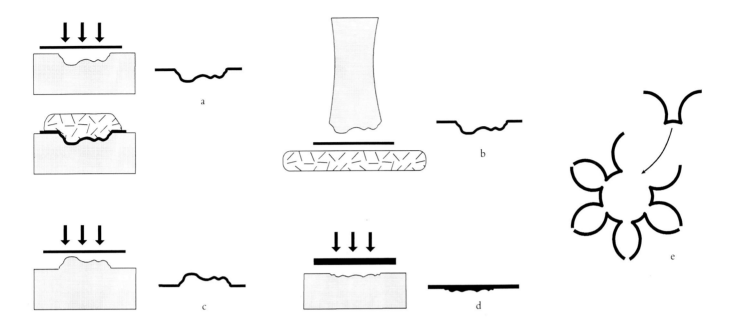

FIGURE 10 Working sheet gold: (a) the gold is pressed down into a metal or wooden die, either using wooden or other tools or by pressing down with a piece of wax, lead or other semi-rigid material; (b) the gold can be placed over wax, pitch or lead and the impression made with a metal punch hit with a hammer; (c) alternatively, the sheet gold can be worked over a raised design in metal or other hard material; (d) if thick sheet gold is hammered over a relatively shallow, sunk design, the result is a struck, flat-backed motif; (e) the repetitive use of die-formed components in Greek jewellery includes the 'paddle-wheels' on some fibulae, which could be made up by soldering together six pieces of die-formed sheet gold, as shown in this cross-section.

down into the die with the aid of simple tools, even of wood, or pressed down by using a block of resin or lead (Fig. 10a lower). Alternatively, a punch might be employed (Fig. 10b), with the sheet gold laid over resin or lead. A similar effect could be produced by using a former (Fig. 10c), where the gold is pressed down over a design made in relief. Sometimes 'striking' was used. Here, thick sheet gold was hammered down onto a sharp but shallow die to produce a solid form with a flat back (Fig. 10d). Even simple forms required in some quantity were produced using dies, punches or formers in this manner. The term 'die-formed' has been used rather loosely in this catalogue, since it is not always possible to determine just which type of tool has been used in a particular case. A series of die-formed units could also be combined to create a larger motif. For example, the 'paddle-wheels' which characterise a northern fibula type are made from sheet gold as shown in Fig. 10e. Each piece of sheet forms the sides of two adjacent 'flanges'.

Hollow sheet-gold objects might be frail and were sometimes filled with plaster or mixtures of wax or resin with ground marble, to add strength. Indeed, such fillings are actually mentioned in connection with some gold wreaths in the inventories of temple treasuries.

Designs could be produced freehand on gold by various means. Chasing tools – such as small blunt chisels – might be tapped with a hammer to produce anything from the dots for an animal's coat to elaborate three-dimensional forms. Punches with variously shaped heads were used to produce repetitive designs. A simple example is the 'ring tool' or 'ring-punch', used to produce the small circles in Fig. 11. This type of tool appears to have been first employed in the Near East in about the sixth century BC and was soon in use in Greece and the Balkans, for

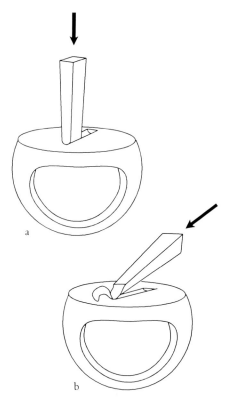

FIGURE 12 The distinction between chasing and engraving: (a) in chasing the gold is displaced, not removed; (b) in engraving the gold is cut out.

example on some sheet-gold earrings from tomb 117 at Sindos. Chasing and punching displaces or dents the gold, but does not remove it (Fig. 12a). Engraving, on the other hand, employs a sharper tool which actually cuts out the gold (Fig. 12b). Engraving is seldom suitable for thin gold sheet and was only used for thicker objects, such as solid gold ring bezels (see Figs 13, 14 and 15). True engraving on gold was employed in the Mycenaean period and recurs in Greece from the early Iron Age onwards, but it was never universal and, generally, the cuts are of the shallow-groove type. Deeper, v-shaped cuts are most typically produced by modern steel tools and are seldom seen on ancient gold. The bezel designs on the gold signet rings in this catalogue are sometimes produced by chasing alone, sometimes by a combination of chasing and shallow-groove engraving. A chisel-like tool can also be 'walked' across a gold

FIGURE 13 Detail of the bezel of the ring from Tharros (no. 153), showing the use of engraving.

Right FIGURE 14 Detail of the bezel of the ring from Phokaia (no. 58), showing part of the engraved figure of a woman.

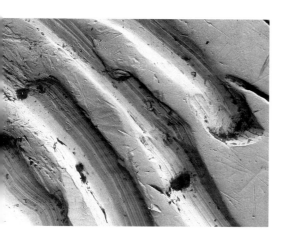

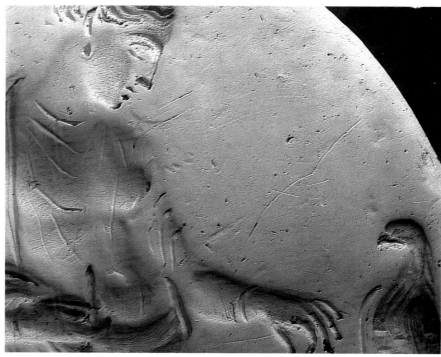

Above FIGURE 15 Detail of Fig. 14: the hand at higher magnification, showing the parallel lines resulting from engraving.

surface, leaving a zig-zag trail which is termed tremolo engraving. This again first occurs in Mycenaean and early Dark Age Greek goldwork, and thereafter sporadically, for example on the ring no. 155. A simpler form of decoration can be produced by simply scratching the design on the gold with a sharp metal point: this is sometimes termed 'incising'.

Above left FIGURE 16 Detail of a chain and pendant from one of the earrings from Kyme (no. 50). The construction of the doubled loop-in-loop chain is clearly visible, as are the spiral 'seam lines' on the wire resulting from the method of manufacture.

Above right FIGURE 17 Filigree work on the single ear stud from Kyme (no. 51), showing palmettes in plain wire, concentric borders of ropes, plain wire and beaded wires and outer lines of gold granules.

FIGURE 18 Filigree work on one of the pair of ear studs from Kyme (no. 52), showing the use of spiral-beaded wire spirals and rosettes, as well as beaded wires and ropes.

Ancient gold jewellery contains much wire in the form of chain or filigree. Round-section wires could be made by hammering and burnishing a thin rod of gold, but smaller diameters – under about 1 mm – were generally made from narrow strips of gold sheet which were twisted along their length and then rolled between two flat surfaces of wood or metal to compact and smooth them into wires. This mode of manufacture tends to leave spiral 'seam lines' along the length of the wire, as can clearly be seen on the chain in Fig. 16 and the palmette filigree in Fig. 17. There is no evidence that the Greek goldsmith ever used the process of wire drawing, in which a rod of wire is pulled through a series of successively smaller holes in an iron draw-plate until a wire of the desired diameter is formed. Wire drawing for jewellery probably does not predate the seventh or eighth century AD.

Two plain wires could be twisted together to form what we call a rope, and two such ropes, with twists of opposite direction, were often placed side by side to produce a herringbone design (Fig. 18). A common type of decorative wire was the so-called beaded wire which first became widespread in the seventh century BC (good examples can be seen in Figs 18 and 19). Here a plain wire was rolled under an edged implement to produce a series of grooves around it. A double-edged tool could be used, as shown in Fig. 20a. Producing narrow-gauge wires by this

FIGURE 19 Plain wire filigree on one of the Cypriot crescent-shaped earrings (no. 162). Its similarity to the ring no. 164 (Fig. 22) suggests that they come from a single workshop.

23

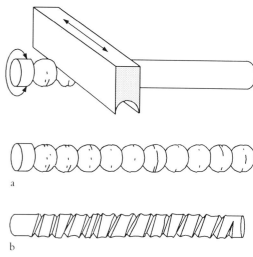

Above FIGURE 20 The manufacture of beaded wires: (a) a double-edged implement used to produce beaded wire; (b) the wire is rolled under a single edge at a slightly oblique angle to make spiral-beaded wire.

FIGURE 21 Detail of earring no. 146, showing the use of spiral-beaded wire filigree, as well as various sizes of gold granulation.

method was fiddly and it was all too easy to cut right through the wire, so an alternative decorative wire type was developed in which the wires were rolled under a single-edged implement held at a slightly oblique angle. This produced a groove spiralling along the wire, rather like a screw-thread (Figs 20b and 21). This is termed 'spiral-beaded' wire and can be found in Etruscan goldwork from the sixth, if not seventh, century BC and perhaps occurs at Sindos in the late sixth to fifth century. However, it was generally all but unknown in Greek or Greek-influenced jewellery – whether from Greece, South Italy, Cyprus, Asia Minor or the Pontic region – prior to about 400 BC, and it does not seem to have become universal for fine filigree until after the middle of the fourth century. When we find spiral-beaded wires they are often in association with thicker, true beaded wires; for example, filigree motifs formed in spiral-beaded wire just 0.2 mm in diameter may be surrounded by a

FIGURE 22 Filigree work on the ring from Kourion (no. 164): compare Fig. 19.

FIGURE 23 Filigree work on one of the earrings from Kyme (no. 50), showing spiral-beaded wire spirals and rosettes. This work is less precise than that seen in Fig. 18 (no. 52), although the overall design is similar.

border of thicker beaded wire (as in Fig. 11). In jewellery before about 400 BC, fine filigree is normally made either from narrow beaded wire or plain, round-section wires. Similarities can suggest workshop links: compare Figs 19 and 22, for example. Even where ornaments share the same techniques and basic designs, variations in precision and placement can lead to very different overall effects, as, for example, in Figs 18 and 23.

A great deal of wire was also used in the manufacture of chains. The simplest chains were of loop-in-loop type. The construction of these is shown in Fig. 24a, but the most common Greek type was that in which each link passes through the previous two, as in Fig. 24b. A typical example can be seen in Fig. 16. Greek and Phoenician jewellers were great masters at producing chains. Elaborate Greek examples may have four sets of links crossing each other, and broad band-like chain forms, known as straps, were particularly popular.

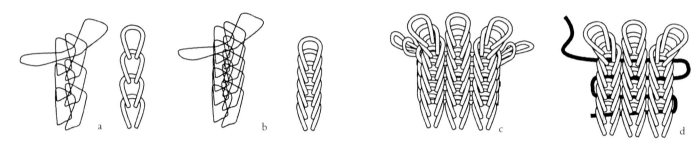

Straps first occur in the Near East in about the eighth century BC, as recent finds from Nimrud have shown, while the earliest Greek example is from Rhodes and dates to the seventh century. The Classical and Hellenistic Greek straps have the appearance of woven bands, and it is easiest to describe them as two or more loop-in-loop chains joined side by side with some type of interlinking. In practice the straps were probably constructed as a single length; in other words, they are really just particularly elaborate multiple loop-in-loop chains with two or more links in one direction and one (or rarely two) links (Fig. 24c), or a single wire (Fig. 24d), across them.

Straps use an extravagant amount of wire: no. 121, for example, contains about 50 metres of gold wire (and about 2,000 separately made and applied grains!). They typically have terminals held in place by wires and rivets, and even the pendants, when present, are held on by mechanical rather than soldered joins (there are several ways of accomplishing this). Loop-in-loop chains were assembled from pre-soldered links and thus did not require potentially damaging soldering during actual assembly. This is not true of the simple link chains generally used today and explains their rarity in antiquity. Indeed, the only example in the present catalogue is the fragment of figure-of-eight chain attached to no. 185: the same type of link is seen on a very similar pendant in the Nicosia Museum.

The individual parts of each jewellery component could be soldered together and the various components then fastened or linked together by mechanical means. The commonest soldering process was probably a version of the so-called diffusion bonding technique, in which the parts are literally stuck together with a mixture of some copper compound

FIGURE 24 The construction of loop-in-loop chain: (a) in the simplest type, each pre-soldered link is passed through the previous one; (b) in doubled loop-in-loop, the commonest Classical and Hellenistic type, each link passes through the previous two. Strap necklaces give the appearance of two or more loop-in-loop chains joined side by side. Most Greek examples are assembled as in (c), with long links passing right across the chains. An alternative method, (d), uses a long length of wire to zig-zag across the chains, in effect sewing them together.

and glue, or even saliva, and the area heated. In the case of the copper compound and glue mixture, the glue burns to carbon, liberating the copper which then alloys with and diffuses into the surrounding gold to fuse the joint. This process results in fine, often almost invisible, joints and was also a satisfactory means of attaching grains.

The skill in granulation lies in the positioning of the grains, not in their production, which is easy but time-consuming. Small particles of gold are heated until they melt and roll up into little spheres. The pre-

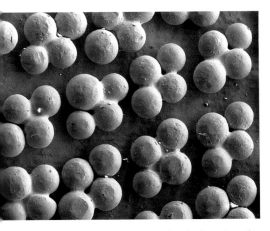

Above FIGURE 25 Precise quadruple clustering of granulation on a boat-shaped earring (*BMCJ* 1655, said to be from Crete; not in catalogue), similar to that seen on nos 70, 89 and 122.

FIGURE 26 Another detail from the same earring as in Fig. 25, showing complex filigree and granulation, including infill granulation (in the pear-shaped motif).

cision achieved in the positioning of granulation can be seen in Fig. 25, with its arrangement of small clusters of four grains, each grain under 0.2 mm in diameter. These linear clusters can be seen on several earrings in the catalogue and may point to at least a limited number of different workshops. Granulation may also be used to fill a filigree motif (Fig. 26). This type of decoration, found on several examples in this catalogue, had appeared in Greece by the late sixth century BC and may derive from, or share a common origin with, Etruscan work. Granulated infill decoration was widespread throughout the Greek world by later Classical and Hellenistic times.

Granulation and fine filigree are usually found only on relatively thin sheet backgrounds. With thicker sheet or solid gold backgrounds more rapid conduction of heat means that the grains or wires are liable to melt before they become fused in place. At best, the result is a very fused appearance (Fig. 22 and no. 99). The extreme fineness of some gold granulation work is not matched in silver jewellery.

Larger gold components could be joined using a conventional solder alloy, that is, an alloy of gold with enough silver or copper added to lower its melting temperature. Fig. 27 shows the soldered seam on the back of a ring hoop.

Classical Greek goldwork is characteristically made up of a series of separately made components. The individual components are constructed from sheet, wire and grains soldered together, but are often attached to the other components by mechanical means rather than by solder. This simplified final assembly retained flexibility and obviated the need for subsequent heating, which could well destroy any enamel and cause surface discoloration. The components could be joined by wire links, rivets and versions of what a modern engineer would call a split- or cotter-pin (Fig. 28). Mechanical joins were also often used in

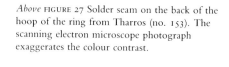
Above FIGURE 27 Solder seam on the back of the hoop of the ring from Tharros (no. 153). The scanning electron microscope photograph exaggerates the colour contrast.

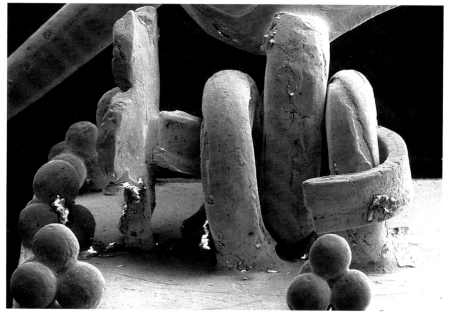

FIGURE 28 The pendant on earring no. 176, from Cyprus, retains flexibility by being attached with a mechanical fastener much like an engineer's cotter-pin. The small pyramids of granulation on the top of the pyramid pendant are also clearly seen.

larger objects, such as for attaching vessel handles and in the construction of pieces such as the massive gold *larnax* found in the royal tomb at Vergina.

Casting, whereby molten metal is poured into a mould of the desired shape, was rarely used in Classical Greek goldwork. Even massive objects such as the signet rings and some fibulae appear to be entirely made from hammered sheet gold, albeit of sturdy gauge. The reasons for this were both technical and economic. Some silver and much copper alloy jewellery was cast, as were, of course, the magnificent copper alloy figures and vessel attachments of the period. Casting, however, was liable to be wasteful of metal, for it was impossible to design a mould to utilise a pre-determined weight of gold, and, in any case, high-purity gold tends not to produce sharp, clean castings.

Once the object was soldered up and assembled it needed to be finished. Plain gold surfaces could be polished with a fine abrasive or, more frequently, burnished, but such treatment was clearly inappropriate for objects with added filigree and granulation. On such pieces, the goldwork was probably cleaned by immersing it in a suitable slightly corrosive mixture. Various solutions of substances such as alum, salt and urine were used; indeed, such 'pickles' have been used by goldsmiths until quite recent times.

Three of the objects in this catalogue are gilded (nos 25, 96 and 194). The overlaying of silver or copper with thin layers of gold dates back to the Early Bronze Age. Various methods could be employed, starting with the use of adhesives or simply folding over the edges. For objects that were likely to receive some use, longer-lasting processes were required. Thin gold foil can be bonded to silver by using heat in conjunction with burnishing, the process which appears to have been used on no. 96. If gold is mixed with mercury a paste-like amalgam results. This can be spread over silver or copper and, when it is heated, the mercury vaporises to leave a gold layer which can be burnished to a compact, shiny gold surface. Such a technique, termed mercury or amalgam gilding, was used for the finger ring, no. 194. This is one of the earliest examples of mercury gilding in the world: the technique did not become common in Classical lands until Roman times.

Gold can be adequately worked with bronze implements and even with wood or bone. The same is true to a slightly lesser extent of silver. The linear and zig-zag tremolo engraving on metal, which seems to occur first on Mycenaean goldwork and then on Dark Age Greek material, might be one of the few techniques that would have benefited from the introduction of iron tools, although these would also have been useful for cutting, or enhancing, the details on bronze dies.

The primary jewellery techniques described above – how the Greeks hammered sheet gold, how they made wire and what sort of solder alloys they used – are generally well understood today and, indeed, were fairly uniform throughout the Mediterranean and Near Eastern worlds by the mid-first millennium BC. What is now of interest to researchers is the implementation of those techniques: how or why the jeweller chose, for example, one particular decorative wire rather than another for the particular work in hand. This type of approach is eminently appropriate for Classical and Hellenistic gold because a great number of examples have survived, often with good provenances, while forms are frequently based on a relatively small number of motifs which may be combined and adapted in many different ways. Typically, there are several ways in which any particular component or decorative motif may be made. For example, a basic filigree rosette design may be produced with the petals bordered in plain, beaded or spiral-beaded wire which, in turn, may either outline each petal separately or all the petals at once with a single length of 'running filigree'. A wing on a figure of Eros or Nike may be made from a single piece of sheet gold which may be either pressed into a die or struck, or it may be made from a die-formed thin front sheet soldered to a flat and slightly thicker backing sheet (Fig. 29). A chain necklet may be fixed into its terminals by a rivet, a wire peg or a longer length of wire twisted back along the sides of the terminal.

We seldom know just why one particular method was used rather than another, and cannot always assume consistency within a single workshop, or even in the work of one jeweller, but comparing several different aspects of the construction of two or more objects can be helpful in assessing their likely interrelationships. This type of research into what we might term the constructional characteristics of Classical jewellery is in its infancy, but it is already beginning to help us to group objects both geographically and chronologically. Stylistic and art-historical study will allow us to link pieces of similar form or with motifs of similar design, and study of their constructional characteristics will then enable us to define their differences. [J.O.]

FIGURE 29 Any given component could be produced in a variety of different ways. For example, the wing from a small figure of Eros or Nike could be made by (a) chasing or die-forming a thin sheet; (b) 'striking' a thicker sheet, or (c) soldering a very thin die-formed sheet over a flat backing-sheet.

BIBLIOGRAPHY: Hoffmann and Davidson, pp. 24–48 (this catalogue, however, contains a good number of forgeries); Higgins *GRJ²*, pp. 11–34; Ogden *JAW*, pp. 34–74, with references; Ogden *AJ*, pp. 41–55. For wire manufacture see the recent summary in J.M. Ogden, *Jewellery Studies* 5 (1991), pp. 95–105.

The Craftsmen

Neither our ancient literary sources nor the jewellery itself tells us a great deal about the identity of Classical Greek jewellers (*chrysochoos*, *chrysourgos*). There are some signatures on rings in the fourth century (no. 97), probably following a trend that is more noticeable on gems, but otherwise the jewellers seem to have been happy to remain anonymous. A rare exception is probably the bracelet from Akarnania with the name Kletios (no. 26).

According to Demosthenes, a goldsmith named Pammenes, son of Pammenes of Erchia, had a goldsmith's shop in the Athenian Agora. He clearly both lived on the premises and carried out his business there. Demosthenes had commissioned him to make some gold wreaths and a *himation* decorated with gold for a procession in honour of Dionysos, but a man named Meidias had broken into Pammenes' shop in order to destroy the items and was only prevented by the owner's return.

This story indicates that Pammenes was a free citizen, and this was probably also true of a number of other jewellers. Some, however, were clearly slaves, as is revealed by the sale in 414 BC of the property of the Hermokipidai (those who mutilated the Herms). On one of the stelai recording this sale, a Carian slave, who was a goldsmith by profession, was sold off for 360 *drachmai*, almost twice the normal price for a slave at that period. We know little more of the social status of jewellers than this; nor is anything recorded of rates of pay in the Classical period, although it has been estimated that for gold vessels there was a 6–7 per cent manufacturing charge.

The jewellery itself can sometimes help in the identification of particular goldsmiths or workshops. It is always worth remembering, however, that, given the extreme scarcity of the raw materials, there were probably relatively few workshops operating in the Classical period. As mentioned in the previous section, there are two main approaches: a stylistic one and a technological one. Both approaches have their weaknesses and they are best used in conjunction. Furthermore, detailed scrutiny often reveals factors which can help to establish a relative chronology; this may then make it possible to relate the material more closely to historical problems, both social and economic.

When jewellery was worn in life it often had to be repaired, as a result of damage or loss. In Aristophanes, for example, we hear of a woman losing an acorn pendant from her necklace. The jeweller might then repair the piece in his shop, or perhaps even visit a wealthy home to carry out repairs there. Many pieces of jewellery in this catalogue show signs of wear and even repair. Sometimes new pieces were added to old jewellery, but it was also quite possible for old pendants or other components to be reused on a new piece, or, of course, the whole might be melted down and remade in the latest fashion.

BIBLIOGRAPHY: Demosthenes, *Against Meidias*, XXII (522). Hermokipidai Stele II, 77ff. Making charge: D.M. Lewis in M. Vickers (ed.), *Pots and Pans* (Oxford 1986), pp. 71–81, esp. p. 79. Aristophanes, *Lysistrata*, 408ff.

The Functions of Greek Jewellery

Greek jewellery was, of course, made to be worn. It was intended to enhance or highlight the beauty of the wearer, but it was also intended to reveal status and wealth, especially when it was of gold. Jewellery was probably given as a gift at births, subsequent birthdays and weddings, and it might become imbued with sentimental or status-value either on account of the donor or because of its previous wearer. It may also have had religious or amuletic significance. In this catalogue there are several examples of heirlooms (one of particular antiquity: no. 82), a priestly sceptre (no. 134) and an official seal (no. 1).

Jewellery was also given to the gods and was an obvious choice for offerings by women. Dedications might have occurred at the time of transition to womanhood; or in thanksgiving for securing a husband or a lover or perhaps in fulfilment of a vow made to Aphrodite to acquire the same; or to a goddess such as Eileithyia on a successful childbirth. Offerings were sometimes made to Asklepios in thanksgiving for a cure, and the inventories of his sanctuary in Athens record diadems, earrings, necklaces and rings. Women might also seek to establish status by such gifts: one thinks of Roxane, the wife of Alexander the Great, who dedicated gold necklaces as well as a gold *rhyton* to Athena Polias in 311/10 BC, and Aspasia, perhaps the lover of Perikles, who dedicated a gold *stlengis* on a wooden backing in the Parthenon. There are also mentions of men dedicating their rings in sanctuaries, and Croesus is said to have dedicated his wife's necklaces and girdles in the sanctuary at Delphi. The officials of a cult might often end their tenure with a joint offering in the form of a wreath. The state itself also made such offerings.

In addition, gold jewellery was actually placed on the cult statues in temples, forming part of the statue's *kosmos* or embellishment. At Athens the statue of Asklepios had a gold wreath, as did Apollo's statue at Delphi, while the statue of Athena Polias in Athens had a diadem, necklaces, earrings and a bracelet. Finds of actual jewellery from sanctuaries are of course very rare, for it was all too easily stolen. Nevertheless, there is some excavated material from sanctuaries which probably represents either offerings by individuals or the *kosmos* of the cult statue. The large amount of late seventh-century BC gold jewellery from the sanctuary of Artemis at Ephesus is an early example of such a phenomenon. There is also the diadem found in 1987 in building B in the sanctuary of Hera Lacinia at Kroton, which combines myrtle leaves and berries with vine leaves, all on a wide band decorated with a guilloche pattern; it probably dates to the later sixth century BC or the early fifth. At an extremely modest shrine in the hinterland of Herakleia in South Italy were found part of a gold necklace and a pair of fourth-century gold ear studs. Since the deposit contained no other items of jewellery, it seems possible that these came from the cult statue of Demeter itself. A still later example is the hoard of jewellery and silver plate from the temple at Tuch el-Karamus in Egypt.

This last find is an example of jewellery in another role, that is as bullion. The inventories of the Athenian temples include huge numbers of gold wreaths, many made by outgoing officials, and very little in the way of coinage, making it clear that the wreaths were a way of storing the wealth of the sanctuary. Private wealth might also be hoarded in the form of jewellery, although it was more commonly kept as coin. The Avola Hoard (nos 142–3), for example, consisted of a large number of gold coins and just a few items of jewellery. It was probably hidden at a moment of danger, never to be recovered by its owner.

The effect of placing jewellery in the tomb was, of course, to remove it from circulation. Some cultures have eschewed the idea entirely, while others have varied their practice according to circumstances. By and large, it seems that the Greeks felt that to place jewellery in the tomb was a proper way of honouring the dead. Nevertheless, there are certain periods in particular areas of the Greek world from which very little gold jewellery has been preserved. This might be the result of a change in either funerary practice or everyday fashion, but it seems likely that any such change would have been driven by an economic factor, whether relative poverty or the scarcity of the metal.

BIBLIOGRAPHY: On temple inventories see especially D. Harris, *The Inventory Lists of the Parthenon Treasures* (thesis, University of Princeton 1991); S.B. Aleshire, *The Athenian Asklepion: The People, their Dedications, and the Inventories* (Amsterdam 1989). For the jewellery from Ephesus see D.G. Hogarth, *Excavation at Ephesus. The Archaic Artemisia* (London 1908), pp. 94–115, pls 3–10. For the small sanctuary near Herakleia see *NSc* 23 (1969), p. 178, fig. 12. Tuch el-Karamus hoard: Pfrommer, FK 6.

The Forms of Greek Jewellery

It should be said straight away that both men and women adorned themselves with gold. In the Classical period Greek men seem normally to have worn only finger rings. On special occasions, however, they also wore gold wreaths, as the story of Demosthenes reveals (p. 30 above). A number of early sixth-century marble sculptures from Attica suggest that men also once wore neck-bands, but this fashion appears to have died out by the middle of the century. In the East Greek cities, probably under the influence of nearby non-Greeks, male jewellery seems to have been more common, and there are representations of men wearing earrings and bracelets. This was normally considered as effeminate by many back in Greece itself. Indeed, in 401 BC a soldier is sent packing from Xenophon's army because he 'has pierced ears just like a Lydian'. In the North Pontic region, amongst the Scythians and their Hellenised neighbours, the display of wealth through gold jewellery and other objects was particularly important. A number of early burials reveal males with necklaces, torques, earrings, bracelets and rings (see nos 71–80).

The most common items of jewellery worn by Greek women were no doubt earrings, necklaces, bracelets and finger rings. However, other more ambitious or showy items included wreaths, diadems and breast pendants. More mundane accoutrements, such as buttons, fibulae and pins, vary according to date and region.

Pollux, a scholar of the second century AD, lists some seventeen names for types of earrings, but the commonest word for an earring, both in the ancient writers and in inscriptions recording the contents of sanctuaries, is *enotion* or *enoidion*. In ancient times to wear earrings meant piercing the ears, for all were passed through holes in the ear: there were no clip-on earrings (Fig. 30). In the Classical period three main types continue from earlier periods, boat-shaped earrings (nos 9, 11, 13, 38, 63, 75, 77, 99, 144), spiral earrings (nos 5, 47, 93, 145, 165, 172–4) and disc-shaped studs (nos 51–2, 109). In addition, one finds discs, rosettes or other floral ornaments from which were suspended a variety of pendants. These pendants may themselves be boat-shaped (nos 70, 88–9, 122, 146)

Above FIGURE 30 Detail of a silver stater of the Lycian dynast Teththiweibi, about 450 BC: inserted through a large hole in the earlobe is a spiral earring with pyramid decoration (British Museum, *BMC* Lycia 82). For the form of the earring compare nos 47 and 93.

FIGURE 31 Bronze mirror with the head of a woman wearing a lion-head earring curving below her earlobe, about 300–250 BC (British Museum *BMCB* 3211).

or in the form of inverted pyramids (nos 12, 49–50), or even figural (nos 19–21, 31, 101, 107, 110, 114). Late in the fourth century a further type developed, a tapering hoop ending in an animal's head (nos 132, 148): these seem to have been worn with the animal head at the front, but upside-down (Fig. 31).

Some seven words for necklaces are to be found in authors such as Homer, Aristophanes and Pollux, as well as in the inventories of temple treasures: *hormos, hormiskos, hypoderis, kathema, halysion, plokion* and *katheter*. The first four seem to refer to necklaces with repeated elements, while a *halysion* consisted of various different elements and a *plokion* was a necklace that was woven. Preserved necklaces of the fifth century are of two main types. The first, which continues sixth-century types, takes the form of repeated beads and pendants in the form of fruit, seeds or buds, sometimes with a central animal-head pendant (nos 7–8, 95, 102, 117, 135; cf. no. 103). The second consists of more two-dimensional elements, either rosettes alternating with lotus-palmettes or corrugated sheet tubes with seed-like pendants (nos 15, 76, 94, 166, 178). This second type continued into the fourth century, when a third type developed, the strap necklace with its woven appearance. The *plokion* is mentioned in connection with Dionysios I and the daughter of Lysander, in other words about 400 BC; it does not, however, occur in temple inventories until 342/1 BC. A variety of pendants were suspended from such strap necklaces, including beech-nut (nos 30, 53, 106, 123) and other seed-like pendants (nos 22, 64, 68, 121), as well as amphoroid pendants (no. 23).

Necklaces were regularly worn tight around the neck, like a modern choker necklace or ribbon, or in a looser fashion, at the base of the neck. They were often worn in multiples, especially a necklace of simple beads with one of more complex form (Fig. 32). It is sometimes assumed that necklaces were also worn across the breast, supported by fibulae at the shoulders. Although long pins seem occasionally to have been used in the sixth century to support necklaces, as is suggested by an image on Kleitias' masterpiece, the so-called François vase in Florence, in the fifth century they only occur linked by chains, as examples from Sindos and the famous pair in Boston indicate. There are no representations of fibulae supporting necklaces and, like the pins, they are only ever found linked by chains (no. 6).

Necklaces of beads or other elements were threaded on one or more cords (*linon*) and even the ends of strap necklaces were tied together by means of a cord, threaded through the ring at either end, as is seen, for example, on the grand black-glazed *krater* in the British Museum decorated with gilded necklaces, wreaths and earrings (Fig. 33). Later necklaces sometimes have hook and eye terminals (nos 23, 149): this type of fastening meant that the necklace had to be made to measure and no doubt indirectly reflects the increase in the amount of gold available.

Bracelets (*pselia*) are of two main forms. The first consists of a penannular rod or strap with animal-head terminals (nos 25, 27, 32, 96, 142, 152, 161, 189; cf. also no. 86 and nos 118 and 124). This form originated in the Achaemenid world and a North Pontic version omits the animal heads (cf. no. 112). The second type takes the form of a spiral, again either a rod or a strap, usually ending in a snake's head (no. 26). Some bracelets were worn at the wrist (no. 83), others near the elbows, but the grandest were worn on the upper arm (no. 37) and are properly

FIGURE 32 Terracotta vase in the form of the head of Athena, about 400–350 BC: she wears two necklaces, the upper one of beads, the lower with pendants (British Museum *BMCT* 1701).

FIGURE 33 Detail from over the handle of an Athenian black-glaze *krater* decorated in gilded relief with two wreaths, two necklaces and an earring, about 340–320 BC (British Museum GR 1871.7-22.3; said to be from Capua). The cords (*lina*) tying the ends of the strap necklaces are quite clear. The earring is of the disc and boat-shaped pendant type with a complex festoon below.

called armlets. A third type is found in the North Pontic area: it consists of an unbroken band, and was worn on the upper arm (no. 82).

Rings (*daktylioi, kirkoi*) were often worn in considerable numbers and different types are often found in a single burial. They can be divided into plain rings, decorative rings and seal-rings. Among the decorative rings are examples with swivel bezels (nos 1, 108, 125–6, 140), fixed elaborate box-bezels (nos 136, 143), and simple fixed bezels, usually made in one piece with the hoop. Decoration may be chased or shallow-groove engraved, in relief, in filigree or in foil on or under glass. In addition, there are rings in the form of snakes (no. 66), miniature versions of snake-bracelets, and occasionally one in which an animal takes the place of the normal bezel (no. 154).

The most elaborate items of jewellery were usually made for the adornment of the head. There were many different types of diadems (*sphendone, ampyx, stlengis*): plain bands (no. 45), bands with a pediment-shaped centrepiece (nos 44, 62, 168–9) and more elaborate constructions, sometimes with a central Herakles knot (nos 18, 131) and sometimes with pendants (no. 46). There were also golden hairnets (no. 197), perhaps the ancient *kekryphalos*. In addition, from the North Pontic area come elaborate tall hats decorated with gold bands (*poloi*), gold combs, such as the famous example from Solokha, and even golden hair-pieces (no. 119).

There were also gold wreaths (*stephanoi*). Examples of gold wreathes of oak (nos 60, 113), olive (nos 105, 115), ivy, vine, laurel and myrtle (no. 10, a spray) leaves are known from burials in Macedonia, South Italy, Asia Minor and the North Pontic area. The inventories of Greek temples and sanctuaries list vast numbers of wreaths of greatly varying weights – in the Parthenon they ranged from 26 to 300 *drachmai* – and could be dedicated by individuals – men, women and foreigners – by officials at the end of their term of office, by the state or by a foreign power. Such gold wreaths were worn in festival procesions, as the story of Demosthenes reveals, and could serve as prizes in competitions, as the temple inventories record. The earliest metal wreath dates from the earlier seventh century BC, but they do not become common in graves until the fourth century BC. The most elaborate wreath to have survived is that from Armento, now in Munich, which combines Nikai and Erotes with a huge variety of floral motifs: it also has a dedicatory plaque, suggesting that it may originally have been part of a temple treasure. The most elaborate to be mentioned in the ancient sources is probably that suspended in the burial chamber of Alexander the Great.

Clothes might be decorated with gold spangles, especially in the eastern regions of the Greek world. These could be circular (nos 56, 91) or rectangular (nos 90, 127–9), in the form of cut-out designs (nos 14, 72–4, 78–80, 92) or elaborate florals (nos 57, 67, 130). Some textiles even had very thin strips of gold woven into their wefts (the idea of casing a thread in gold was a later development). There were gold fibulae, especially in Macedonia and South Italy, and pins (much rarer), as well as gold brooches and buttons. Some belts or parts of belts have also been preserved, both of gold and silver.

Finally, gold was used for objects of status, not in themselves true items of jewellery, although they were no doubt made by jewellers. These include sceptres (no. 134), fans, scabbard covers (no. 112) and bow-case covers.

BIBLIOGRAPHY: Attic sculpture with neck-bands: I. Blanck, *Studien zum griechischen Halsschmuck der archäischen und klassischen Zeit* (Cologne 1974), pp. 62–3. Soldier with earrings: Xenophon, *Anabasis* III, 1, 31. François vase: A. Furtwängler and K. Reichhold, *Griechische Vasenmalerei* (Munich 1904), pl. 1/2 (one of the Moirai). Munich wreath from Armento: *L'oro dei Greci*, pls 119–20. Alexander the Great's funeral wreath: Diodorus Siculus, XVIII, 27, 5. In general, see also Higgins GRJ², *passim*, and his article in Barr-Sharrar and Borza.

The Iconography of Classical Greek Jewellery

As has already been noted, men in the sixth century BC and, in general, men in the eastern part of the Greek world, under the influence of eastern peoples, wore some jewellery. Greek jewellery was normally made, however, for women and was intended to make them more attractive to the opposite sex. It should not be surprising, therefore, to find that the iconography of Greek jewellery centres around women and 'Golden Aphrodite', the goddess of love.

The figures that inhabit Greek jewellery are mostly female deities, and Aphrodite indeed takes pride of place. She appears in all her beauty on a number of rings (nos 17, 126); indeed, rings with their flat field are the most iconographically rich items of normal jewellery. The goddess also appears in less clearly defined form as a female head on necklaces and earrings (nos 91, 145, 157, 160, 177, 190). Her son, the young Eros (Love), frequently accompanies her (nos 126, 155, 158) or even substitutes for the goddess (nos 29, 43, 138, 140). Eros also multiplies into what are regularly called Erotes, as on the Kyme (nos 49–50) or Madytos earrings (no. 63; also nos 20, 170), but may have been identified more precisely by the wearers as Himeros and Pothos (both words mean desire or yearning). He regularly holds a *iunx*, a magic love charm intended to arouse desire (nos 43, 49–50, 194), the precursor of Cupid's bow and arrow.

Artemis, too, is a popular figure. She may be seen in her huntress guise (no. 4) or as an Olympian (no. 125), and by extension in related deities of vegetation (no. 85), the animal world and the darker powers of the sky and underworld (no. 10). On a series of reliefs from northern Greece a female head appears wearing a lion-skin over her head (no. 33). She may be Artemis, who is sometimes shown wearing a lion-skin, or Omphale, the Lydian queen to whom Herakles was sold as a slave and for whom he performed a series of labours, an interesting role reversal which was made much of by Roman poets such as Ovid.

Demeter and Persephone also occur, no doubt because of the importance of their cults to women. We see both on a series of plaques from the Great Bliznitza (nos 127–8), together with Herakles (no. 129). His presence suggests that the fact that Greek-speaking outsiders could be initiated into the Mysteries was important to the far-off Hellenised peoples of the Crimea. The other important aspect of the cult in that region was its association with crops, in particular corn, for cities such as Athens relied on imports from the Black Sea. Both these factors can also be seen to have played a part in the contemporary surge in the worship of Demeter in South Italy.

Athena finds a place too, although she is usually shown as a cult-statue, whether in the form of a detail from the Athena Parthenos (no. 87) or as a seated figure (no. 133), when she is perhaps intended to be Athena Polias. Athena was an important deity for Greek women, as well as for the city of Athens, for she was the goddess of all handicrafts. The frequency of her appearance at the outer reaches of the Greek world, both east and west, testifies to her importance as a symbol for those wishing to demonstrate their Hellenisation.

The only male divinity to appear on Greek jewellery with any frequency is Dionysos. He may be alone, often in the form of a mask, or occasionally accompanied by Ariadne, as on the Madytos diadem (no. 62), but most commonly he is represented by his followers, both maenads and satyrs (nos 116, 143, 197). The popularity of Dionysiac imagery on female jewellery may be linked with the freedom allowed to women in his rites. Helios occurs on the jewellery of Rhodes (no. 41), but this is local homage to the island's patron deity. The river-god Acheloos may be found in both western and eastern contexts. On no. 94, he is perhaps best understood in association with Dionysos, for there his head alternates with a fennel seed (see below), suggesting the story that Acheloos provided the first water to be mixed with wine. Acheloos is, however, also connected with Herakles. They fought for the hand of Deineira and Herakles broke off his horn, which then became associated with the 'horn of plenty'. Herakles himself was connected, as noted above, with the Eleusinian Mysteries, but above all he was the most important of the Greek heroes.

Among the lesser female deities is Thetis, the daughter of Nereus. She was, of course, a special archetype for women at the time of marriage: her abduction by Peleus (no. 82) was one of the images used to symbolise the removal of the woman from the home of her parents to the bridegroom's house. Thetis' sisters, the Nereids, are also shown riding dolphins or *kete* (sea monsters) and carrying new armour for Achilles, commissioned by his mother Thetis from Hephaistos (nos 42–3, 88, 120). Although Achilles may have been regarded as the worthiest of sons, and thus an archetype, this theme occurs most frequently in the jewellery from the Black Sea and is probably to be thought of as having particular local significance. According to some sources, after his death at the hands of Paris, Achilles lived immortal on the island of Leuke in the north-west Black Sea.

Among the other female figures that appear are winged women. These are usually described as Nikai, daimons of victory, and this is what they clearly are in most cases, for example the Nike holding a trophy (no. 21), the Nike on Athena's palm (no. 133) and the Nikai driving chariots (nos 14 (Fig. 34), 70, 156; cf. also 107). Nevertheless, they are sometimes closely associated with Erotes: for example, on the earring from Kul Oba, Nikai are seen tying their sandals (no. 89), a motif derived from the frieze of the temple of Athena Nike on the Athenian Acropolis, but also recalling the task regularly performed by Eros for Aphrodite; and on one of the pairs of earrings from Kyme (no. 50) they are shown playing knucklebones or dice and are placed above a pair of Erotes, each

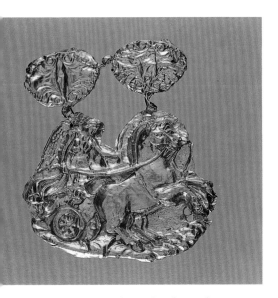

FIGURE 34 Nike driving her chariot, from a necklace (no. 14).

of whom holds a *iunx*. The clear implication is that they were thought of as being involved in the game of love and the victory of amorous conquest.

A further winged female occurs on one of the Kul Oba bracelets (no. 82). She is carrying off a naked boy and is usually identified as Eos, the goddess of the dawn, abducting a youth called either Kephalos or Tithonos. This is an inversion of the norm: a male deity seducing a young mortal woman. As such, it may be linked with the representations of Zeus in the form of an eagle carrying off the young Ganymede (no. 31). These scenes, like the rape of Thetis, are closely linked with Greek conceptions of marriage.

The Muses with their variety of accoutrements on the diadem from Madytos (no. 62) introduce another theme, that of music (also no. 63). Eros is sometimes seen with *auloi* (no. 140) or a kithara, and the same is true of the sirens (nos 19, 114, 131). The music of the sirens is, of course, closely linked with a specific myth, that of Odysseus and his sailors: their music induced irresistible longing, which drove sailors onto the rocks. Indeed, Odysseus' ship, surrounded by sirens, is juxtaposed with three Erotes flying over the sea on a vase in the British Museum and one of the sirens there is actually named Himeropa (face of desire).

A number of heroines and priestesses are also to be found. The long-suffering Penelope is one of these (no. 98). She is a model of the patient and resourceful wife, left alone for many years by Odysseus to fend off the growing attentions of local nobles. Kassandra seeking refuge from the vicious attack of Ajax at the statue of Athena is another Trojan War motif to be found on rings (no. 16). Ariadne, who was deserted by Theseus and found by Dionysos, is also represented (no. 62). Finally, there is the beautiful Io, priestess of Hera, who was pursued by Zeus and then turned into a heifer by the jealous goddess (no. 135).

This concentration on female deities and themes of love, however, takes no account of the jewellery made for men. Greek men, as we have noted, normally seem to have avoided wearing jewellery, apart from rings and wreaths, at least in the Classical period, but in some areas on the margins of the Greek world they did adorn themselves with gold. The most obvious examples occur in the Bosporan kingdom, where the possession and display of wealth through gold seems to have been a requirement for the élite of the society. The male in the Kul Oba burial was adorned with a torque and bracelets (nos 81–3), while in some early burials from Nymphaion and Seven Brothers the corpse was also decked with necklaces and earrings (nos 71–80).

The iconography of male jewellery is very different. There is none of the emphasis on Aphrodite and other goddesses. Instead, one finds remarkably detailed studies of men, both Scythian (no. 81) and Greek

(Solokha comb-ornament), riding horses and fighting. Fierce animals and monsters connected with strength and death, such as lions (no. 104) and sphinxes (no. 83), predominate. The North Pontic necklaces and earrings are without any iconography (nos 71, 75–7), while the earrings worn by men in Asia Minor similarly avoid all figural decoration (cf. no. 47).

Animals are, of course, also frequently found on female jewellery. These include lionesses (no. 124), rams (nos 25, 32, 118, 161), bulls (nos 72, 100), stags (nos 76, 86, 110–12), antelopes and goats. When worn by women they may have served as sympathetic magic for the opposite sex; when worn by men they may have been seen as direct symbols of their power and potency. Snakes are particularly favoured and it is often thought that this is because of their connections with the underworld. They do, however, make perfect twining ornaments for arm and finger or a neat end to a hammered earring hook. The twining property also led, no doubt, to the inclusion of *kete* (nos 37 and 108) and tritons (no. 37), which belong in the marine world. From that sphere also come fish and dolphins, as well as shells, of both cockle (no. 9) and horn varieties (no. 122). From the air were drawn birds (no. 86), bees (nos 60, 110, 170) and cicadas (no. 60, Fig. 35). Animals that span two realms, such as the frog (no. 154) and the scarab beetle (no. 126), have more complex religious and magical connotations. Mythical beasts and monsters, such as griffins (nos 1, 33, 86, 112), horned lions or griffin-lions (nos 165, 171–4) and Pegasoi (nos 24, 33, 63–4, 123) are even more frequent.

Two large, openwork lunate pectorals deserve a mention here. They adorned the breasts of women in two particularly rich burials: Great Bliznitza and Tolstaya Mogila. The Great Bliznitza example shows a frieze of animals in a rustic setting; the Tolstaya Mogila piece is more elaborate, with a frieze of griffins fighting horses, a floral frieze including birds and a frieze of quiet domesticity with animals being milked. This interest in rural activities recurs in the far west on a ring from Tharros on Sardinia (no. 153).

Intertwined with the figural iconography discussed above, there is floral decoration. Wreaths of oak (nos 60, 113), olive (nos 105, 115), ivy, vine, laurel and myrtle are all regular accompaniments of funerals. Sprigs or sprays are also sometimes found (no. 10), as are ears of wheat. These were probably placed in the hands of the deceased or in their hair or diadems. Both wreaths and sprays, however, were used in cult ceremonies as well as at funerals, and are recorded as offerings in the temple inventories. The trees and bushes selected by the Greek jewellers all had their places in Greek cult: the oak was sacred to Zeus, the olive to Athena, the ivy to Dionysos, the laurel to Apollo and the myrtle to Aphrodite. Many myths and folk-tales were associated with them. For

FIGURE 35 Gold cicada from an oak wreath (no. 60).

example, the nymph Daphne was turned into a laurel in order to escape the advances of Apollo, Hera anointed herself with sacred olive oil when she wished to seduce Zeus, and when Aphrodite rose from the sea she hid her naked beauty behind a myrtle bush.

Many of the fruit or seeds of these trees and bushes are to be found as pendants on necklaces and earrings. Acorns were particularly favoured (no. 166; cf. Fig. 2) and myrtle seeds also occur (no. 7). Olives are probably to be identified on two late fifth-century necklaces from Eretria, now in Athens.

Beech nuts (Fig. 36) also became popular (nos 30, 49, 53, 106, 123), but modern scholars have tended to identify them as spear-heads because of the mention in some temple inventories of necklaces with pendants in the form of *logchia* (spear-heads) or *hormoi logchotoi*. Spear-heads, however, have only two lobes. Arrow-heads have three lobes, but are of a different shape, with pointed shoulders. It is possible that the necklaces mentioned in the inventories with spear-head pendants in fact resembled the strap necklaces with beech-nut pendants which are preserved, for the officials who made these lists, just like modern commentators, may not have realised what the jewellers intended. Beech nuts make much better sense than spear-heads in the context of all the other pendants designed by Greek jewellers. It is interesting to note that the beech tree was, and is, common in northern Greece, and not in the south; this may suggest that the idea for this type of pendant first occurred in the north, presumably in a Macedonian workshop.

FIGURE 36 Beech-nut pendants (detail of no. 30).

Two necklaces from the Bosporan region (nos 76 and 94) have simple seed pendants with vertical ribs. These may be fennel seeds. They also occur, together with acorns, on the fine gold *phiale* in New York and they may be the *karyota* mentioned in the Delian inventories. The giant fennel was sacred to Dionysos, and his followers carried *thyrsoi* made from its stalks. Ivy leaves are also found on many pieces in this catalogue, even together with bunches of grapes (no. 32): they may also be connected with Dionysos.

Pomegranates appear on the ends of the chains of the tie-necklace from Kyme (no. 55; cf. also no. 35). Such pendants can be traced back in Greek jewellery to the middle of the ninth century BC. Pomegranates are, by reason of their numerous fleshy seeds, symbols of fertility and sacred to Aphrodite, as well as being connected with Persephone.

The remarkable sceptre from Taranto is topped by a green glass fruit which may be identified as a quince (no. 134). This fruit was known from the time of Homer and is usually called a *milo Kydonion* (Cydonian apple). It was sacred to Aphrodite and was connected in ritual with marriage: the newly weds had to eat some before the wedding night.

In addition to seeds and fruit a number of flowers may be recognised amid the foliage of Greek jewellery. These include the dog-rose flowers from the Madytos find (no. 67), although it is not always easy to be sure of the difference between dog-roses and myrtle flowers. More stylised rosettes are particularly common. Amid the scrolls of a number of pieces (e.g. no. 137) appear bell- or trumpet-shaped buds and flowers: these may well be bindweed. Finally, the very fine granulation sometimes used both to fill pear-shaped or tongue-like forms in the centres of flowers and to decorate elaborate boat-shaped pendants is clearly intended to imitate pollen. The groups of four granules set in curving lines on some of the most elaborate boat-shaped pendants recalls the similar arrangement of the pollen-bearing anthers of flowers such as the golden elecampane, a northern Greek plant with important medicinal properties which has been identified as the *panakes to Cheironeion* (the all-healing of Cheiron) noted by Theophrastos.

The most common elements of the floral decoration of Greek jewellery are the leaves. Two forms are regularly found: the palm, heavily stylised as a palmette, and the acanthus. The palm was closely associated with the twins Apollo and Artemis, who were said to have been born under its shade. An acanthus growing by a vase for offerings in a cemetery in Corinth was said by Vitruvius to have inspired the fifth-century sculptor Kallimachos to create the Corinthian-style capital. Its introduction into the iconography of jewellery seems to date to the fourth century. The forms to be found in the jewellery most closely correspond to the *acanthus mollis*, which is only found wild in northern Greece. As with the beech nut, therefore, the form of floral motifs may suggest where particular types of jewellery ornamentation perhaps originated.

Many other elements in Greek jewellery were no doubt inspired by the plant world, but precise identification usually proves elusive. For example, the flat, lunate earrings from Cyprus (nos 162 and 175) recall the seeds of leguminous plants such as the so-called medick tree, while the 'paddle-wheels' of northern Greek fibulae (no. 33) suggest the fruit of the smyrnium, but it is difficult to be sure. Jewellers seem rapidly to have developed the ribbed fennel seeds noted above into more fanciful specimens with a dog-tooth calyx (Fig. 37), which is at first only decorated with granules but later covered with feather patterns. The greatest elaboration of these seed-like pendants occurs on the large necklace from the Great Bliznitza (no. 121).

Both the world of myth and religion and the natural world of plant and animal life were, thus, clearly important sources of iconography. There is, however, one other source of inspiration, and that is textiles. The gold wire on which so much Greek jewellery is based can be used very like thread. This is most obviously seen in the strap necklaces which imitate woven bands, but simpler rows of decorative wires may also

FIGURE 37 Various forms of seed-like pendants (detail of no. 64).

produce textile effects, such as the herringbone pattern created by laying rope wires next to each other with their twists in opposite directions. The twisted ribbons of the Melos diadem (no. 18) may also be inspired by small textiles.

Finally, there is the so-called Herakles knot. This was closely connected with marriage. It tied a bride's garment and was untied by the groom. The tying of knots marks a moment of transition in many cultures, whether from maiden to married woman or from the living to the dead. The undoing of knots is also connected with the easing of childbirth. The Herakles knot is found in Greek jewellery as early as the Mycenaean period, but it became particularly popular in the second half of the fourth century BC.

BIBLIOGRAPHY: On the mythological iconography of Greek jewellery see Hoffmann and Davidson, pp. 12–13. Siren vase in London: *BMCV* E 440. Great Bliznitza and Tolstaya Mogila pectorals: *Scythian Art*, pls 255–6 and 118–21. For comparisons on floral iconography see especially H. Baumann, *Greek Wild Flowers and Plant Lore in Ancient Greece* (English trans., London 1993). New York gold *phiale*: *BMetrMus* 42 (1984), p. 50. Corinthian capital: Vitruvius, *De Architectura* IV, 1, 9. On Herakles knots see K. Keyssner in *Paulys Real-Encyclopädie der classischen Altertumswissenschaft*, *sv* nodus; J. Boardman in *LIMC* IV, p. 729 and Pfrommer, pp. 4–6.

Greek Jewellery as Sculpture

We occasionally read in our ancient literary sources of gold and silver sculpture. It is not always clear, however, what the scale of such figures was, nor whether such statues were solid or only coated with sheet metal. The gold lion given by King Croesus to Delphi was presumably of solid gold, since a weight is given, but parts of a roughly contemporary chryselephantine statue (that is, one combining ivory with sheet gold), also of East Greek style, have been found at Delphi, and this was probably the norm. It was certainly the technique used by Pheidias for his colossal statues in the Parthenon and at Olympia.

The pendants suspended from some Classical Greek earrings, such as those of Ganymede and the eagle (no. 31, Fig. 38), the various sirens (nos 19 and 114), the Nike with a trophy (no. 21) and the Nike in a chariot in Boston are all miniature sculptures of great power. The Ganymede pendants may be associated with a famous bronze group, mentioned by Pliny, of Ganymede and the eagle, a work of the first half of the fourth century BC by Leochares and the first to show Zeus as an eagle. Pliny describes the statue as follows: 'Leochares represented the eagle which feels what a treasure it is stealing in Ganymede, and to whom it is bearing him, and using its talons gently, though the boy's garment protects him.' The earrings are surely not miniature copies of Leochares' sculpture, but they do seem to reflect it in basic conception and in mood.

In addition to such miniature pendant figures, usually constructed

FIGURE 38 Earring with Ganymede and the eagle (no. 31).

from sheet gold but occasionally solid like the Ganymede earrings, Greek jewellers produced many three-dimensional representations on a larger scale. Most common among these are the numerous animal-head terminals, originally of Achaemenid inspiration, and such larger-scale sculpture became particularly fashionable and highly developed in the North Pontic region. Lion-head and ram-head terminals were transformed into complete, leaping animals (nos 118 and 124); sphinxes became majestic creatures with huge wings, veined horse-like flanks and jewellery-bedecked heads, necks and ears (no. 83). Most remarkable of all, however, was the appearance of human figures fully worked in the round. The masterpieces are the Kul Oba torque with Scythian riders (no. 81), the Solokha comb with its warring Greeks and Scythians and the openwork pectorals from Great Bliznitza and Tolstaya Mogila. On these the modelling of both human and animal forms and the treatment of mood and movement vie with the best work in bronze, marble or terracotta.

Finally, the technique of working gold into a die has produced many examples of relief scupture in Classical jewellery from all parts of the Greek world. Some examples are on quite a large scale, such as the various series of clothing appliqués from the North Pontic region, others are smaller, like the more delicate appliqués from the East Greek workshops or the Tarentine box-bezel rings with their tiny reliefs.

BIBLIOGRAPHY: C. Vermeule, *Greek and Roman Sculpture in Gold and Silver* (Boston 1974). Pliny on Leochares, *Natural History* XXXIV, 79. Solokha comb: *Scythian Art*, pls 122–3. Great Bliznitza and Tolstaya Mogila pectorals: *Scythian Art*, pls 255–6 and 118–21.

Greek Jewellery as Drawing and Painting

The use of filigree wire on large flat fields, as on the Santa Eufemia diadem (no. 137) or the Patras brooch (no. 24), to create complex scrolls punctuated by flowers and rosettes strongly recalls the art of drawing. Indeed, Benvenuto Cellini was to write in the sixteenth century that

> those who did the best work in filigree were the men who had a good grip of drawing, especially designing from foliage and pierced spray work, for everything that you set to work upon requires first of all that you think it out as a design. And though many have practised the art without making drawings first because the material in which they worked was so easily handled and so pliable; still those who made their drawings first did the best work.

We do not know whether ancient Greek jewellers made preliminary sketches, but it would seem quite likely for the more complex products. Athenian vase-painters made preliminary sketches on their vases, probably in charcoal, and ancient jewellers could well have used some easily removable substance.

'Drawing' on Classical Greek jewellery employed wires of different thickness and of different reflective qualities engendered by the surface of the wires – plain, beaded or spiral-beaded. Figured designs were not attempted, only floral (Etruscan jewellers had attempted both and had preferred silhouettes within areas of granulation to outline work in filigree). The middle of the fourth century BC seems to have witnessed the development of a new floral style in large-scale painting, which, to judge from the comments in the ancient writers, may be associated with Pausias of Sikyon. Nothing of his work, of course, is preserved, but in South Italian vase-painting and Macedonian mosaics in the second half of the fourth century there is a proliferation of flowers and of elaborate scrolls and a new, vivid three-dimensionality in their representation, all no doubt under Pausias' influence. This same increase in floral elements and in their plasticity may be observed in contemporary jewellery.

In addition to the graphic use of filigree, jewellers in the Classical period employed colouristic effects. The most common of these was coloured enamel surrounded by filigree wire to produce pools of colour in·the gold. The usual palette consisted of blue and green, with the addition of black and white. Jewellers also realised that red was particularly effective with gold, but, finding that they could not produce red enamel, were forced to use cinnabar pigment. This red they also used to highlight elements of their three-dimensional work, such as the ears and mouths of lions (Fig. 39). Since it was not enamel it has sadly proved extremely fugitive.

BIBLIOGRAPHY: B. Cellini (trans. C.R. Ashbee), *The Treatises of Benvenuto Cellini on Goldsmithing and Sculpture* (New York 1967, unabridged republication of the 1888 edition), p. 10. On Pausias see M. Robertson, *A History of Greek Art* (Cambridge 1975), p. 486.

FIGURE 39 Detail from a bracelet said to be from northern Greece, showing the use of black and white enamel for the eyes and red cinnabar in the mouths and ears of the lions' heads (New York 57.11.9).

1   The Greek Mainland and Islands

The bright world of Bronze Age Greece, with its palace-based civilis-
ation and the golden splendour of its Shaft Graves at Mycenae, collapsed
at the end of the twelfth century BC. Initially there was severe depopu-
lation, and it was really only in the eighth century that numbers began
to rise again. In artistic terms much of the impetus came from the east.
This began as early as in the eleventh century, as the new finds at Lef-
kandi on Euboea have revealed, and continued intermittently until the
beginning of the sixth century BC. The Euboeans were, indeed, the first
adventurers to cross the sea. In about 800 BC they went east to the
northern shores of Syria, to Al Mina, and possibly at about the same
date began to travel westwards, soon to found a colony at Pithekoussai
on Ischia just off the coast of central Italy.

In mainland Greece a network of fiercely independent city-states
(*poleis*) developed. They were each dominated by a body of free male
citizens that wielded military, political and religious power. Athens,
Corinth and Knossos on Crete were early centres of wealth, and it
is possible that, alongside a continuing local tradition, some eastern
craftsmen, perhaps Phoenicians, emigrated to these cities and produced
jewellery of high quality there. By the seventh century the focus of
jewellery-making seems to have passed to the islands, and important
finds have been discovered on Melos, Thera and Delos. There were
close links at this period with some of the cities of East Greece, notably
those on Rhodes.

The sixth century was a period of artistic brilliance, but there is little
early Archaic jewellery from which to form an opinion of the craft's
status, except perhaps a small group of gold pieces in the Stathatos
collection which are said to be from Argos. They are usually dated to
the mid-seventh century BC, but are more probably works of the early
sixth century, as is part of a similar bronze earring from Olympia.
Representations on sculpture, vases and terracottas give us some insights,
although it should be noted that we cannot really be sure whether we
are looking at representations of gold, silver or bronze jewellery, or
even at items of more perishable material. Certainly, if there was much
gold jewellery around during the sixth century in mainland Greece, it
must almost all have gone back into the melting pot.

The second half of the sixth century, however, is marked by a sudden
blossoming in northern Greece. The cemetery at Sindos, near Thessaloniki, has produced a wealth of gold jewellery to match recent finds
from Lydia in Asia Minor. Grave 28 at Sindos belongs to about the
middle of the century, while graves 20, 48 and 67 date from the last
quarter. Similar jewellery has been found elsewhere in Macedonia, in
particular at Aiani, and all these examples have connections with material
from further north, especially Trebenishte.

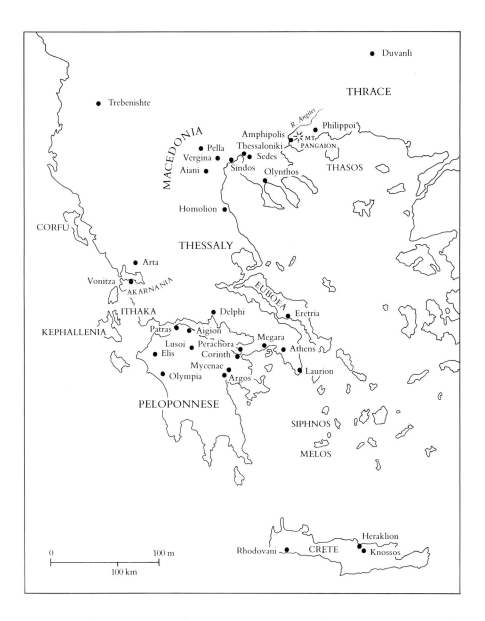

The fifth century saw the Persian invasion and its repulsion. It saw, too, Athens move from being the leader of a group of allies with a common enemy to become the ruler of a tribute-paying maritime empire. The wealth of this empire was made visible by Perikles' building programme, which culminated in the Parthenon. There seems, however, little evidence for such wealth in the private sphere, at least as it is represented by gold jewellery placed in tombs. The reason may be that there was no surplus of gold in the private sector, or that the apparent sumptuary restrictions on elaborate funerary monuments extended to the offerings of gold jewellery placed within the tomb. That gold was available for jewellery, at least in the north, is demonstrated by the series of tumuli at Duvanli in central Bulgaria, which date from the second quarter of the century to its end. There, the forms seem local, although the workmanship might suggest an original impetus from Greek craftsmen.

Whatever the cause, it is really only in the second half of the fifth century that we begin to find groups of jewellery in Greece itself. This is usually of bronze or silver, such as the material from Olympia, Halae and Elis (no. 6). From the end of the fifth century comes a particularly rich series of graves at Eretria, now divided between Athens, London (nos 3 and 9) and Berlin, which included necklaces, earrings and rings. In addition, there are some scattered finds, such as the pair of spectacular pins said to be from Patras or Aigion and now in Boston, an earring in Berlin which is said to be from Corinth and a pair of earrings from Koutsomita near Arta in central Greece.

These pieces give us only a very imperfect idea of what fifth-century Greek gold jewellery might have been like. Although it is difficult to explain this widespread dearth of gold jewellery, one might seek to understand the rich finds at Eretria in the light of the small colony that seems to have been sent out from Athens, following continued opposition from the oligarchs there. This might explain the high number of Athenian white-ground *lekythoi* from the cemetery, for such vessels are very rare outside Athens itself, and might indicate that the jewellery preserved in the tombs was made for the Athenian settlers.

The Peloponnesian War slowly brought Athens to her knees. Her surrender in 404 BC, although it no doubt brought economic hardship, fostered the determination to regain what had been lost. It also provided the impetus for a general diaspora of Athenian craftsmen, including architects, sculptors, potters and goldsmiths. The results of this may perhaps be seen in the establishment of goldsmiths' workshops at Taranto in South Italy, in the eastern Greek cities on Rhodes and the mainland opposite, and at Pantikapaion in the Bosporan kingdom on the northern shore of the Black Sea.

The first half of the fourth century found the principal Greek cities still locked in struggle and the old hatred of Persia still unspent. The rise of Macedon, however, was to change all that, as its rulers Philip II and Alexander the Great altered for ever the balance of power. Philip came to the throne in 359 BC. Already by 356 he had secured the gold-rich mining area of the Angites river and Mount Pangaion by the founding of Philippoi, a colony on the site of an earlier city called Krenides. This was to release an explosion of goldworking in northern Greece. The results are evident in the numerous finds of Greek gold jewellery from Macedonia (nos 17, 30–34) and Thessaly (37). It seems very probable that many Greek jewellers were drawn to the Macedonian capital to work for Philip and his successors. It is, indeed, quite likely that the Macedonian court now became the leader in jewellery fashions. New and improved motifs which began to appear in the second half of the fourth century are very likely to have been developed in these workshops, for example the beech-nut pendant, the acanthus leaf and the Herakles knot.

Fourth-century jewellery from elsewhere in mainland Greece, however, is scarce. There is the myrtle spray and necklace from Athens (nos 10 and 14), a fine necklace from a hoard at Corinth which may in fact be a product of a Macedonian workshop, a brooch from Patras (no. 24), a diadem and necklace said to be from Melos (nos 18 and 22), and earrings said to be from Crete (no. 24). No clear picture, however, really emerges, and it is difficult to identify any individual goldsmiths or workshops.

BIBLIOGRAPHY: In general see Higgins *GRJ²*, pp. 121–34 and 153–72; Higgins in Barr-Sharrar and Borza, pp. 141–6; Deppert-Lippitz, *passim*. Stathatos group from Argos: *Stathatos*, nos 42–5, pl. 10. Olympia earring: *Olympia* XIII, no. 415. Sindos: *Sindos, passim*. Aiani: G. Karamitrou-Mentesidi, *Aiani of Kozani* (Thessaloniki), figs 29–32. Trebenishte: L. Popovic, *Katalog nalaza iz Nekropole kod Trebenista* (Belgrade 1956). Duvanli: B.D. Filow, *Die Grabhügelnekropole bei Duvanlij in Südbulgarien* (Sofia 1934). Olympia: *Olympia* XIII, esp. nos 416–21. Halae: *AJA* 19 (1915), p. 425, fig. 2. Boston pins: Hoffmann and Davidson, nos 69–70. Corinth (Berlin): Greifenhagen II, pl. 38, 12–13. Koutsomita: *ArchReps*, 1955, p. 19, fig. 16. For the jewellery from Eretria see the introduction to no. 9; *AA* 1931, p. 114, fig. 4 (Athens); Greifenhagen II, pl. 4, 1–2 (Berlin); Higgins *GRJ²*, pl. 26 (Athens). Corinth necklace: *Corinth* XII, pl. 109.

1 Gold ring with movable circular box-bezel

Probably from Corfu
About 500 BC
Diameter of box 1.3 cm, height of box 0.6 cm, width of hoop 2.8 cm; weight 9.8 g
British Museum GR 1866.5-4.57; bequeathed by James Woodhouse

This large, man-sized ring consists of a drum-like box-bezel which is free to rotate on the gold rod hoop. The top face of the bezel bears a plain wire rosette with a central grain and has a beaded wire border. The underside of the bezel has a chased depiction of a griffin, skilfully rendered to fit the circular form precisely. Across the griffin is the inscription DAMO, written in reverse. The side wall of the bezel has a serpentine pattern in plain wire. The ring is equipped with a plain hoop; a wire passes through the box-bezel and wraps around the ends.

1

1

This is the earliest box-bezel ring in gold. The idea gained particular popularity in the fourth century BC (nos 136 and 143). The direction of the script and the inscription itself, Doric Greek for 'the people', suggests that the ring was an official seal.

BIBLIOGRAPHY: *BMCR* 41; J. Boardman, *AK* 10 (1967), P 9, pl. 7; Boardman *GGFR*, p. 157, pl. 443.

2

2 Gold pendant in the form of an amphora

Said to be from Melos, 1819; Thomas Burgon collection
500–450 BC
Height 2.0 cm; weight 2.3 g
British Museum GR 1842.7-28.107

This pendant of sheet gold takes the form of a handleless pointed amphora. The neck is pierced laterally and there is a tiny lid on top. The lid has a spiral-beaded wire edge and a granule in the centre. There are plain wire tongues on the shoulder and at the base of the amphora, as well as spiral-beaded and plain wires at the top and bottom of the neck. The pointed base is decorated with a spiral-beaded wire and a granule.

The pendant shows signs of wear. It may have been the centrepiece of a simple cord necklace or even the pendant from a ring earring. Other examples of this type of pendant with a separate lid are from Taranto and Athens. There are also Cypriot versions (nos 181–2). Many examples are known in bronze from Olympia and Perachora: these give us an insight into the more ordinary jewellery of the later sixth and fifth centuries BC.

BIBLIOGRAPHY: *BMCJ* 2026. Information on find-spot from drawings by Burgon in the Ashmolean Museum, Oxford. Taranto pendant: Deppert-Lippitz, fig. 64. Athens pendant: *Stathatos*, pls 10 and 51. For amphora pendants as earrings see Deppert-Lippitz, fig. 76; and in sculpture (e.g. Berlin *kore* from Keratea), J. Boardman, *Greek Sculpture: The Archaic Period* (London 1978), fig. 108. Bronze pendants: *OlF* XIII, pp. 366–70; *Perachora*, pp. 176–7.

3 Gold ring with filigree florals

Said to be from Eretria
450–400 BC
Length of bezel 1.7 cm, height of hoop 1.8 cm; weight 4.9 g
British Museum GR 1907.5-1.905; bequeathed by Sir A.W. Franks, 1897

The narrow, pointed bezel of this ring is decorated with a filigree palmette and spirals in fine plain wire. The borders are of beaded and plain wires. The hoop is hammered from the same piece of gold as the bezel and tapers towards the back.

This ring may be compared with a series of fine late fifth-century rings found at Eretria at the end of the last century and the beginning of this. An example from Kourion on Cyprus (no. 164) is also comparable, but it has coarser filigree.

BIBLIOGRAPHY: *BMCR* 905. Eretria rings: K. Kourouniotis, *AM* 38 (1913), pl. 16, 7–10, esp. 9–10.

3

4

4 Gold ring engraved with a figure of Artemis

450–425 BC
Height of bezel 1.8 cm, height of hoop 1.6 cm;
    weight 4.0 g
British Museum GR 1914.10-17.2

On the pointed oval bezel is engraved the standing figure of the goddess Artemis. She is dressed in a short *chiton* and an animal skin, with one breast left bare. There seems to be a *chlamys* over the back of her shoulders. She also wears soft boots and a necklace with pendants. She holds a pair of spears in her right hand and a *phiale* over the corner of an altar. There are two simple ground lines. The hoop, which appears to be a separate piece of gold soldered to the ends of the bezel, tapers towards the back.

BIBLIOGRAPHY: Higgins *GRJ*, pl. 24c; Boardman *GGFR*, p. 216, pl. 662 (Waterton Group, shape I); *LIMC* II, pl. 519, Artemis no. 981.

5 Gold spiral earring with a rosette

425–400 BC
Height 2.3 cm; weight 4.1 g
British Museum GR 1917.6-1.1648; bequeathed by
    Sir A.W. Franks, 1897

This earring consists of a wire spiral, the ends of which have been worked into a series of mouldings. Set near the top of the spiral is a single large rosette with convex petals and spiral-beaded borders.

This form of earring is a simplification of the type popular on Rhodes in the later seventh century BC. A somewhat similar

5

earring, in silver and possibly later, is in Athens. There the rosette has been replaced by a disc decorated in relief with the head of Athena.

BIBLIOGRAPHY: *BMCJ* 1648; Higgins *GRJ*², pl. 25H. Athens earring: Hadaczek, fig. 23.

6 Pair of silver fibulae and chain

Said to be from Elis
420–400 BC
Length of chain and loops 54.0 cm, length of
    fibulae 7.5 cm; weight 156.5 g
British Museum GR 1904.7-7.1

The fibulae are bow-shaped and have four cog-wheel beads on the arc; each cog-wheel has ten blades. The catch-plates are surmounted by two capstans and decorated with two rows of imitation twisted wire. The hinge-plates are incised with a palmette with an imitation twisted wire above. Traces of the bronze pins remain. Apart from the capstans, the fibulae are solid. The basic forms were possibly cast, but the details and surface are all hand-worked.

The fibulae are linked by a large figure-of-eight loop to a doubled, two-fold loop-in-loop chain with a snake-head terminal at either end. The collars are decorated with two friezes of filigree tongues in plain wire.

Such fibulae are normally found in fours or sixes, and this pair was in fact acquired with a second pair of fibulae to which a snake-head chain was also attached, although all of this chain is lost. It should be noted that the two fibulae exhibited here are not mirror images of each other. This indicates that both were worn near the same shoulder in a complex arrangement probably somewhat similar to that of an elaborate set, complete with all its chains and pendants, from Bukjovci. A somewhat simpler set was recently found at Sindos.

This type of fibula is typical of northern Greece and, if the reported find-spot is correct, these examples would appear to be imports to the western Peloponnese. The form is also found in the fourth century in gold (no. 33).

BIBLIOGRAPHY: *BMCJ* 2845–6; Jacobsthal, *Greek Pins*, fig. 647; *Stathatos* III, fig. 116. Bukjovci fibulae: *Thracian Art*, pls 210–12. Sindos set of four fibulae: *Sindos*, nos 351–2.

Opposite: 6

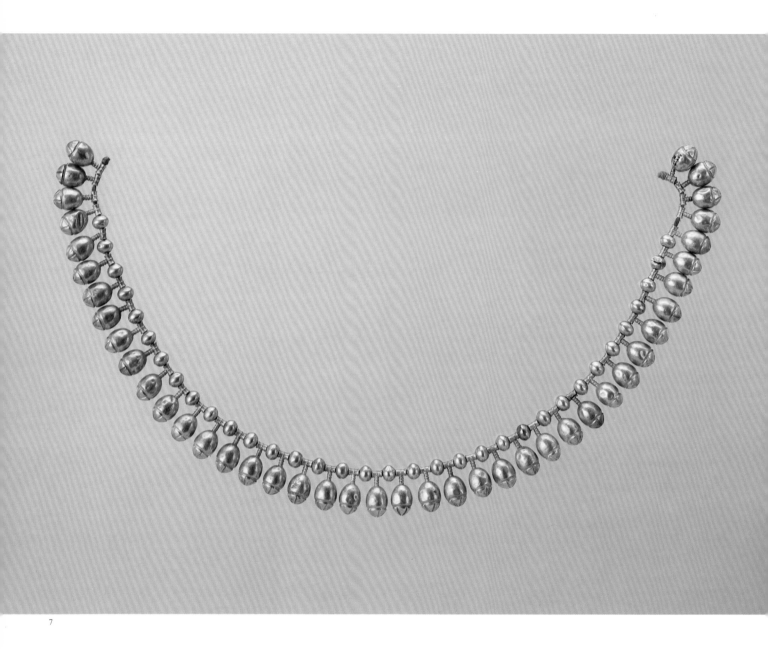

7

7 Gold necklace with myrtle buds

Said to be from Akarnania
450–400 BC
Strung length *c.* 27.0 cm, height of pendant
    1.1 cm; weight 22.2 g
British Museum GR 1919.6-21.2

This unusual necklace consists of forty-two myrtle-bud pendants and thirty-four small, plain spherical beads. The myrtle buds are made from sheet gold, in two halves, and are attached by means of a beaded tube to a horizontal suspension tube. The biconical beads are made in left and right halves.

Buds, as well as flowers, sometimes appear on myrtle wreaths. A necklace with myrtle-bud pendants has been found at Iasos.

BIBLIOGRAPHY: Unpublished. Myrtle wreaths with buds: *Grèce d'Asie*, pl. 19; *BMCJ* 1632 (from Kyme); also the wreath from the Halikarnassos tomb ('Ada', see p. 86). Iasos necklace: *BdA* 49 (1964), p. 208 and pl. 1, 4. Cf. also *Brooklyn*, no. 19.

8

8 Gold lion-head pendant

Said to be from Akarnania
450–400 BC
Height 2.3 cm, diameter of back-plate 1.4 cm;
    weight 2.8 g
British Museum GR 1919.6-21.1

The lion-head is made from sheet gold in die-formed left and right halves. The tongue and teeth have been added separately. The circular back sheet has a round hole in the centre and the joint with the lion-head is decorated with beaded wire. The horizontal suspension tube is mounted on the back of a palmette complex consisting of a cut-out gold sheet decorated with beaded wire palmettes on plain wire spirals.

This lion-head pendant from a necklace may be compared with examples from Rhodes (no. 39) and Cyprus (no. 187). The colour of the gold might suggest that the pendant does not belong to the myrtle-bud necklace acquired with it (no. 7), but the method of suspension is similar and one cannot rule out the possibility that the jeweller might have recycled another piece of jewellery with a different gold content to produce it. Both this pendant and the necklace might, in fact, be products of an East Greek workshop.

BIBLIOGRAPHY: Unpublished.

Eretria Tomb *(no. 9)*

In 1893 the British Museum purchased a small group of objects that were said to have come from a tomb at Eretria. A note in the Departmental Register reveals that above the tomb was said to have been a structure in four steps, the lowest of limestone, the upper ones of marble. Such a structure would most probably have been surmounted by a carved grave relief. The offerings in the tomb included a pair of earrings, an Athenian red-figured *pyxis* that has been placed in the Manner of the Meidias Painter and an ivory stylus.

BIBLIOGRAPHY: The vase is *BMCV* E 775; the stylus, GR 1893.11-2.1. On Classical tombs at Eretria see G.A. Papabasileios, *Peri ton en Euboiai archaion taphon* (Athens 1910), pp. 72–86, and K. Kourouniotes, *AM* 38 (1913), pp. 296–319.

FIGURE 40 Eretria tomb group: Athenian red-figured *pyxis* (British Museum *BMCV* E 775) and ivory stylus (British Museum GR 1893.11-2.1).

9 Pair of gold boat-shaped earrings

Said to come from a tomb at Eretria
420–400 BC
Height 5.6 cm, width of boat 2.2 cm; weight 11.4 and 11.4 g
British Museum GR 1893.11-3.1

The boats are decorated, front and back, with tightly packed filigree designs, consisting of two friezes of double spirals separated by three twisted wires flanked by a beaded wire. The top and bottom contours are bordered with beaded and plain wires, while the terminals have a beaded wire and a row of granules surmounted by a rosette. In the hollow of the boat is a siren, constructed from a die-formed front sheet and a flat back sheet. Suspended from the bottom of the boat by means of rings and loop-in-loop chains are four cockle-shells, made in die-formed front and back halves. Above the boat is a large two-tiered rosette, which is attached to the terminals of the boat by means of a forked wire. The large outer petals are convex; the smaller inner ones are concave and filled with enamel, alternately light and dark (presumably green and blue), and there is a central granule. All the petals have beaded wire borders.

Of the several other elaborate boat-shaped earrings with figures set in the hollow, including no. 11, only the pair from Mogilanskata Mogila has a disc above. The cockle-shell pendants can be paralleled in both the west and the east. As one of the more popular attributes of Aphrodite, the bivalve is a particularly suitable pendant for jewellery.

BIBLIOGRAPHY: *BMCJ* 1653–4; Becatti, no. 295; Miller, pl. 3d; Higgins *GRJ*², pl. 24e; Deppert-Lippitz, fig. 128. Mogilanskata Mogila earrings: *Thracian Art*, pl. 196. For cockle-shell pendants see one in Hamburg (said to be from Ephesus), Deppert-Lippitz, fig. 104; a pair of earrings from South Italy once on the market, Deppert-Lippitz, fig. 126; fragments from the Santa Eufemia Treasure, *BMCJ* 2120.

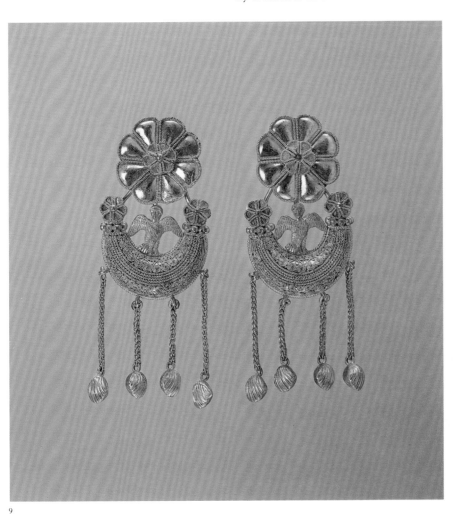

9

The 'Tomb of Aspasia' *(no. 10)*

In 1804 Giovanni Battista Lusieri excavated a tumulus near the Piraeus for Lord Elgin. Elgin himself was later to give it the fanciful name of the Tomb of Aspasia. The tumulus had a circumference of about 250 feet (76 m) and a height of 80 feet (24 m) and was made of fine, tightly packed sand. About 10 feet (3 m) down from the existing top was a large, roughly finished, egg-cup shaped marble vase, which had a plain marble cover (broken in fragments) and contained a large bronze *dinos*. Inside the *dinos* were some burnt bones (returned to the soil by the finders), on which rested a myrtle spray. Outside the marble vase was a large alabaster *alabastron* (not in the British Museum, perhaps still at Broomhall). The *dinos* bears the inscription 'I am one of the prizes of Argive Hera'.

BIBLIOGRAPHY: E. Dodwell, *A Classical and Topographical Tour through Greece*, vol. 1 (London 1819), p. 446; A.H. Smith, *JHS* 36 (1916), p. 258, and *JHS* 46 (1926), pp. 253–7. For the marble vase see *BMCS* III, no. 2415; for its lid, *A Description of the Ancient Marbles in the British Museum*, vol. IX (London 1842), frontispiece and reverse of title page. The bronze *dinos* is GR 1816.6-10.115; for the inscription see L.H. Jeffery, *The Local Scripts of Archaic Greece* (Oxford 1961), p. 170, no. 43 (dated 450–425? BC), and M.L. Lazzarini, *Atti e Memorie della Società Magna Grecia* 1 (1992), pp. 95–7.

FIGURE 41 'Tomb of Aspasia', Athens: bronze *dinos* (British Museum GR 1816.6-10.115).

10 Gold myrtle spray

Said to be from near the Piraeus
400–350 BC
Height as preserved *c.* 9.0 cm; weight 7.2 g
British Museum GR 1960.11-1.48

The stem is made from gold sheet over a bronze core. There are three sizes of leaf: the two larger pairs are pushed into holes in the stem, the smallest pair inserted into the end of the tube. Inserted beside the pair of middle-sized leaves are myrtle flowers on long wire stems. These consist of a cup with a serrated top, a six-petalled flower, and a central rod holding a ring of twenty-four blob-ended stamens and capped with a disc. The discs have an inner and an outer ring of fine spiral-beaded wire, both of which were presumably once filled with enamel.

The end of the spray is crimped, indicating that it was once inserted into something. The presence of a bronze core, however, may suggest that the spray was not part of a full-scale wreath, for these are usually constructed from a hollow gold tube without a bronze core.

Another myrtle spray of similar construction, but with myrtle fruit as well as flowers, was found in central Macedonia. Unfortunately it was a chance find, so nothing more is known of its function.

BIBLIOGRAPHY: A.H. Smith, *JHS* 46 (1926), p. 255, fig. 2. Spray from Macedonia: *Makedonia*, no. 210.

11 Gold boat-shaped earring with a sphinx

375–350 BC
Width 1.6 cm, height 2.5 cm; weight 3.5 g
New York 41.160.418; bequest of W. Gedney Beatty, 1941

This single earring consists of a boat-shaped body decorated with filigree and surmounted by a small seated sphinx. The boat and the sphinx are both made of sheet

10

11

gold in two halves. The two sides of the sphinx, and probably the boat also, were made in dies. The boat is decorated with spiral-beaded filigree forming a central circumscribed palmette below which are spirals and three-leaf palmettes. In places pairs of filigree 'straps' pass over other wires, producing a three-dimensional effect. The joint between the two sides of the boat is concealed by two wires, and the outer edge bears a row of large grains each capped by a smaller grain. The boat

terminals are embellished with filigree collars of plain and beaded wires and pointed tongues. A hollow ribbed bead of spherical shape and topped by a rosette is loosely fitted into the top of one terminal. It probably does not belong.

There are a number of other elaborate boat-shaped earrings of similar date with added figural decoration in the curve of the boat. The most elaborate has a winged hippocamp with a bird on top, but others have a gorgon, a siren (no. 9), a sphinx

or a hippalektryon (part horse, part cockerel). They come from a wide area, but the nearest parallels would seem to be from Greece.

BIBLIOGRAPHY: Unpublished. For earrings with figures above cf. Miller, pls 2 and 3a–b (Homolion J1) and pl. 3e (Boston 60.1508, from Athens); *Baltimore*, no. 237 (Baltimore WAG 57.1733a); *Stathatos* pl. 52 (Athens St. 283); (London market) Christie's, 8 June 1988, lot 94 (said to be from Yugoslavia). See further under no. 9.

12   Pair of gold earrings in the form of an inverted pyramid

Said to have been found in Greece
400–350 BC
Height 3.7 cm; weight 4.0 and 4.1 g
British Museum GR 1920.12-21.5-6

On top of the front of the pyramid is a cut-out sheet in the form of a palmette with spiral-beaded leaves, and on each corner a pile of four grains. The box-like upper section of the pyramid is decorated with a frieze of pairs of running spirals bordered above and below with spiral-beaded and plain wire. Below this are two levels of four globes with grains in the interstices and a vertical strip between pairs of globes. The cone-shaped base is constructed from a coil of spiral-beaded wire and terminates in two small globes separated by three grains. The hook ends in the front with a snake's head.

The basic form of these earrings has a long history, probably from the early sixth century down into the Hellenistic period. The simpler, and often earlier, pieces lack a disc or other element above. Many simple bronze examples have been found at Lusoi, Olympia and Olynthus (cf. Fig. 1). A pair of gold earrings from Amphipolis and a pair once on the Geneva market are particularly close to the pair exhibited here.

BIBLIOGRAPHY: Sotheby's, 7 December 1920, lot 248; Higgins *GRJ*[2], pl. 25f. On the form of earring see Hadaczek, pp. 27–31. Bronze examples: (Lusoi) *ÖJh* 4 (1901), p. 54, fig. 91; (Olympia) *OlF* XIII, pp. 120–25; (Olynthus) *Olynthus* X, pp. 79–81. Gold earrings from Amphipolis: *Thesauroi*, no. 381. Geneva market: Habsburg, Feldman, 14 May 1990, no. 266.

13   Gold boat-shaped earring with a rosette

400–350 BC
Height 3.3 cm; weight 4.8 g
British Museum GR 1917.6-1.1659; bequeathed by
    Sir A.W. Franks, 1897

This boat-shaped earring is formed in two halves from sheet gold and is decorated with a central vertical spiral-beaded wire flanked on either side by a plain wire. Two large granules are soldered onto the bottom of the hull of the boat. A large

12

two-level rosette, the lower level being really an amalgam of a rosette with a lotus at the top and bottom, is attached to the outer side of one terminal, making it the front of the earring. The petals are all bordered in spiral-beaded wire. The boat has plain and spiral-beaded wire collars; the hook is now missing.

There is a virtually identical earring in Berlin (ex Gans collection) and Greifenhagen wondered if it might be the pair to the London example. There is, however, another singleton in the Heraklion Museum on Crete, which could equally be the pair, for Franks bought jewellery from T.B. Sandwith, one-time Consul on Crete.

BIBLIOGRAPHY: *BMCJ* 1659; Greifenhagen II, figs 4–5. Berlin earring (ex Gans): Greifenhagen II, pl. 38, 10–11. Heraklion Museum earring: unpublished.

13

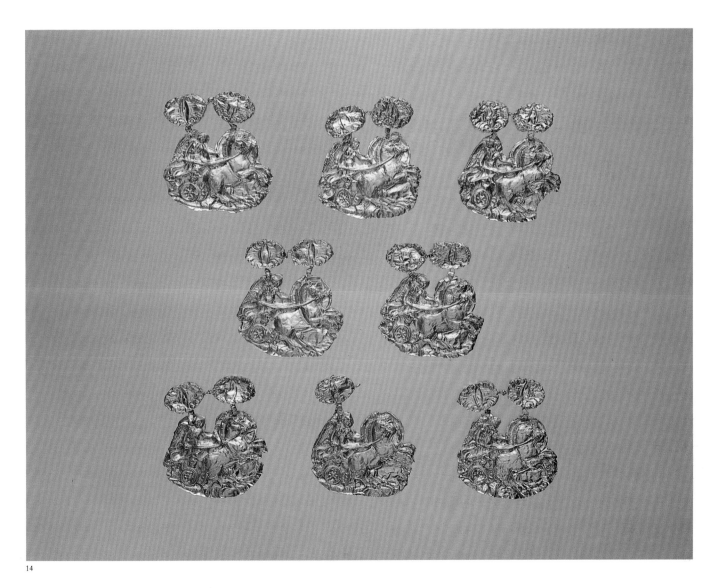

14

14 Gold necklace with pendants showing Nike in a chariot

Said to be from Athens
400–350 BC
Length of each chariot pendant 4.0 cm, length of each oval unit 1.5 cm; weight of each section 2.2 g
British Museum GR 1909.7-10.1 a–h; presented by Sir Henry Howorth, KCIE, through the National Art Collections Fund

Eight units of this unusual necklace have been preserved. Each consists of a cut-out gold sheet with a die-formed design of Nike wearing a *chiton* and driving a two-horse chariot, suspended by gold ribbon wires from two die-formed oval box-like units (sides bent over, but no backs) decorated with a pair of addorsed palmettes. A gold wire links the two ovals together and similar wires probably linked the complete units to each other.

The Nike reliefs have a number of tiny additional attachment holes: behind the chariots, between the horses' back legs and the chariot wheel, between the horses' front and back legs, in front of the horses' chests, above the horses' heads and behind Nike's head. These suggest that they were originally stitched directly onto leather or fabric, like the many East Greek (nos 56–7) and North Pontic appliqués (nos 72–4, 78–80, 90–92, 127–9). They were perhaps converted into a necklace at the time of the death of their owner by the addition of the flimsy palmette units above.

BIBLIOGRAPHY: *BMCJ* 1983*.

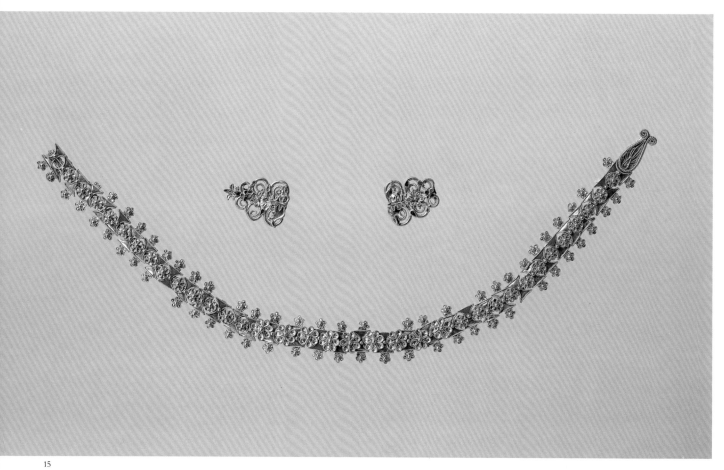

15

15 Gold rosette and 'double axe' necklace and two floral ornaments

400–350 BC
Present length 22.5 cm, height of florals 1.9 cm; weight of necklace 14.6 g, weight of spiral units 1.8 and 1.8 g
British Museum GR 1891.6-27.1 a and b

The necklace consists of rosettes alternating with 'double axe' units. The latter are rimmed with spiral-beaded wire and filled with green enamel. At the centre is a grain, and attached to the edge of each 'blade' is a small rosette. The rosette units are, as preserved, of two sizes (nine units of seven petals; twenty-five units of six petals). All have concave petals with spiral-beaded wire borders, and all a central grain. There are traces of blue enamel in one of the smaller type. One terminal-like element is preserved, attached to a 'double axe' unit. It is of droplet shape and is decorated with a filigree palmette bounded by spiral-beaded wire ending in spirals. Both the rosettes and the 'double axes' have double threading tubes on the back.

The two floral elements do not belong to the necklace, nor do they have any clear means of attachment. Nevertheless, they were acquired with the necklace, and the wire and condition suggest that they may belong to the same *parure*. Each consists of three pairs of spirals topped by a small palmette, the heart of which is blue and the leaves green. At the bottom are acanthus leaves, the central one filled with green enamel, the outer ones with blue. In the centre is a rosette, and at the top a smaller one with alternately green and blue petals. There are also droplets on either side of the central rosette, the lower pair blue, the upper pair green. The filigree, rosettes and spirals are of spiral-beaded wire.

This beautiful and delicate necklace is a variation on the rosette and lotus-palmette scheme (nos 94 and 135), the lotus-palmettes here being replaced with 'double axes'.

BIBLIOGRAPHY: *BMCJ* 1951; M. Pfrommer, *IstMitt* 36 (1986), p. 67, n. 41.

16 Gold ring with intaglio of Kassandra

Said to be from Greece
400–380 BC
Height of bezel 2.0 cm, width 1.5 cm; weight 16.1 g
New York 53.11.2; Rogers Fund, 1953

This heavy gold ring is elegantly proportioned, with a rounded hoop of triangular section which rises to a flat oval bezel. It is decorated with a finely chased and shallow-engraved depiction of Kassandra kneeling before the Palladion, the cult statue of Athena in Troy.

Kassandra, the daughter of King Priam, has taken refuge in the sanctuary of Athena. She has one arm round the

15

16

statue's lower legs, while the other hand holds up her cloak, which is delicately stippled. She wears a belted *chiton* and her left breast is bare. The latter is the most direct allusion to her imminent rape by Ajax the Locrian, but her upturned face and loose cloak add to the sense of her vulnerability. Athena wears a helmet with a triple crest, her aegis over her chest and a shield with a star as its blazon, and wields a spear. From the shield hangs a remarkable stiff fillet which terminates in a tripartite form that calls to mind a trident. There is a hatched ground line, and Kassandra's name is inscribed behind her head. The reversed lettering indicates that the ring was intended to be used as a seal.

Rings with such elaborate narrative scenes taken from mythology are very rare.

BIBLIOGRAPHY: Richter, no. 80, pl. 14; Boardman *GGFR*, pl. 709 and p. 222 (shape v, Kassandra Group); *MMA Greece and Rome*, p. 78, no. 58.

17

17 Gold ring with intaglio of a naked woman

Said to be from Macedonia
400–380 BC
Height of bezel 2.0 cm, width of bezel 1.9 cm,
    height of hoop 2.3 cm, width 1.9 cm; weight
    15.80 g
New York 06.1124; Rogers Fund, 1906

This elegant heavy gold ring has a flat, oval bezel which is chased and engraved with a naked girl who stands facing right, her hands behind her head, stretching back. Behind her stands a *klismos*, over which is slung some drapery. Her hair is tied up in a top-knot; her right foot is seen in three-quarter view; one breast is frontal, the other in profile. The hoop is diamond-shaped in section.

This type of ring was typically hammered out of solid gold, not cast. Although seemingly of simple form, the production of such rings required as much, if not more, technical mastery than elaborate sheet-metal and filigree ornaments. There is a platinum-group metal inclusion between the woman's ankles.

BIBLIOGRAPHY: *BMetrMus* 2 (1907), p. 123, no. 4, fig. 2; Alexander, fig. 119; Richter, no. 77; Boardman *GGFR*, pl. 710 (shape v, Kassandra Group: cf. no. 16). The inclusion consists of 45% ruthenium, 31% osmium and 24% iridium (analysis by Dick Stone).

18

18

18 Gold diadem of twisted ribbons with a Herakles knot

Said to be from Melos
300–280 BC
Length 27.9 cm; weight 32.7 g
British Museum GR 1872.6-4.815

The arms of this unusual diadem consist of three long sheets of gold twisted to form ribbons. The central ribbon has a rosette on each frontal plane: the petals are convex with spiral-beaded wire borders and contain traces of enamel. The terminals take the form of simple sheet-gold caps with spiral-beaded and plain wires around the edge. The rings attached to the top edge of the terminals are modern: the remains of the original loops have been filed off.

In the centre is a Herakles knot with a circular garnet in the very middle. The bands of the knot are decorated with seven twisted wire ropes and six small rosettes, their petals filled alternately with green and blue enamel. A spiral of thick plain wire lies at each corner of the joint between knot and collar. The collars are decorated with spiral-beaded, plain and rope filigree. In addition, there are three rows of scales, alternately filled with green and blue enamel (see Fig. 6). At the junction with the twisted ribbons there is a row of cut-out darts. The garnet may be a replacement.

This is a particularly remarkable diadem. The twisted ribbons are most closely paralleled on what are normally con-sidered to be a pair of armbands in the British Museum. They are in fact most probably the flanking parts of a very similar diadem, bent to form bracelet-like elements, with consequent deformation of the ribbons (the lion-head terminals probably belong and may have framed a central Herakles knot, as on no. 131). Single twisted ribbons also occur on a series of armbands.

BIBLIOGRAPHY: *BMCJ* 1607; Higgins *GRJ*², pl. 45A; *Seven Thousand Years of Jewellery*, fig. 186 (opp. p. 85); Pfrommer, pl. 9, 3 (HK 31). Bracelets: *BMCJ* 1991–2. Single twisted ribbons: (Mottola armband) Deppert-Lippitz, fig. 168; (Mt Pangaion armband) Greifenhagen I, pl. 12, 2, now lost; (von Aulock hoard armbands) *Baltimore*, no. 267.

19

two square sheet-gold plates separated by grains and decorated on the upper part with small pyramids of grains.

The numerous components of this earring are all soldered together without recourse to mechanical joints, except for the strings, which are merely twisted into place. This type of construction differs from that of such pieces as the elaborate boat earrings (e.g. nos 88–9). This earring has often been compared with the Ganymede earrings (no. 31) and even attributed to the same workshop.

BIBLIOGRAPHY: E. Robinson, *BMetrMus* 4 (1909), pp. 44–5; Alexander, fig. 61; B. Segall, *BMusFA* 40 (1942), pp. 50–54 with figs 4 and 6; Hoffmann and Davidson, p. 82, fig. 12e; *Search for Alexander, NY Suppl.*, no. S 61.

20 Pair of gold earrings with disc and Eros

Said to be from Rhodovani, Crete (found *c.* 1902)
About 300 BC
Height 10.4 and 9.5 cm; weight 5.85 and 5.75 g
New York 30.116.1-2; gift of Mrs Albert M. Lythgoe, 1930

The disc has a flat rim decorated with concentric circles of decorative wires (beaded, plain and twisted) and a central bowl in which is set a large, central two-tier rosette made up of thin rounded leaves. In the very centre is a wire ring that originally held an enamel inlay.

The Erotes, which are mirror images of each other, are suspended from a thick beaded wire hoop soldered to their heads. They are shown naked, with wide, fluttering cloaks behind them, and wear their hair tied up in a knot on the crown of the head. Each holds a jug in one hand and a *phiale* in the other. They are each made of sheet gold in two halves (front and back); the arms, long raised wings and cloaks are added separately. The wings are each made from a thin sheet of gold with an impressed and chased feather design, soldered onto a flat sheet-gold backing plate.

The earrings have been repaired in modern times and have new wire hooks. At the end of the last century and the

19 Earring in the form of a palmette and a siren playing a kithara

330–300 BC
Height 4.4 cm; weight 7.3 g
New York 08.258.49; Rogers Fund, 1908

This single earring is a masterpiece of miniature sculpture, its static pose giving it much power and presence.

The upper part consists of a two-tier palmette. In the centre is a rosette, behind which is a nine-leaf palmette, and behind that a ten-leaf palmette with a small rosette on the central leaf. The palmette leaves and rosettes are of sheet metal bordered by spiral-beaded wire and may once have been enamelled, although no traces now remain. To the back of the palmette complex is soldered a gold wire hook terminating in a simply formed snake-head.

The gold figure of the siren is made in two halves, front and back, from sheet gold. Details such as the tail, legs, diadem, grain earrings, plektron and kithara are made separately and soldered in place. Even the kithara on the siren's left arm, with its integral beaded cross-piece, is made in thin sheet gold from back and front halves. The three surviving kithara strings are separately made gold wires just 0.1 mm in diameter – about the thinnest Greek gold wire recorded. The siren's large wings are each made from sheet gold. There are chased feathers on her legs, and her feet have three claws and a spur. She stands on a plinth composed of

20

beginning of this, a number of rich tombs containing jewellery were discovered in the western part of Crete.

BIBLIOGRAPHY: C. Alexander, *BMetrMus* 26 (1931), pp. 22–3; Oliver, fig. 17.

21 Gold earring pendant in the form of a Nike with a trophy

About 300 BC
Height 3.4 cm; weight 7.1 g
British Museum GR 1917.6-1.1851; bequeathed by
    Sir A.W. Franks, 1897

The figure of Nike is made up from several components soldered together. She wears a *chiton* belted at the waist and with an overfold that reaches to the groin. Her left breast is bare and the *chiton* is split from the upper thigh. In her right hand is the end of a pole to which a cuirass is attached; her left hand is raised, perhaps steadying the helmet that is now missing from the top of the trophy and that partially hid the link to the upper part of the earring. The thick, chased sheet-gold wings are soldered into slots cut into the shoulder-blades of the figure.

This is a particularly fine earring pendant. The sensitive modelling of the forms beneath the drapery and the vital twist in the figure's pose are both very effective. Another earring with a pendant in the form of Nike holding a trophy is in Oxford: it is rather later.

BIBLIOGRAPHY: *BMCJ* 1851. Oxford earring: *LIMC* VI, *sv* Nike, no. 423, pl. 592.

21

22

22

22 Gold strap necklace with seed-like pendants

Said to be from Melos
330–300 BC
Length 33.6 cm; weight 66.4 g
British Museum GR 1872.6-4.660

This necklace consists of a gold 'strap' chain of three doubled loop-in-loop chains interlinked. Attached alternately along the lower edge of the strap are two-tier rosettes and ivy leaves filled with green enamel and with a blue disc below. These support a festoon of small and large seed-like pendants. The small pendants are plain; the large ones are ribbed and have a grain at the apices and interstices of the zigzag calyx on the top. Above the smaller pendants are discs which have a blue enamel outer zone and perhaps green centres; above the large pendants are rosettes.

This necklace was repaired by Alessandro Castellani in the 1860s or 1870s. He reattached the terminals and replaced missing rosettes, leaf motifs, chains and pendants. His work can be identified on the basis of the techniques used and by the way in which his elements have discoloured.

This necklace is very close to the example from Asia Minor (no. 68): they may even be from the same workshop.

BIBLIOGRAPHY: *BMCJ* 1947; Ruxer, pl. 20, 5; Higgins *GRJ*[2], pl. 49b.

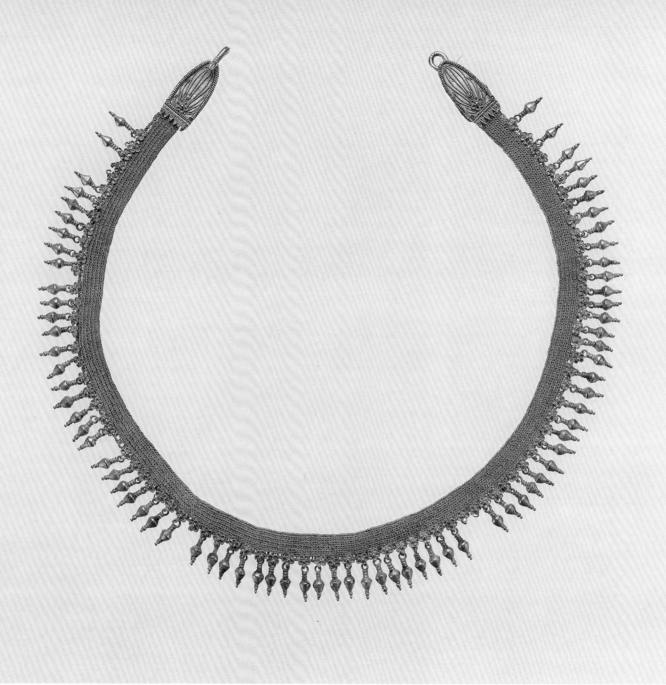

23

23 Gold strap necklace with seed-shaped pendants

From the de Massoneau collection
About 300 BC
Length 25.3 cm, length of terminal 2.2 cm;
    weight 42.4 g
New York 22.139.47; Rogers Fund, 1922

The strap is formed from five doubled loop-in-loop chains with double interlinking. The wires forming the links are just 0.2 mm in diameter, exemplifying the astonishing intricacy and complexity of strap assembly. To the lower edge of the strap is attached a fringe of rosettes from which hang simple seed-shaped pendants.

Eighty-three rosettes and seventy-five seeds are preserved. The seeds have corrugated necks and their bases terminate in two grains. As is usual, the rosettes are attached to the strap by mechanical means, not soldered.

The terminals, which have a hook and eye fastening, are of the usual tongue shape with beaded wire borders, and are decorated with palmettes in spiral-beaded wire filigree with pointed, incurving leaves and a central rosette with a small disc above. There are two small discs at the base, and a row of cut-out darts projects over the strap. The terminals are

attached to the strap by means of gold wires which pass through the terminals and bend back along their sides.

Areas of the strap have a very fused surface, suggesting that this necklet was once in a fire – probably a funerary pyre.

Much of the jewellery in the de Massoneau collection came from the North Pontic region, but not all. Necklaces with similar pendants are known from several regions of the Greek world, including Greece and South Italy.

BIBLIOGRAPHY: Alexander, fig. 10.

24 Gold pediment-shaped brooch

Said to be from Patras
340–320 BC
Length 7.8 cm; weight 16.68 g
New York 06.1159; Rogers Fund, 1906

This remarkable object gains most of its effect from the calligraphic use of filigree wire on its large flat surface. There are now no traces of enamel, but this may well have added the further dimension of colour.

The pediment is decorated with a group of three acanthus leaves from which spring spiral tendrils supporting five palmettes and two flowers. The main spirals are made from round wires doubled back on themselves, soldered together and then hammered slightly flat prior to attachment. The upper border of the pediment, the *sima*, takes the form of a row of large grains surmounted by small grains with an ovolo pattern below. The architrave below the pediment consists of a frieze of spirals made up from double wires with omega-shaped bud infills, framed above and below with plain and heavy beaded wires.

The central *akroterion* bears a similar floral complex, but less elaborate. The corner *akroteria* take the form of the foreparts of a winged horse supported by a three-cornered Ionic volute capital, only one of which remains. The horses are made in left and right halves, with legs and wings added separately (a corrugated tube separates the legs).

The back sheet is plain, and there are remains of the silver spring and clasp. The presence of column capitals under the bodies of the Pegasoi suggests that there might have been a full façade beneath the pediment, but there are no traces of attachment for any such structure.

BIBLIOGRAPHY: *BMetrMus* 2 (1907), p. 123, no. 7, and p. 125, fig. 6; Alexander, fig. 92; Richter *Handbook*, fig. 128g; Jacobsthal *Greek Pins*, p. 69, n. 3; *Search for Alexander, NY Suppl.*, no. s 57. From Patras (or Aigion) are also said to come the two elaborate gold pins in Boston: see Hoffmann and Davidson, nos 69–70; for the vases found with them, Jacobsthal *Greek Pins*, figs 280–81.

24

25 Silver ram-head bracelet

Said to have been found near Pella
About 350 BC
Width 5.8 cm, height 5.0 cm; weight 94 g
New York 1989.281.73; gift of Norbert
 Schimmel Trust, 1989

This beautiful little bracelet was probably designed for the wrist of a small woman, rather than a child. It consists of a hoop which is seemingly in one piece but chased to represent three silver rods twisted together. At either end are rams' heads with plain collars. Traces of gilding remain on the heads, but apparently not on the hoop; the fleece is indicated by small lunate punch marks. The hoop was once decorated with lengths of beaded silver wire which lay along the valleys, but only one short piece is now preserved; the recesses drilled into the ends of the hoop at the collars for the attachment of these wires also remain.

A somewhat similar silver bracelet, and of similar dimensions, is in the Stathatos collection in Athens.

BIBLIOGRAPHY: H. Hoffmann (ed.), *The Beauty of Ancient Art: Classical Antiquity, Near East, Egypt* (Mainz 1964), no. 34; Hoffmann and Davidson, no. 58; O. White Muscarella (ed.), *Ancient Art: The Norbert Schimmel Collection* (Mainz 1974), no. 70; J. Settgast and U. Gehrig (eds), *Von Troja bis Amarna: The Norbert Schimmel Collection, New York* (Mainz 1978), no. 95; Deppert-Lippitz, fig. 141; Pfrommer, TA 133; *BMetrMus* 49 (1992), p. 61, no. 68. Stathatos bracelet: *Stathatos*, no. 275, pl. 51.

25

26 Silver snake-head bracelet

Said to be from Vonitza, Akarnania
350–300 BC
Diameter *c.* 7.0 cm; weight 131.8 g
British Museum GR 1905.11-1.2

This bracelet consists of a silver rod twisted into nearly six complete turns. Its incised decoration includes a scale-like pattern, an ivy chain and, in the centre, a pair of addorsed palmettes. It is also carefully inscribed with the name KLETIOS. The spacing of the letters and their decorative character suggests that the inscription was added by the jeweller at the time of construction. Kletios might be the pur-

26

chaser's name, but the wearer of such a bracelet is very unlikely to have been a man and the nominative case is commonly used by gem engravers for their signatures. It is therefore probable that this is a very rare example of a jeweller's signature.

BIBLIOGRAPHY: *BMCJ* 2775.

27/28

27 Silver serpentine bracelet

Said to be from Akarnania
350–300 BC
Width 7.4 cm; weight 52.25 g
New York 06.1085; Rogers Fund, 1906

This most unusual bracelet is made from
one piece of hammered silver, the ends of
which have been turned into snakes that
form a Herakles knot at the back and
slither forwards along the hoop. The front
is decorated with silver filigree applied to
a separate sheet. The filigree work takes
the form of a pair of addorsed circumscribed palmettes, with a further pair of
palmettes beyond. All the spirals end in a
granule of silver. At the very centre is a
ball of silver which has been gilded.

Far less silver than gold jewellery has
been preserved, making this bracelet by
its very nature exceptional. Nevertheless,
nothing else in silver of such complex
design has survived, except a pair of lion-
head bracelets in the Metropolitan
Museum of Art. Most of the known silver
jewellery has come from northern Greece;
perhaps it was more popular there, or it
may be related to the abundance of silver
coinage in the area.

BIBLIOGRAPHY: BMetrMus 2 (1907), p. 124,
no. 9; Alexander, fig. 79. New York bracelets
(06.1163–4): Alexander, fig. 78.

28 Plain silver ring with gold stud

Said to be from Akarnania
350–300 BC
Height 2.2 cm; weight 7.50 g
New York 06.1083; Rogers Fund, 1906

This plain ring of silver, with its gilded
ball in the centre, is clearly from the same
workshop as no. 27. The two pieces are
also linked by their condition and reported
find-spot.

BIBLIOGRAPHY: BMetrMus 2 (1907), p. 124,
no. 10.

29 Gold ring with a flying Eros

Said to be from Kephallenia
330–300 BC
Width of bezel 1.2 cm, width of hoop 1.5 cm;
    weight 4.9 g
British Museum GR 1867.5-8.414

This small ring, suitable for a girl or a
small woman, has an almost circular,
slightly convex bezel and a D-section
hoop. The bezel shows Eros flying to the
left, holding a wreath out in both hands.
There is a dotted ground line, below and
above which is written CHAIRE (rejoice).
The ring appears to be hammered from
a single piece of gold and has occasional
platinum-group metal inclusions.

Rings of this form are characteristically
engraved with a figure of Eros, and it is
probable that they were designed as love-
gifts. The typically shallow engraving and
the direction of the inscriptions, when
present, show that they were not intended
as signets.

BIBLIOGRAPHY: BMCR 102.

29

The Ganymede Group *(nos 30–34)*

The pieces which make up this group of jewellery were said to have been found together in Macedonia, in the hinterland of Thessaloniki, some time before 1913. The group first surfaced in the hands of the dealer Ritsos, who sold it to E. von Gans; it then passed to the Galerie Bachstitz, from which it was acquired for the Metropolitan Museum in 1937.

The assemblage in New York forms an impressive *parure* – earrings, necklace, fibulae, bracelets and a ring – but one cannot really be sure that the pieces belong together, for they do not show a clear stylistic uniformity. Another pair of fibulae, however, formerly in the Gans collection, very probably does belong to the group, for such fibulae seem to have been worn in sets of six. One is in Berlin, the other remained with the Gans family.

BIBLIOGRAPHY: R. Zahn, *Amtliche Berichte* (Berlin Museums) 35 (1913–14), p. 73; R. Zahn, *Galerie Bachstitz* 2 (1921), pp. 25–7, pls 22–3; G.M.A. Richter, *BMetrMus* 32 (1937), pp. 290–95; Becatti, pl. 105; Segall, pl. 45; *Search for Alexander, NY Suppl.*, nos s1–10; Higgins in Barr-Sharrar and Borza, p. 144, fig. 9; Pfrommer, FK 106. For the other fibulae see no. 33.

30 Gold strap necklace with beech-nut pendants

Said to be from near Thessaloniki
About 300 BC
Length 33.0 cm, height 2.1 cm, length of section
   with beech nuts 23.0 cm; weight 37.8 g
New York 37.11.8; Harris Brisbane Dick Fund,
   1937

The strap is made up of three doubled loop-in-loop chains with double interlinking and a fringe of beech-nut pendants. The terminals take the form of an ivy or vine leaf and have a border of beaded wire and a rosette in the centre. They end in plain wire loops for attachment and are joined to the strap by means of transverse gold wires, which are bent back along the terminals' sides. The pendants each consist of a rosette with a three-lobed beech nut below. Fifty-nine beech nuts are preserved, of a probable total of sixty-six.

The unusual shape of the terminals is similar to those on a pair of necklaces perhaps from Mottola and a necklace in Naples. Strap necklaces with beech-nut pendants have been found in many areas of the Greek world, including South Italy, Asia Minor (no. 53) and the North Pontic region (nos 106 and 123).

BIBLIOGRAPHY: See introduction to group. Mottola necklaces: *Taranto*, no. 151; Pfrommer, pl. 10, 1. Naples necklace: Siviero, no. 88, p. 33.

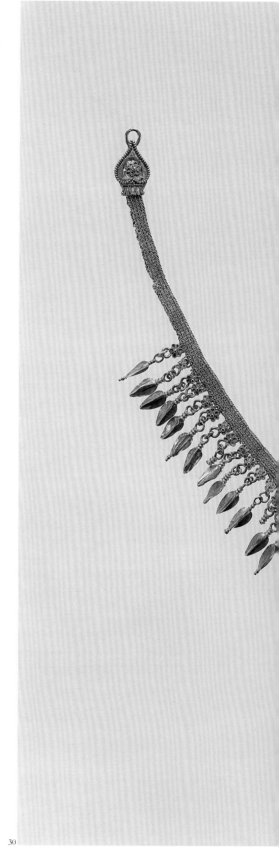

30

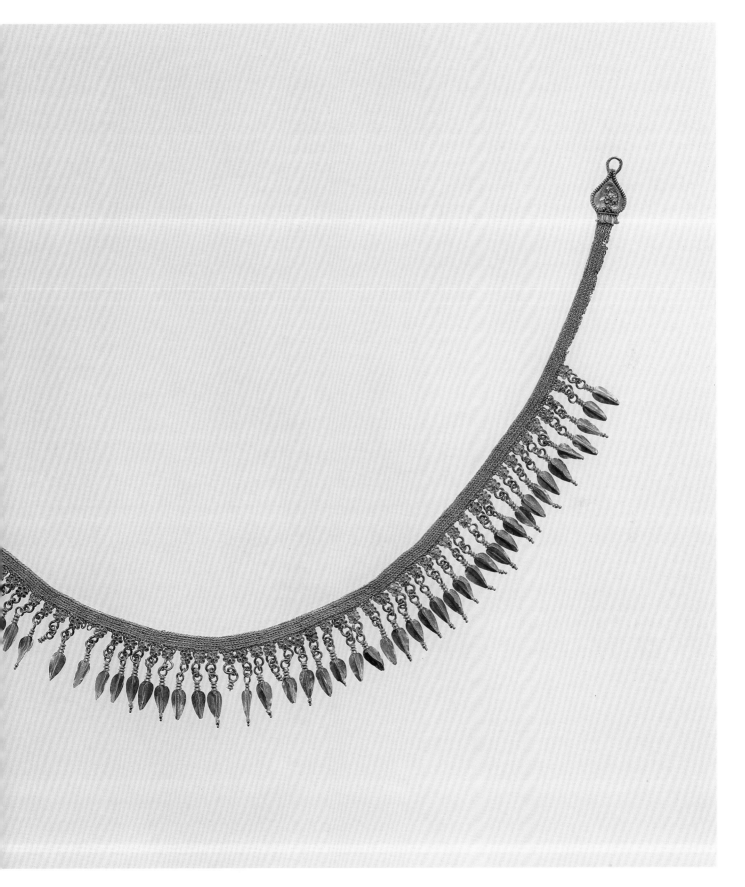

31 Pair of gold earrings with Ganymede and the eagle

Said to be from near Thessaloniki
330–300 BC
Height 6.0 cm, height of rosette 2.5 cm, height
of Ganymede group 3.0 cm; weight 15.1 and
16.5 g
New York 37.11.9–10; Harris Brisbane Dick
Fund, 1937

These superb earrings consist of a large honeysuckle palmette below which hangs a finely worked three-dimensional figure of Ganymede in the clutches of Zeus, who

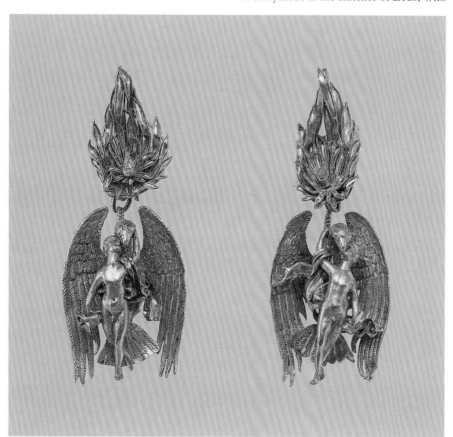

31

has assumed the guise of an eagle. The pointed-leaf palmette is in two levels and has a drop-shaped heart with infill granulation. A plain wire ring acts as a support and reinforcement for the arrangement of the leaves. The hooks for attachment to the ears end in a snake-head.

Ganymede and the eagle seem almost to kiss, while one eagle's claw rests lightly on the boy's hip. A wisp of drapery passes over Ganymede's forearms and down his back. The figures of Ganymede are solid, but the eagles are constructed of sheet gold. Their tails and legs were separately made, and the wings are of sturdy sheet gold with chased details on the front. Ganymede is attached to the eagle by solder at strategic points. A long beaded wire hook links the group to the back of the palmette.

The pendants are sculptural masterpieces in miniature. There are a number of similar groups, from both Italy and the east: for example, a pair in Berlin and a pair in Naples, as well as a pair once in the Nelidow collection. Pliny (*Natural History* XXXIV, 79) mentions a famous bronze group of Ganymede and the eagle, a work of the first half of the fourth century BC by Leochares and the first to show Zeus as an eagle. The miniatures in gold no doubt reflect Leochares' sculpture in their basic conception.

The honeysuckle palmettes may be compared with those on the siren earring in the Metropolitan (no. 19), the famous Nike earring in Boston and a pair of Erotes earrings in the Benaki Museum in Athens. Robert Zahn suggested that they were all works of the same jeweller; Segall, Hoffmann and Davidson have disagreed. To this list of honeysuckle palmettes should now be added the diadem from the antechamber of the so-called tomb of Philip II at Vergina.

BIBLIOGRAPHY: See introduction to group; Jacobsthal *Greek Pins*, fig. 289; Hoffmann and Davidson, fig. 12g; Higgins *GRJ*[2], pl. 48a. Berlin Ganymede earrings: Greifenhagen II, pl. 40, 3. Naples: Breglia, pl. 19, nos 116–17. Nelidow: Paris sale, May 1911, lot 297, pl. 11. On Ganymede see H. Sichtermann in *LIMC* IV, pp. 154–69. Boston Nike earring: Hoffmann and Davidson, no. 12. Benaki Erotes earrings: *Benaki*, no. 57, pl. 21. Diadem: *Vergina*, figs 158–9.

32

32 Pair of bracelets with rock-crystal hoops and gold ram-heads

Said to be from near Thessaloniki
330–300 BC
Width 8.0 cm, height 7.8 cm; weight 60.5 and
   60.1 g
New York 37.11.11–12; Harris Brisbane Dick
   Fund, 1937

The hoops of these bracelets are carefully cut, carved and polished from clear rock crystal to produce a twisted appearance, which is highlighted by the addition of the spiral-beaded wire bindings fitted into the valleys. The ram-heads are of sheet gold, probably die-formed with hand-chased details, including the finely stippled fleece. The heads extend into long, elaborate collars which are decorated with three friezes enclosed within bands of darts and bordered by plain and beaded wires. The upper frieze consists of an ivy chain on a vine which is tied with a Herakles knot at the centre and bears four bunches of grapes; the middle frieze has palmettes with pointed leaves, and the third frieze a palmette complex, with a central palmette flanked by small palmettes, flowers, quatrefoils and open spiral wires (corkscrews).

The filigree work on the collars of these bracelets is somewhat reminiscent of South Italian work.

BIBLIOGRAPHY: See introduction to group; Higgins *GRJ*[2], pl. 51a (one); Pfrommer, TA 131, pl. 21, 1.

33

33 Two pairs of gold fibulae of Macedonian type

Said to be from near Thessaloniki
330–300 BC
Width 5.0 cm, height 3.8 cm; weight 16.5, 17.0, 17.3 and 16.5 g
New York 37.11.13–16; Harris Brisbane Dick Fund, 1937

Each fibula consists of an arched bow which terminates at one end in a hinge-plate to which the pin is attached and, at the other end, a catch-plate into which the sharp end of the pin locates. These four fibulae form two mirror-image pairs, but the precise similarities of construction and decoration and the near constant weights suggest that they were worn as a set together with a pair still in Europe (Berlin).

Each bow is made from a section of curved gold rod over which are threaded five 'paddle-wheels' with spiral-beaded and plain wire separators. The individual 'paddle-wheels', each with six 'paddles', are made up from six identical sheet-gold components which were probably produced with a die. Each of these components forms one side of a 'paddle', part of the hub, and then the adjacent side of the next 'paddle' (see Fig. 10e).

The hinge-plates are made from two squares of sheet gold separated by a spool-like hinge over which the end of the pin could be looped. The plates have a relief on either side, surrounded by a border of flattened spiral-beaded wire and relief dots. Both sides are decorated with the head of a woman wearing a lion-skin (either Omphale wearing Herakles' lion-skin or Artemis), all produced with the same die.

Each of the catch-plates has, on the side opposite the pin, the foreparts of a griffin between two large domes or capstans. Three of the four fibulae preserve the fore-parts of a horse in front of, and below, the griffin. The griffins and horse protomes were made in left and right halves, and their wings are supported and separated by short beaded struts. The domes flank-ing the griffins are made in two halves from sheet gold and are supported on cir-cular collars of beaded wire. The backs of the catch-plates are decorated with two spirals of wire above a separately applied sheet embossed in low relief with a rosette set on two acanthus leaves. The hinge-and catch-plates, like the bow itself, are of sturdy gold sheet to permit frequent use.

This type of fibula has a long history in northern Greece and is found in silver (no. 6) as well as gold. A fibula in Berlin and a more damaged piece still with the

34

Gans family very probably come from the same group. A similar pair has also been found in a tomb at Veroia. From a tomb at Derveni come three pairs (lion-skin on the catch-plate). A variant form has biconical beads decorated with a tongue pattern instead of 'paddle-wheels'.

Rectangular reliefs decorated with lion-heads and heads of Omphale or Artemis have been found in a tomb near Katerina in Macedonia.

BIBLIOGRAPHY: See introduction to group; *Stathatos*, p. 208, fig. 113d–f. For the type in general see *Stathatos* III, pp. 202–12, and Greifenhagen II, pp. 89–90. For Berlin 30219.453 see Greifenhagen II, pl. 65, 1, 3 and 7; for the Gans piece, *Stathatos* III, p. 208, fig. 113g. Derveni, tomb E: *ADelt* 18 (1963), pl. 229, 3. Veroia 991 a–b: *Search for Alexander*, no. 55. Katerina tomb: *Makedonia*, nos 168–9.

34 Gold ring set with an emerald

Said to be from near Thessaloniki
330–300 BC
Height 2.1 cm, width 1.9 cm, diameter of bezel
  1.4 cm; weight 3.75 g
New York 37.11.17; Harris Brisbane Dick Fund,
  1937

This gold ring is set with a fine-coloured but flawed oval cabochon emerald. The emerald is held in a dog-tooth setting bor-dered with plain wire. Below are rows of plain wire and rope. The setting has a plain sheet back. The hoop consists of a pair of wire ropes set side by side, with a fine spiral-beaded wire soldered in the centre on the outer side of the hoop.

Emeralds first appear in jewellery in early Hellenistic times and most probably came from the mines in the eastern desert of Egypt, although it is possible that some came from the Urals. The Egyptian emer-alds tend to be very flawed internally, but some are of fine colour. A similar ring was found in a late fourth-century tomb at Derveni.

BIBLIOGRAPHY: See introduction to group. Ring from Derveni, tomb E: *ADelt* 18 (1963), pl. 229, 4 (left). Cf. also *Brooklyn*, no. 8.

Mount Aeto Tomb, Ithaka *(nos 35–6)*

John Fiott (he later changed his name to Lee), an English traveller, and John Foster, a young architectural student from Liverpool, seem to have learnt of the possibility of excavating tombs on Ithaka by the middle of December 1812. After calling on the commandant of the island, Captain Guiterra, to gain permission, they hired labourers at Vathy on 26 December. The following day they were joined by Jacob Linckh, an artist from Württemberg, Baron Carl Haller von Hallerstein of Nüremberg and Francesco Luz of Swabia, and began excavations near the remains of an ancient building, now called Palaiokastro, on Mount Aeto. Here, 'in a tomb near to the wall, on the outside, were found the female ornament of worked gold . . . ; and the gold ring with the bone of part of a thumb, still within it.'

On 30 December they paid off their workmen, divided the spoils into five lots and, after the division, made exchanges and purchases among themselves. Lee then went to the north of the island and, on New Year's Day 1813, he, Foster and Haller began new excavations. These were stopped, however, by Guiterra and they returned to Aeto, where they were joined by Otto Magnus, Baron von Stackelberg of Estonia. Here they resumed excavations on 3 and 4 January, only to be stopped again by Guiterra. The new finds were then also divided.

BIBLIOGRAPHY: T.S. Hughes, *Travels in Sicily, Greece and Albania* I (London 1820), pp. 144–71; Stackelberg *Gräber*, pp. 26–7; J. Lee, *Archaeologia* 33 (1849), pp. 35–64; M. Fraenkel, *Antike Denkmäler* I (1891), pl. 12; A. Oliver in *Brooklyn*, pp. 79–83; Christie's, 12 December 1989, lots 56–7.

35 (detail)

35 Gold cross-strap diadem with a Herakles knot

From a tomb on Mt Aeto, Ithaka; from the collections of General Sir James Campbell, H.E. Bunbury and David L. Davis

300–250 BC

Width as mounted 42.5 cm, total height as mounted *c.* 7.0 cm, length of straps *c.* 19.0 cm, length of Herakles knot 6.6 cm, height of Herakles knot 2.7 cm; weight of knot 11.9 g

New York 58.11.5; Pulitzer Bequest Fund, 1958

The Herakles knot is made of cut-out sheet gold. Its contours are defined by beaded and plain wires, and it is decorated with four rosettes and four small circular garnets set in beaded wire frames. In the centre, a faceted garnet in a dog-tooth mount is set on a sheet on top of a 'palmette' bed. The garnet appears to be a natural crystal, the faces of which have been slightly polished. The rectangular terminals are decorated with a central rosette on a palmette and discs at the corners. A row of pointed tongues projects over the straps, which are held onto the backs of these terminals by means of wire hooks through the centre.

From either side of the Herakles knot hangs a small die-formed sheet-gold satyr's head, from which are suspended three chains ending in biconical pomegranate pendants.

The back of the Herakles knot bears a modern incised inscription in two parts: 'of Saphpho' and 'of Laodamia'.

This type of diadem is a translation into gold of the ribbons often seen tied round the head. Another example, but with more elaborate straps, is in the British Museum. Such diadems are sometimes called breast-bands; although breast-bands are definitely attested, they would have required longer and more flexible 'arms' than those provided here.

BIBLIOGRAPHY: Hughes, op. cit., p. 164; Stackelberg *Gräber*, p. 50, pl. 73; *Benaki*, p. 35, no. 3; Sotheby's, 1 June 1939, lot 189; J. Chittenden and C. Seltman, *Greek Art* (London 1947), p. 43, no. 288; Münzen und Medaillen AG, 1958, lot 152: Hoffmann and Davidson, pp. 57–8; Oliver, pp. 275–6, figs 12–13; *Haller Catalogue*, p. 183, no. 9.1 (Foster's share); Pfrommer, HK 32. On the inscription see J. Lee, *Archaeologia* 33 (1849), pp. 35–64. London diadem: *BMCJ* 1984. Garnet analysed by Dick Stone.

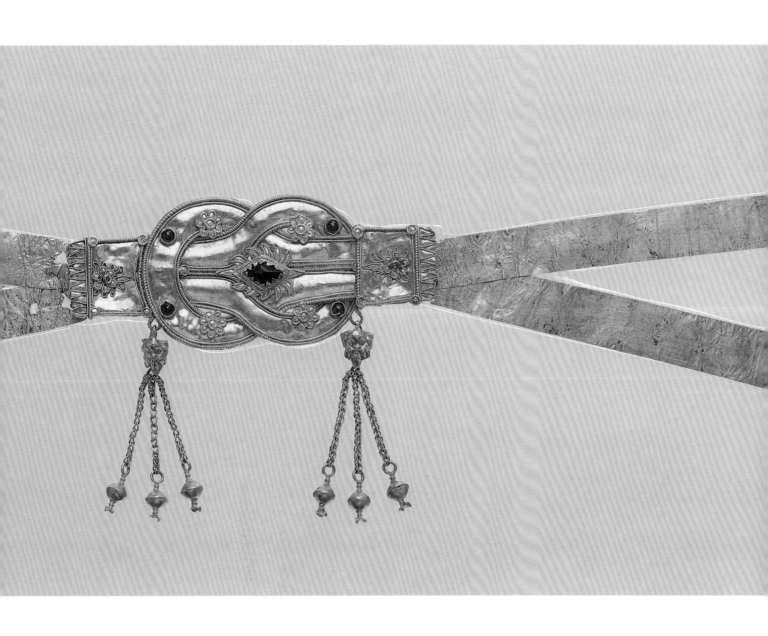

36 Gold ring with a garnet

Found in the same tomb as no. 35 and preserved with part of a finger (61.89 B), not shown here
300–250 BC
Height of bezel 2.0 cm, width of bezel 1.6 cm, height of hoop 2.0 cm; weight 6.9 g
New York 61.89 A; gift of David L. Davis, 1961

This ring is made of sheet gold with a plain strap hoop. The bezel is roughly oval in shape, and in the centre is set a large oval garnet of the same composition as that in the centre of the diadem found with it (no. 35).

The simplicity and flimsiness of both the ring and the diadem suggest that they were most probably made for the tomb.

BIBLIOGRAPHY: See introduction to group.
Garnet analysed by Dick Stone.

36

37 Pair of gold armbands with terminals in the form of a triton and a tritoness

Probably from northern Greece
About 200 BC
Present height of triton armband 25.0 cm, present
    height of tritoness armband 26.5 cm; weight
    of each 186.5 g
New York 56.11.5–6; Rogers Fund, 1956

These imposing armbands – between them they contain well over a third of a kilo of gold – represent two tritons carrying Erotes. The bearded triton faces to the right, his right arm raised behind his head, his left hand supporting a small baby Eros. The tritoness holds her left arm behind her head and similarly cradles a baby Eros in her right arm. Both have naked torsos, but drapery flares out behind their heads and shoulders. Their eyes have a dot to indicate the pupil. Below the hips, the torsos are set into acanthus-like ornaments that also suggest legs but in fact form the transition to the lower, fishy portion of their bodies. These fishy bodies disappear into an ornamental band of dotted cross-hatching and an acanthus leaf surrounded by dots. The central part of each armband is chased with scales. The lower terminals begin after a second ornamental band and, although they are damaged, seem to take the form of sea-monsters (*kete*).

These lower terminals are made in one with the bands, but with a sheet back. The bands, which are concave in section, are located and soldered into the hollow bodies of the tritons, which are worked from sheet gold and have flat gold-sheet backs.

Three suspension hoops are soldered to the tops of the figures, presumably for attaching the armbands to the sleeves of a garment. The inside of both hoops bears the dotted inscription, ZOI, upside-down.

This inscription appears on several pieces from the so-called Carpenisi Group (found in 1929): it may be the abbreviated name of either the maker or the owner. However, since the inscription ZOI or ZOILAS is found on five pieces from the Carpenisi Group, of differing form and style (two rings, a necklace, two bracelets and a medallion), it seems more likely that it refers to the original owner, a woman called Zoïla.

Elaborate armbands often end in snakes or even *kete*, but these are the only known examples to employ tritons. The inclusion of Erotes is perhaps intended to suggest that the tritons are in love or are married.

BIBLIOGRAPHY: J.J. Rorimer, *BMetrMus* 18 (1959), pp. 30, 34 and 36; Coarelli, pl. 48; Oliver, fig. 20; Higgins *GRJ* [2], p. 168, pl. 51b (tritoness); *Search for Alexander, NY Suppl.*, no. s 63; Deppert-Lippitz, fig. 202; *MMA Greece and Rome*, p. 83; Pfrommer, sr 65–6. On the Carpenisi Group see *Benaki*, pp. 31–50; *Stathatos*, pp. 89–135; Pfrommer, FK 21.

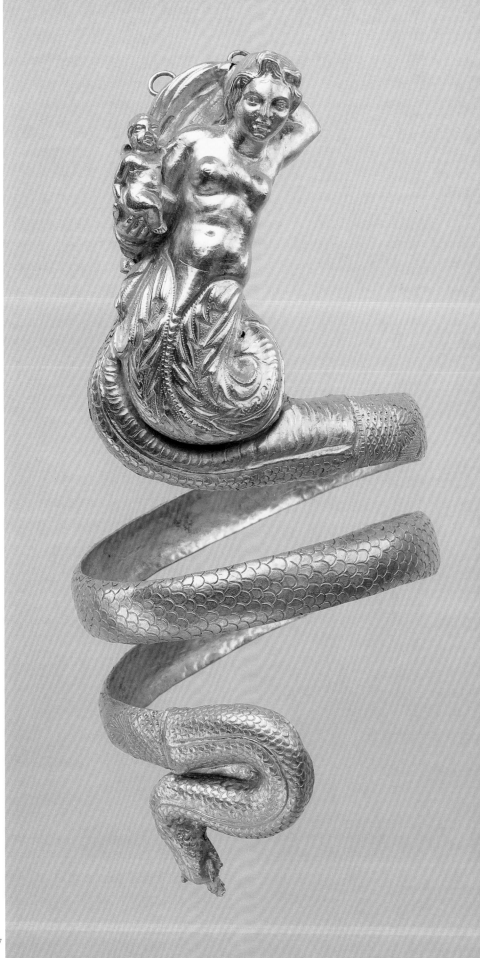

2 The East Greek Cities

The Greek cities on the islands and coast of ancient Asia Minor (modern Turkey) had a long and rich history. There is evidence of contact with the Greek mainland from the end of the Middle Bronze Age and in the Late Bronze Age a strong Mycenaean Greek presence has been discerned on the islands of Rhodes, Kos and Kalymnos, as well as on Samos, Chios and Lesbos. There was also a good deal of trading contact with the coastal region of the mainland opposite. This almost all came to a close at the end of the Bronze Age, but reoccupation and contact were rapidly restored, probably before the end of the tenth century BC.

The Greeks of Rhodes and the nearby islands and promontories, who maintained the Dorian dialect, formed themselves into a group called the Doric Hexapolis. On the mainland between the rivers Hermos and Maeander were the Ionic Greek cities. These were organised, perhaps by the end of the ninth century BC, into a league which also included the islands of Chios and Samos. North of the Hermos were the Greek cities where the Aeolian dialect was spoken. There were twelve Aeolian cities: the best known are Mytilene on Lesbos and Kyme on the mainland.

Of the local populations around and inland from these Greek settlements, the Carians in the south had had close contacts with the Greeks even in the Mycenaean period. The Phrygians, centred on Gordion, were immensely important in the ninth and eighth centuries but the power of Midas I was broken by the first of the Cimmerian invasions from the north in the early seventh century. The political initiative then passed to the new dynasty of Gyges the Mermnad and the Lydians. Between 675 and 546 BC the Lydians were the main threat to the Greek settlements. Indeed, it was probably this barrier to further expansion to the east that drove the Greeks to explore northwards, first to the Dardanelles and the Propontis and finally around the Black Sea itself.

The seventh and sixth centuries were periods of great prosperity in these East Greek cities, but in 561 BC Croesus came to the throne of Lydia and quickly conquered them. Although Croesus was in many ways a generous conqueror, it was barely fourteen years before he rode east to challenge Cyrus of Persia. As a result, Lydia fell to the Persians and Sardis eventually became the capital of the Persian west. The Greek cities in turn soon began to fall to the Persian satrap. But at the beginning of the fifth century the East Greeks were to revolt and, although the uprising failed, it finally brought Persia into direct conflict with Greece.

The Greek defeat of Persia and the development of the Athenian maritime empire resulted in the drawing of all resources to Athens and the effective stifling of East Greek culture and life. This Athenian domination, however, came to an end in the closing decades of the fifth century. The consequent rise of city independence led to a new phase

of grand urban planning, for example on Rhodes, where in 408 BC the three large cities agreed to amalgamate, creating one great modern city on the northern tip of the island. It affected the fringes of the East Greek world too, as seen in the rise of Mausolos at Halikarnassos and his systematic programme of Hellenisation. Alexander the Great's passage through the East Greek world in 334–333 BC and the final lifting of the Persian threat led to further increases in wealth and prosperity. Despite the conflicts which followed his death and the subsequent shifts in the balance of power, the East Greek cities remained vital and prosperous in the third century BC.

The history of East Greek jewellery begins with the eighth-century material from Rhodes. In the second half of the seventh century, to judge from the preserved material, two major centres of production seem to have arisen, one at Ephesus, the other on Rhodes. The former is clearly linked to the workshops of Phrygia and Lydia. The Rhodian school, however, was closely allied to developments in the Greek islands, especially Melos.

The evidence for the sixth century is disparate, but what glimpses there are reveal spectacular goldwork. A very fine assemblage of Ionian relief work comes from a mid-sixth-century votive deposit at Delphi, and a number of acorn-shaped necklace pendants on granule rings and a pair of lion-head bracelets were found in a tomb at Gordion of similar date. From Lydia comes a wealth of objects in precious metals of the later sixth century, some purely Greek in style, some that merge Greek styles with Lydian and Achaemenid fashions.

From the fifth century preserved material is very scarce (nos 38–40). The reasons for this are obscure: one might have imagined that the defeat of Persia by the Greeks would have released a huge amount of wealth, but Athenian domination may have meant that the reserves of gold went to Athens and particularly to her sanctuaries.

It was only in the fourth century BC, when the East Greek cities began to enjoy a new sense of independence and perhaps when a new influx of craftsmen entered the area, that the quantity of gold jewellery increased. Rhodes is particularly visible as a centre of production in the first half of the fourth century (nos 41–3), but Greek jewellers working in Caria were also to leave their mark, as the jewellery found at Halikarnassos in 1989 reveals. There, in an intact sarcophagus, was found the skeleton of a woman of about forty years of age, who had had more than one child. On the skeleton were found an elaborate gold myrtle wreath with a large central rosette, a pair of antelope-head bracelets of Achaemenid type, two necklaces (one with round beads and seed-like pendants, the other with discs alternating with twin addorsed palmettes, from which hang beech-nut pendants), three rings (a chalcedony engraved with the standing figure of a Persian satrap; an agate engraved with a female head; a thin box-bezel ring with filigree decoration), and a series of twenty-four rosettes which probably decorated her silk garment or shroud. It has been suggested that she might be Ada I, sister of Mausolos and wife of Idreus, but apart from the jewellery the offerings were meagre.

This wealth of Greek gold jewellery seems to have increased further in the second half of the fourth century. From this period date some rich tombs at Iasos, a group in Pforzheim which is said to be from Sardis, much of the Kyme Treasure (nos 44–5 and 48–57), tomb groups from Pergamon, and material from the Dardanelles, including the Madytos jewellery (nos 62–7) and the oak wreath (no. 60).

It is in this last phase that we begin to be able to identify workshops. Given the size of the Kyme Treasure, this is an obvious place to start. It does, indeed, seem possible to link other pieces with the fine disc and pyramid earrings, including the pair in Berlin, and with the ear studs (nos 49–52), especially a pair of ear studs from Galata, although a pair from Zagazig and a pair once in Missouri are also very close. There are further links with other pieces from the group, especially the pair of tie-necklets (nos 54–5), and with pieces from elsewhere, including the two other known tie-necklets, one perhaps from Mytilene (no. 69) and the other said to be from Sardis. It is likely that this Kyme workshop operated in the Aeolian and Ionian sphere, although some objects, which are possible exports from it, seem to have travelled much further afield.

BIBLIOGRAPHY: For seventh-century jewellery see R. Laffineur, *L'Orfèvrerie rhodienne orientalisante* (Paris 1978) and Higgins *GRJ*[2], pp. 95, 111–18 (Rhodes) and 118–20 (Ephesus); Deppert-Lippitz, pp. 92–114. Sixth century: (Delphi) *L'oro dei Greci*, pl. 96, 1–9; (Gordion tomb) R.S. Young, *Archaeology* 3 (1950), p. 199, figs 5–6. Late sixth-century Lydian jewellery: *MMA Greece and Rome*, p. 45, figs 29–30; Calendar of Lectures at the Museum of Anatolian Civilisations (Ankara 1994). Iasos, tombs X and Y: *BdA* 49 (1964), pp. 205–13, with pl. 1 and figs 10–16. Sardis group (Pforzheim): Segall, *passim*. The jewellery from the so-called tomb of Ada has received a number of preliminary notices and is now on show in the museum at Bodrum. Berlin Kyme earrings: Greifenhagen II, pl. 40, 1–2. Galata studs: Greifenhagen II, fig. 2. Zagazig (Dresden ZV 789): Hoffmann and Davidson, p. 99, fig. 21b. Once Missouri (coll. D.M. Robinson): Segall, pl. 34. Sardis tie-necklet (Pforzheim): Segall, pls 6–7, 16–17, 18b.

38 Pair of gold boat-shaped earrings decorated with a palmette

Said to be from Kalymnos
450–400 BC
Width of boat 1.8 cm, height with pendants
  c. 4.0 cm; weight 2.1 and 2.3 g
British Museum GR 1901.2-26.1

Each boat is made in two halves from sheet gold. The decoration consists of a plain wire flanked by a row of granules along the lower contour and across the middle of the front and back. In the centre is a three-petalled palmette of plain wire filigree, on spirals with added granules. The terminal of each boat has a band of large granules flanked by plain wire. The hoop is of plain tapered wire. From a ring on the base of each boat hangs a pair of chains with pendants. On one earring there are two ribbed seeds each made from two die-formed halves, but on the other is an open seed-pod and a repaired seed with a filigree ivy leaf and a long petal below on either side; these two did not perhaps originally belong.

The simple pendants under these boat-shaped earrings may be paralleled on pieces from South Italy (no. 144) and Greece (no. 9). Boat-shaped earrings with various central pendant forms are well known in Phoenician goldwork, and the plain wire filigree palmette recalls some Cypriot pieces (nos 164 and 181–2).

38

BIBLIOGRAPHY: *BMCJ* 1660–61; Higgins *GRJ*[2], pl. 25a. For simple pendants below boat-shaped earrings cf. *Taranto*, nos 60 and 68; also, from Metaponto, see J.C. Carter, *Ancient Crossroads: The Rural Population of Classical Italy, Guide to an Archaeological Exhibition* (n.d.), fig. 31a; and Deppert-Lippitz, fig. 126. On finds of jewellery from Kalymnos see C.T. Newton, *The Archaeological Journal* 13 (1856), pp. 14–37. Cf. also the later pair of earrings and a ring from Kalymnos in Berlin (Greifenhagen II, pls 40, 4 and 55, 7–9), as well as a group of simple funerary jewellery in the National Museum in Athens (nos 23, 32, 158, 160 and 258). For this type of earring from Syria see A. de Ridder, *Collection de Clercq: Catalogue*, vol. VII (Paris 1911), no. 709.

39

40

39 Gold lion-head pendant

From excavations on Rhodes (Biliotti sale)
450–400 BC
Height 2.1 cm, width 1.7 cm; weight 3.8 g
British Museum GR 1885.12-13.45

The lion's head is made from one piece of sheet gold, but with separate teeth. The muzzle is stippled. The joint with the back-plate is ornamented with a beaded wire and there is a triangular 'trapdoor' in the back sheet to allow for air-expansion during soldering. The suspension hoop is made from a ridged strip, and a rosette with fine beaded wire petals is added at the front for decoration.

Such simple animal-head pendants were particularly popular over many centuries: lion- and bull-heads are the most common

forms. They could be combined with other necklace elements or worn singly on a linen cord.

BIBLIOGRAPHY: *BMCJ* 1208; Ruxer, pl. 4, 31.

40 Pair of gold ear reels

420–400 BC
Diameter 2.2 cm, thickness *c.* 1.1 cm; weight 4.1 and 4.3 g
British Museum GR 1872.6-4.845–6

Each of these spool-shaped ornaments is made up from two end-plates, a spool-shaped side sheet and an open central tube which is turned over at the ends to hold the piece together. The die-formed faces are decorated with eight concentric rings.

These spools were worn in the ears, as

can be seen from contemporary and earlier representations in terracotta. They seem to have been particularly popular in East Greece, both in gold and a variety of other materials, but they also occur on Cyprus. An example with an open central tube has been found at Sardis. In addition, there are numerous ancient Egyptian ante-cedents for the shape, mainly in faience, and in India the use of such ornaments (some with remarkably similar concentric decoration) as earrings is well attested from before 500 BC up to recent times.

BIBLIOGRAPHY: *BMCJ* 2065–6. Sardis reel: *Sardis*, no. 85, pl. 8, figs 5–6. For similar spools see G. Jacopi, *Clara Rhodos*, vol. III (Rhodes 1929), pp. 153–8, tombs 153 and 155 (tomb 153 contained an Athenian red-figured *lebes gamikos*

41

42

in the manner of the Meidias Painter: *ARV²*, p. 1322, no. 14). For the Indian spools see M. Postel, *Ear Ornaments of Ancient India* (1989), *passim*.

41   Pair of gold ear reels

Said to be from Rhodes
400–350 BC
Diameter 1.6 cm, thickness c. 0.7 cm; weight 1.3 and 1.3 g
British Museum GR 1908.4-16.2–3

This pair of spool-shaped ornaments is similar to no. 40 but lacks the central tube. The front face of each takes the form of a die-formed sheet decorated with the head of Helios in relief. The die-formed backs have six concentric rings and a separately made rosette with spiral-beaded wire petals and traces of enamel soldered to the centre.

The rosette and rings recur on the New York reel (no. 42) and on a pair once in the Nelidow collection.

BIBLIOGRAPHY: F.H. Marshall, *JHS* 29 (1909), p. 165, fig. 18; *BMCJ* 2068–9; Higgins *GRJ²*, pl. 24a; *LIMC* v, *sv* Helios, no. 161. For the Nelidow reels see *Nelidow*, no. 523.

42   Gold ear reel

400–350 BC
Diameter 2.0 cm, thickness 1.0 cm; weight 5.1 g
New York 25.78.89; Fletcher Fund, 1925

This earring is made up from two end-plates and a spool-shaped side sheet. On the front is a die-formed relief showing a Nereid riding on a dolphin to the left. She holds a helmet, part of the new panoply made by Hephaistos for Achilles. Around this are three concentric grooves: in the third is a beaded wire. The die-formed back-plate is decorated with five concentric grooves and a separately made central rosette.

The ear spool shows signs of wear and damage. Inside it was found a fourth-century bronze coin of Kranai in Laconia.

The motif of Thetis or one of the other daughters of Nereus carrying the new arms for Thetis' son Achilles seems to have been particularly favoured in the eastern part of the Greek world.

BIBLIOGRAPHY: Richter *Handbook*, p. 157, fig. 128f; *Search for Alexander, NY Suppl.*, no. s 56.

Rhodes Tomb Group *(no. 43)*

In 1862 Auguste Salzmann and Alfred Biliotti opened a tomb at Kamiros on Rhodes. It contained a fine Athenian red-figured *pelike* attributed to the Marsyas Painter and datable about 360–350 BC, as well as a marble *pyxis*. Inside the *pyxis* were found a gem engraved with a heron with antlers, and a pair of gold ear reels. One of the reels came to the British Museum, but the other was sold to the Louvre.

This tomb is roughly contemporary with some of the North Pontic burials, such as the Pavlovsky kurgan (nos 106–8). The objects are of the same quality, but the quantity of jewellery placed with or owned by the deceased is far less in the East Greek burial.

BIBLIOGRAPHY: C.T. Newton, *The Fine Arts Quarterly Review* 2 (January 1864), pp. 1–8; C. Torr, *Rhodes in Ancient Times* (Cambridge 1885), pl. 1 with caption on p. x and see pp. 115–16. For the vase see *BMCV* E 424 and *ARV²*, p. 1475, no. 4. The *pyxis* is GR 1862.5-30.7; the gem *BMCG* 553.

FIGURE 42 Rhodes tomb group: Athenian red-figured *pelike* showing Peleus seizing Thetis as she bathes (British Museum *BMCV* E 424).

FIGURE 43 Rhodes tomb group: marble *pyxis* (British Museum GR 1862.5-30.7) and gem (British Museum *BMCG* 553).

43

43

43 Gold ear reel

From Rhodes
350–330 BC
Diameter 2.3 cm; thickness *c*. 1.1 cm; weight 4.1 g
British Museum GR 1862.5-30.8

This gold ear ornament consists of two end-plates and a spool-shaped side sheet. The end-plates are die-formed and have figures against a background of concentric circles. One side shows a naked Eros leaning against a pillar as he plays with a *iunx*. The other side has a Nereid wearing a *chiton*, with one breast bare. She rides on a dolphin and holds Achilles' new helmet in one hand.

The pair to this ear reel is in the Louvre. The motif of a Nereid carrying new arms for Achilles recurs on the pair of ear reels in New York (no. 41) and frequently in the North Pontic region (nos 88 and 120).

The *iunx* is a magic toy often seen in the hands of Eros (cf. no. 194): it was intended to arouse erotic desire.

BIBLIOGRAPHY: *BMCJ* 2067. Louvre ear reel: A. de Ridder, *Catalogue sommaire des bijoux antiques du Musée du Louvre* (Paris 1924), no. 17.

The Kyme Treasure *(nos 44–57)*

This group of gold jewellery, nearly a hundred pieces in all, was said to have been found in a tomb at Kyme in Aeolis, on the coast of Asia Minor. It was acquired for the British Museum in three lots between 1876 and 1878. The first lot had been sold by Alfred Lawson, Director of the Ottoman Bank at Smyrna, to the dealer P. Lambros in Athens. The second lot came directly from Lawson and is mentioned in a letter of 27 May 1875, which is worth quoting in detail since it gives a good picture of the antiquities market in Turkey in the later nineteenth century. Lawson wrote:

A short while ago I bought the remaining fragments of the gold ornaments I had sold to Mr. Lambros. . . . The holder of this portion has had it put by ever since the time the tomb containing the jewellery was opened by himself & another man and has only now consented to part with it, through an agent of mine.—Owing to the commotion made at the time of the find, I have been compelled to pay a relatively high price – but it was so necessary, for considerations I will explain, that other buyers should not be attracted to the spot that I was obliged to come to terms with the possessor the moment he reluctantly showed the jewellery and named his price.— The reason why I acted so promptly in this matter is owing to the fact that this man's property includes several other tombs, quite as ancient, which, from considerations of personal safety, he must open in such a way as not to attract the attention of his neighbours, as his life might be endangered by any extravagant reports; and the country about is not very secure.—I expect that by winter he will be enabled to work, and his 'discoveries' will then come to me.

The Kyme Treasure is said all to have come from the same tomb. This seems, however, to be impossible, since the 'treasure' contains a pair of later fifth-century earrings (no. 47), a large group of late fourth-century material (e.g. nos 44–5, 48–57), a group of early third-century pieces (e.g. no. 46), some later Hellenistic items, two Roman pieces and two tiny items that may even be as late as the nineteenth century. Nevertheless, the homogeneity of both the late fourth-century group and the early third-century group suggests that these pieces might well have come from a large hypogeum with perhaps four or more female corpses of the late fourth century and one of the early third. Given the uncertainty surrounding this group as a whole, only a selection of objects is included, concentrating on the later fourth-century material.

BIBLIOGRAPHY: *BMCJ*, p. xxxviii; Segall, p. 28; Higgins *GRJ*², pp. 156 and 160; I. Ondrejova in J. Bouzek *et al., The Results of the Czechoslovak Expedition: Kyme II* (Prague 1980), pp. 125–6; Pfrommer, p. 241, FK 71; D. Williams in A. Calinescu and W. Rudolph (eds), *Ancient Jewelry and Archaeology* (papers of the Bloomington congress, 1991, forthcoming).

44 Gold pediment-shaped diadem

Said to be from Kyme
330–300 BC
Present length 22.5 cm, height in centre 5.8 cm
British Museum GR 1877.9-10.60

This diadem is made of thin sheet gold with a die-formed design. In the centre is a palmette complex, on either side of which sits a winged figure. That on the right is female, that on the left possibly male. Beyond are spirals and large rosettes. There is a line border and an outer border of dots. A single die, probably of copper alloy, was used to form the entire design in one operation, except for the dotted border which was added afterwards by hand.

The Kyme Treasure contained fragments of at least eleven such diadems, with a variety of decorative schemes. It is quite possible that a single burial contained more than one diadem, for there are several examples of multiple pairs of earrings and multiple wreaths. This type of diadem is especially common in the eastern part of the Greek world, with a particularly high concentration in the Greek cities of Asia Minor. The best-known example is that from Madytos, the finest of the series (no. 62).

BIBLIOGRAPHY: *BMCJ* 1612. The other diadems are *BMCJ* 1611–1614**; some fragments join each other. For this type of diadem see further under no. 62.

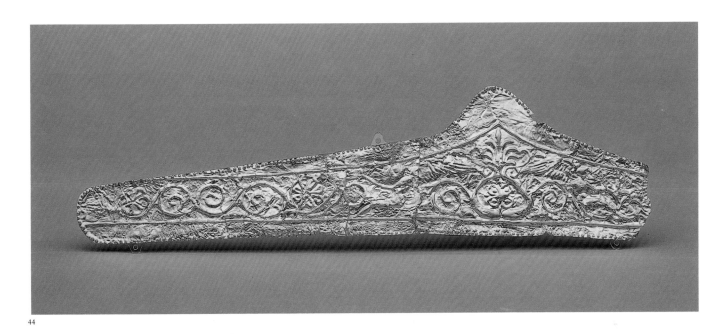

44

45 (detail)

45 Gold strip with gorgoneia

Said to be from Kyme
330–300 BC
Length 32.2 cm, height 1.3 cm; weight 2.5 g
British Museum GR 1877.9-10.37 and 40

This narrow band is decorated with twenty-eight gorgoneia within circles of dots, all made by the repeated use of the same die. There is a pin-hole at either end for a cord.

A similar strip (although employing different dies) in Berlin has a small pediment in the centre: it probably came from the island of Chalki, near Rhodes. Both were no doubt intended to bind the hair. The Kyme Treasure also contained two other long gold strips of this type, one decorated with stars and one with frontal lion-heads.

BIBLIOGRAPHY: *BMCJ* 2097–8. Berlin band: Greifenhagen II, pl. 2, 7. Other Kyme strips: *BMCJ* 2099–2100 (lion-heads), *BMCJ* 2101 and 2102–3.

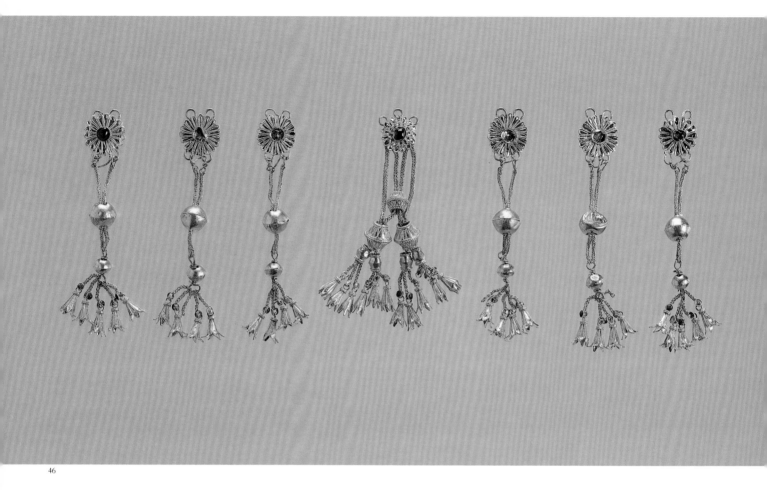

46

46 Gold pendants from a diadem

Said to be from Kyme
300–280 BC
Height of six of the pendants 7.0 cm and diameter
of their rosettes 1.5 cm, height of the other
pendant 6.5 cm and diameter of its rosette
1.2 cm; weight of the elaborate pendant 11.2 g,
weight of each of the others 4.4 g
British Museum GR 1877.9-10.2-8

Of the seven pendants, six are the same,
while the seventh is more elaborate. The
simpler type is made up of a large sheet-
gold rosette with details in spiral-beaded
wire and a central garnet in a plain setting
(some missing). At the top and bottom of
the rosette are two rings. From each of
the bottom rings hangs a chain. Half-way
down these chains is threaded a large,
plain spherical bead, made in top and
bottom halves pinched together over the
chain to hold it in place. The ends of both
chains are attached to a ring on top of a
smaller plain spherical bead (also in top
and bottom halves), from the bottom of

which hang five short chains. On the end
of each of these chains is a disc with blue
enamel and an open seed-head, inside
which is a rosette.

The more elaborate pendant consists of
a large two-tier rosette with a central garnet in a plain setting. There are three rings
above and two double tubes on the back.
From the double tubes hang four long
chains. At the end of the chains are two
large biconical slip-beads: these are decorated with tongues, and the joint between
the upper and lower halves is covered by
a beaded wire flanked by plain wires.
Further up the chains, holding the two
inner chains together, is a third slip-bead,
smaller but similarly decorated. Below
the two large beads are two much smaller
biconical slip-beads (plain, with only a
beaded wire at either end), from each of
which sprout three short chains. Each of
these ends with a disc filled with blue
enamel and, below, an open seed, prob-

ably an asphodel seed, inside which is a
small rosette.

These pendants may well have hung
from some complex diadem as represented on a later terracotta from Myrina,
but the multiple suspension loops above
are puzzling. Were they needed because
the band of the diadem was made of fabric
rather than metal, or was there some sort
of network of chains above?

The use of asphodel seed-pods recurs
on the tie-necklet perhaps from Mytilene
(no. 69). Stylistic and floral elements link
this diadem with other East Greek
jewellery.

BIBLIOGRAPHY: *BMCJ* 1936–41 and 1942 (the
elaborate example); Higgins *GRJ*[2], p. 158;
Pfrommer, p. 241 with n. 1871. Myrina
terracotta: S. Mollard-Besques, *Catalogue
raisonné des figurines et reliefs en terre-cuite grecs et
romains, II: Myrina* (Paris 1963), pl. 38b, no. 661.

47

48

47 Pair of gold spiral earrings with copper alloy cores

Said to be from Kyme
420–400 BC
Height 3.3 cm; weight 15.0 and 15.2 g
British Museum GR 1877.9-10.56–7

The sheet gold over the copper alloy spirals is decorated with small applied lozenges and triangles of granulation, larger triangles of granulation below beaded and plain wires, and pyramids of grains on the terminals and at either end of the two lower loops. The lozenges, triangles and pyramids were each built up on a sheet-gold backing and then soldered as a unit to the spiral. This avoided potential problems in soldering numerous separate grains onto thin gold foil overlaying a copper alloy core.

This type of earring has been discussed by Hadaczek and Silantyeva, who suppose that the earrings were hung from a missing hoop. However, the coins of the Lycian dynast Teththiweibi of about the middle of the fifth century, noted by Hadaczek, clearly show this type of earring being worn through a large hole in the earlobe.

The closest parallel in form and style was found at Xanthos in Lycia, near the Lion Tomb. A simpler pair, without the granulation on the shanks, comes from Marion and has been dated from its context to the first half of the fourth century. A further pair, with simpler granulation on the shanks and without the pyramids on the crests, comes from a burial at Duvanli of about 450 BC. There were very probably several centres of production of this type, including one in the North Pontic region (no. 93): the Kyme pair was no doubt made somewhere in Asia Minor. These earrings are the earliest objects in the Kyme Treasure.

BIBLIOGRAPHY: Hadaczek, p. 15, fig. 24; BMCJ 1585–6; Higgins GRJ², pl. 25e. On the type see Hadaczek, pp. 13–16; P.F. Silantyeva, Trudyi Gosudarstvennogo Ordena Lenina Ermitaja 17 (1976), pp. 123–37. On the coins see G.F. Hill, Catalogue of the Greek Coins of Lycia, Pamphylia, and Pisidia (London 1897), pl. 5, 8. Xanthos earring: P. Demargne, Fouilles de Xanthos, vol. 1 (Paris 1958), pl. 4. Marion (tomb 60) earrings: Pierides, pl. 20, 9. Duvanli earrings: Deppert-Lippitz, fig. 80.

48 Gold earring with spherical bead

Said to be from Kyme
350–300 BC
Diameter 2.0 cm, length of bead 1.7 cm; weight 2.1 g
British Museum GR 1877.9-10.27

The plain tapering hoop of circular section is decorated at one end with a spherical bead. The bead is soldered in place and has an opening at its extremity into which the other end of the hoop could locate. The bead is made from sheet gold in two halves and is decorated with applied filigree double spirals in plain wire, with granules at the centre and in the interstices. The central seam of the bead has an applied beaded wire flanked on either side by a plain wire.

An identical pair of earrings was excavated by Epaminondas Baltazzi at Myrina in 1874: they are now in Berlin. The type seems to be a local variety, although the concept of a bead on a plain hoop recurred far later in Dark Age European, Byzantine and Islamic jewellery.

In addition to this earring, there are parts of at least two necklaces in the Kyme Treasure that consist of spherical beads with filigree double spirals. Such necklaces are known from Greece, Thrace and the North Pontic region (no. 117).

BIBLIOGRAPHY: BMCJ 1844; Higgins GRJ, pl. 53c. Berlin earrings: Greifenhagen II, pl. 39, 8. Kyme necklaces: BMCJ 2036–9 (terminals), 2044 (beads). For this type of bead see further under no. 117.

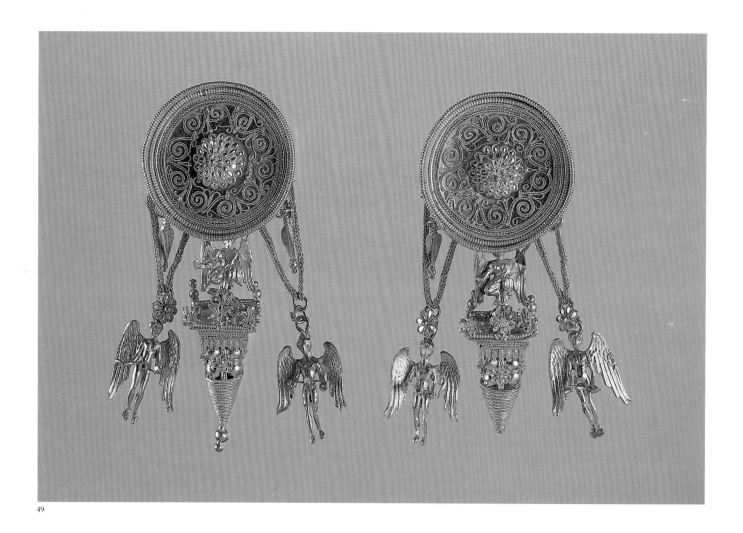

49

49 Pair of gold disc and pyramid earrings

Said to be from Kyme
330–300 BC
Diameter of disc 2.4 cm, height *c*. 6.0 cm; weight
16.7 and 17.4 g
British Museum GR 1877.9-10.16–17

These elaborate earrings consist of a decorated disc below which hangs a central inverted pyramid pendant flanked by hanging figures of winged Erotes. The disc is pan-shaped and its rim is edged in precisely made beaded wire. The field of each disc has concentric rows of plain, beaded and rope filigree surrounding a band of spiralling vegetation in spiral-beaded wire and granulation and a large central four-tiered flower-head. Each tier of the flower-head consists of a rosette supported on a small gold tubular collar. The petals are convex, and thus were probably not enamelled originally, and there is a large gold granule at the apex of the flower.

Between each disc and the central pyra-mid pendant is an intervening supporting member in the form of a winged Nike in *chiton* and *himation*, crouching to the left and holding out her right hand. Each Nike is die-formed in front and back halves in sheet gold; the wings are separately made and soldered in place. Below the Nike, and attached by a split-ring fastener, is the pyramid pendant. At the top, masking the linking rings, is a rosette with concave petals and some remaining enamel; there are three palmettes along the front edge, large granules at the back corners and clusters of grains at the centre of the sides and back. Below this, the pyramid tapers downwards in a series of bands of beaded, spiral-beaded and plain wires and two tiers of four large, hollow gold spheres with granulated, filigree and rosette decoration. The lower half of the pendant consists of a cone of sheet gold over which are coiled a plain and a spiral-beaded wire side by side. The base is decorated with a large and a small granule (now missing on one earring).

On each side of the central pendant, pairs of loop-in-loop chain support figures of Eros holding a *iunx* which retains traces of enamel. Each Eros is surmounted by a rosette with convex petals, and between the supporting chains is a small beech-nut pendant surmounted by a disc. The figures of Eros are made in front and back halves from sheet gold, and their wings from thin, die-formed sheet over a flat gold-sheet backing. The wings and the Erotes vary slightly, and it would appear that the left-hand Eros on each earring in fact matches the right-hand one on the other.

The hook behind the disc for insertion in the ear is a plain tapered wire without the snake-head terminal found on some other earrings.

Disc and pyramid earrings are widely found throughout the Greek world: in addition to the East Greek examples, they have been discovered in the North Pontic region (no. 116), on Cyprus (no. 176), in Greece and in South Italy (no. 147). The

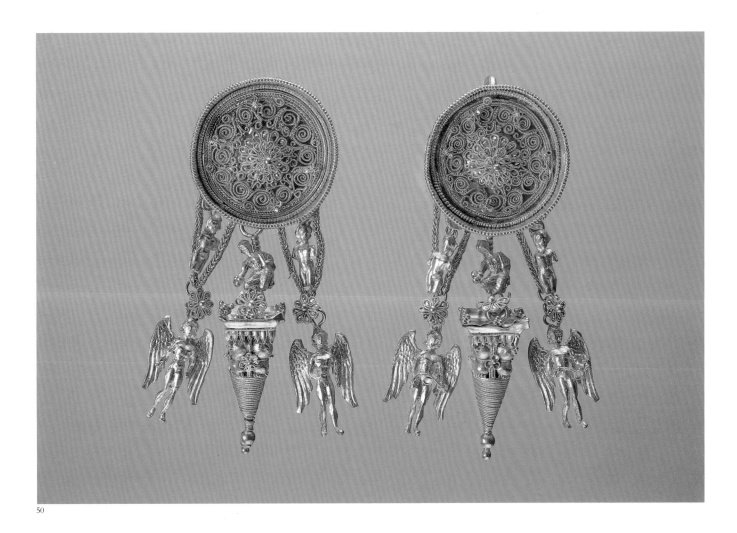

50

East Greek jewellers seem to have been particularly fond of pendants in the form of Nikai, Erotes and dolls. The decoration of the discs is closely related to that of the series of ear studs (nos 51–2), and one pair from Galata in Thrace is surely by the same jeweller as the Kyme earrings.

BIBLIOGRAPHY: *BMCJ* 1672–3; Segall, pl. 21a; Deppert-Lippitz, fig. 131. Galata studs: Greifenhagen II, fig. 2.

50 Pair of gold disc and pyramid earrings

Said to be from Kyme
330–300 BC
Diameter of disc 2.4 cm, height *c.* 6.0 cm; weight 14.9 and 15.3 g
British Museum GR 1877.9-10.18–19

These earrings are very similar to no. 49, but there are a number of differences. The filigree in the field of each disc has a more crowded and vibrant scheme, including tiny quatrefoils raised on rectangular blocks, but is, if anything, slightly less precise (see Fig. 23), while the central

flower-heads have only three tiers instead of four. The arrangement of the pendants is the same but here the beech nuts are replaced by die-formed figures of truncated naked dolls. The flanking Nike figures share the same wing dies with the two Nikai on the other pair, thus confirming a common workshop origin for the two pairs. The crouching figures in the centre are now wingless, but hold out three tiny balls, perhaps intended to be knucklebones. The inverted pyramids are surmounted by tiny piles of granules instead of palmettes, and the elaborate filigree bands are omitted below.

Differences in workmanship between the two pairs include the choice of different types of decorative wire in certain places and the way in which the loops are attached to the backs of the earrings. However, the common wing dies and the fact that odd bits of spare spiral-beaded wire were often used to make attachment loops point to their being produced in the same workshop.

Much of a third pair of similar earrings was also preserved. It has winged Nikai, like the first pair (but they hold three balls), and tiny dolls and simplified tops to the pyramids, as in the second pair. A further pair of earrings, now in Berlin, is also said to come from Kyme: it was bought from Lambros in 1876, like the British Museum's first Kyme lot. It combines the elaboration of the disc and pyramid pendant of the first pair with the tiny doll pendants of the second, but replaces the crouching link figure with a sheet decorated with a circumscribed palmette. All four pairs of earrings were clearly made in the same workshop and have many stylistic links with other items from the find.

BIBLIOGRAPHY: *BMCJ* 1670–1. The third pair consists of *BMCJ* 1662–3 and 1664–5, together with three Erotes previously attached to the necklace *BMCJ* 1946: see Williams, op. cit., forthcoming. Berlin pair: Greifenhagen II, pl. 40, 1–2. On the tiny truncated dolls see further Segall, pp. 37–8, and O. Cavalier, *Revue du Louvre* 1988, 4, pp. 285–93.

51 Gold ear stud

Said to be from Kyme
330–300 BC
Diameter of disc 2.8 cm, diameter of stud 1.4 cm; weight 7.5 g
British Museum GR 1876.6-17.4

The outer edge of this particularly elaborate stud is formed from a corrugated gold strip (see Fig. 7) which is soldered onto the upturned edge of the pan-like disc. The top rim bears a row of granules which, in at least two places, are attached to an inserted wire loop rather than being soldered in place. These loops may once have supported pendants. The decorated field of the disc bears concentric bands of beaded, plain and rope filigree and a frieze of palmettes (alternately circumscribed and uncircumscribed) in plain wire filigree (Fig. 17). In the centre of the disc is an upright tubular pillar, over which are four tiers (perhaps more originally) of gold rings with radiating wires. The tiers bear, in turn, rosettes of six petals, rosettes of four petals, a gold granule and ivy leaves. Originally, the top of the tube would have borne a rosette or other motif. Since such elements were often simply fixed in place by a tight push-fit, its loss is not surprising.

The back stud is plain with a beaded wire border and an attachment loop, perhaps for a safety link to the front section, where the attachment loop is now missing. The tube on the back stud locates precisely into the tube on the reverse of the disc.

BIBLIOGRAPHY: *BMCJ* 2059; Deppert-Lippitz, fig. 134 (left).

51

52 Pair of gold ear studs

Said to be from Kyme
330–300 BC
Diameter of disc 2.5 cm, diameter of stud 1.25 cm; weight 8.7 g with stud, 6.8 g without
British Museum GR 1877.9-10.21 and 1878.10-15.1

The disc is pan-shaped with an upturned edge rimmed with beaded wire. Within the disc are concentric bands of spiral-beaded, plain and rope filigree, and friezes of simple filigree running spirals and complex spirals with omega fillers, all in spiral-beaded wire (Fig. 18). In the centre of the disc is a three-tiered flower-head, its convex petals bordered in spiral-beaded wire, surmounted by a large central granule.

One disc retains its back stud, which has a die-formed star-burst within a spiral-beaded and plain wire border. There are no signs of any safety chain or cord, as on no. 51.

Such ear studs were particularly common in burials in Asia Minor and on Cyprus, but they also occur in South Italy, in Thrace, in the North Pontic area (no. 109) and even in Egypt. Representations of the type may be found in northern Greece and South Italy.

BIBLIOGRAPHY: *BMCJ* 2060–1; Deppert-Lippitz, fig. 134 (right). Cypriot examples: Pierides, pl. 20, 1–2 and 3–4. Thracian studs (from Galata): Greifenhagen II, fig. 2. South Italy (S. Maria d'Anglona, near Herakleia): *NSc* 23 (1969), p. 178, fig. 12. Egyptian example in Edinburgh: Ogden, forthcoming.

52

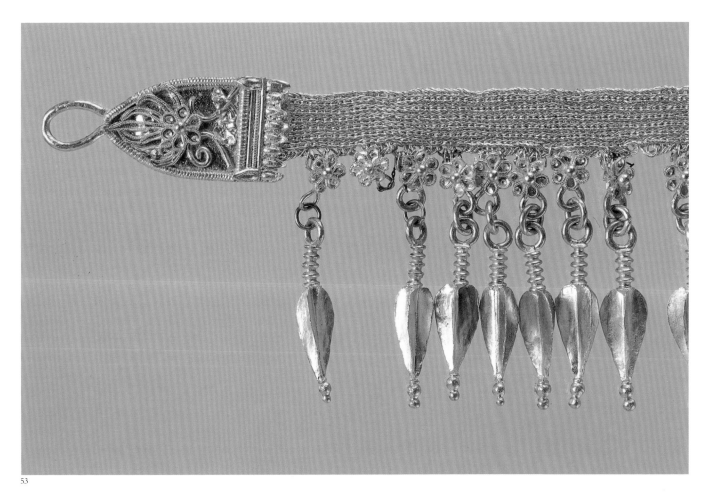

53

53 Gold strap necklace with beech-nut pendants

Said to be from Kyme
330–300 BC
Present length 29.2 cm, height of beech-nut
    pendants 1.6 cm; weight 35.2 g
British Museum GR 1876.6-17.1–2

The strap consists of a six-fold loop-in-loop chain with doubled cross linking. Along its length are rosettes, fifty-five of which are preserved from a probable original total of about seventy-five. From the rosettes hang beech-nut pendants (forty-nine preserved). The terminals are of box-like construction, the strap being held in place by transverse wires (the originals now missing). The top of each terminal is decorated with a palmette with pointed leaves on a spiral base, with three acanthus leaves and a rosette with concave petals set on top. At the base is a sequence of plain and spiral-beaded wires and a row of darts.

This necklace had previously been wrongly restored with three Erotes pendants that actually belonged to a pair of earrings. Its original length cannot now be determined, for several repairs have been

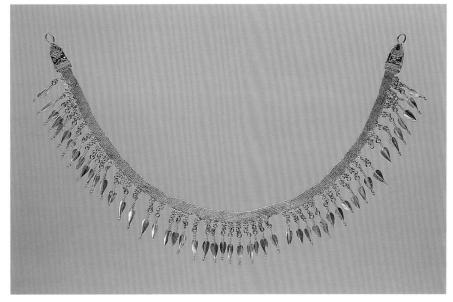

53

made to the strap. The Kyme Treasure included fragments of two other strap necklaces of decreasing sizes: all may have formed a set.

This type of necklace is well known from many other regions (Greece, no. 30; North Pontic, nos 106 and 123), but there are particularly close examples from northern Greece as well as Asia Minor.

BIBLIOGRAPHY: *BMCJ* 1946; Ruxer, pl. 20, 3. Other necklace fragments: GR 1876.6-17.2 and 1877.9-10.20 (part *BMCJ* 1945); GR 1877.9-10.10 (*BMCJ* 1944). Close parallels: (Pella) *Thesauroi*, pl. 15, no. 79; (Derveni) *ADelt* 18 (1963), pl. 229.

54 Gold tie-necklet

Said to be from Kyme
330–300 BC
Length *c*. 25.0 cm, length of long chains
   c. 20.0 cm, length of larger bead 1.3 cm,
   length of smaller 1.2 cm; weight 30.0 g
British Museum GR 1876.6-17.3

This unusual and complex necklet consists of two long chains, both of which pass through a single large biconical bead and then through smaller beads to split into five short chains terminating in myrtle flowers. The main chains are two-fold double loop-in-loop, with simple loop and ring terminals (only one surviving). The large biconical bead is made of sheet gold in two halves and has plain and beaded wire collars and equator, and spiral-beaded filigree in the form of cir-cumscribed palmettes with traces of enamel fill. The chains are not held in this bead by wire ties but cross inside it, and are prevented from moving freely by the slight flattening of the bead's opening. The smaller biconical beads have plain and beaded wire collars and equators, spiral-beaded filigree spirals and quadruple clus-ters of grains. These beads conceal the expansion of the chains from a single strand to five strands, and are prevented from sliding further down the ornament by the greater thickness of the five chains.

The terminating myrtle flowers are of complex construction. Each is essentially in the form of a sheet-gold funnel ending in a flat flower-head into which is soldered a small gold tube. Over this tube are located gold rings to which are soldered radiating wire stamens, arranged in pairs and terminating in gold grains. The open end of the tube is closed by a small rosette mounted on a gold peg, which is a simple push-fit into the open tube end. Only nine of the original ten flowers remain, and the central rosettes and stamens are missing on several others.

There are fragments of another such necklet among the Kyme material: they seem very slightly later in date. A some-what similar necklace, perhaps from Mytilene (no. 69), employs straps instead of chains. Yet another example, in Pforz-heim and perhaps from Sardis, has chains and myrtle-flower pendants, but the slip-beads have been replaced by a palmette on a leaf-shaped sheet which in some ways recalls the central element of the Kyme earrings in Berlin.

BIBLIOGRAPHY: *BMCJ* 1954. Kyme fragments: *BMCJ* 2011–12 (flowers), 1953 (chain). Pforzheim necklet: Segall, pls 16–17. Berlin earrings: Greifenhagen II, pl. 40, 1–2.

Opposite: 54

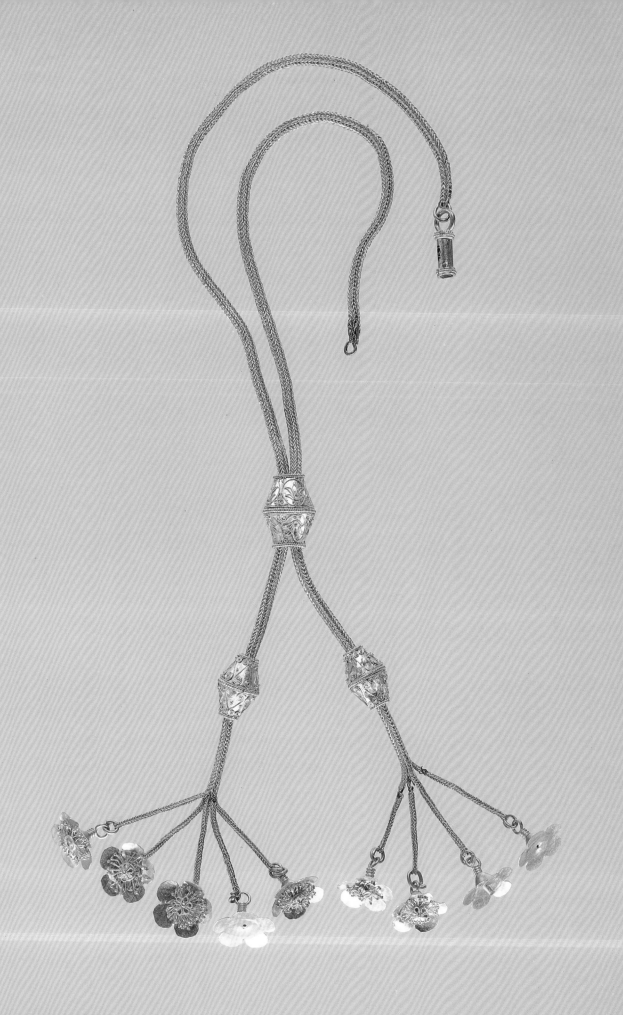

55 Gold tie-necklet

Said to be from Kyme
330–300 BC
Length *c.* 24.5 cm, length of biconical beads 0.8,
    1.0 and 1.3 cm; weight 34.4 g
British Museum GR 1877.9-10.9

This elaborate necklet consists of two pairs of long chains linked by passing through a single large biconical bead; they then pass through further beads to divide into a festoon of finer chains, each with a pomegranate-like terminal.

Each of the main chains is two-fold doubled loop-in-loop. Only one terminal is preserved: it has a loop end and is decorated with simple imbrocated filigree patterns in spiral-beaded wire. The large central biconical bead is decorated with linked palmettes in spiral-beaded wire, with applied triangular sheet-gold hearts. The collars and equator are decorated with plain and beaded wires. This bead has sheet-gold patches around pairs of holes that once held wires to secure it in place. The other, smaller, biconical beads are of similar construction but are decorated with spiral-beaded wire spectacle spirals.

The smaller biconical beads conceal the place where the single chains divide into four. The small chains end in spherical beads with spiky sheet collars in imitation of pomegranates. It should be noted that the innermost chains are linked and share a final bead. These beads are decorated with filigree spectacle spirals, but here in plain wire, and their attachment to the chains is concealed behind small discs bor-

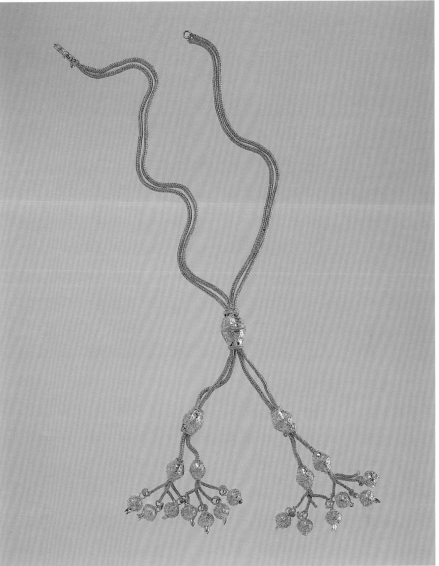

55

dered by spiral-beaded wire and containing remains of enamel.

Although this necklet reveals different solutions to constructional problems from no. 54, the style of the filigree work clearly links both with other pieces in the Kyme complex.

BIBLIOGRAPHY: *BMCJ* 1955; Ruxer, pl. 35, 4; Deppert-Lippitz, fig. 121.

Opposite: 55

56

56 Gold discs with female head

Said to be from Kyme
330–300 BC
Diameter 1.05 cm; weight of each 0.1 g
British Museum GR 1877.9-10.15

These discs all bear within a border of dots the die-formed three-quarter head of a woman wearing earrings with amphora-like pendants and a necklace with similar large pendants. There are four pin-holes for attachment in each disc. Thirty-six of these dress ornaments were acquired.

The designs on these discs are remarkably sharp and detailed. Many other such discs have been found in the eastern part of the Greek world, both in western Asia Minor and in the North Pontic region (nos 91–2).

BIBLIOGRAPHY: *BMCJ* 2084. Cf. *Brooklyn*, no. 22, from Asia Minor; GR 1899.12-1.36–62, from Phokaia.

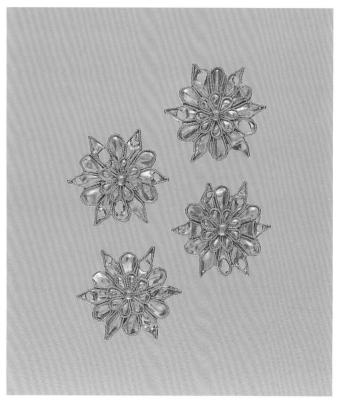

57

57 Gold rosettes

Said to be from Kyme
330–300 BC
Maximum width 1.05 cm; weight of each 0.2 g
British Museum GR 1876.5-17.11

These cut-out rosettes consist of twelve alternately rounded and pointed petals with spiral-beaded wire borders and a smaller rosette and a grain in the centre. Each rosette has five or six pin-holes for attachment. Sixteen such rosettes were acquired.

BIBLIOGRAPHY: *BMCJ* 2087.

58 Gold ring engraved with a woman at an altar

Said to be from Phokaia; bought by Sir A.W.
Franks from Alfred Lawson in 1893
About 350 BC
Height of bezel 2.0 cm, height of hoop 1.7 cm;
weight 11.3 g
British Museum GR 1917.5-1.59; bequeathed by
Sir A.W. Franks, 1897

On the oval bezel is engraved the figure
of a woman at an altar. She wears a *chiton*,
himation, sandals and simple droplet earring; her hair is tied up at the back. In one
hand, fingers downwards, she holds out
a small seed or piece of incense (see Figs
14 and 15), which she is presumably about
to place on top of the altar before her. The
altar is seen in three-quarter view from a
low angle of vision, and has hooks on the
corners. On top of it sits an eagle, which
may indicate that the offering is being
made to Zeus or Apollo.

The hoop is slightly bevelled and is
hammered from the same piece of gold
as the bezel. The gold shows occasional
platinum-group metal inclusions.

BIBLIOGRAPHY: *BMCR* 59; A.B. Cook, *Zeus*,
vol. III (Cambridge 1940), fig. 579; Richter
EGGE, no. 243; Boardman *GGFR*, pl. 739
(Salting Group; shape VIII).

58

59 Gold ring with the head of the gorgon Medusa

Said to be from Smyrna
350–330 BC
Length of bezel 1.9 cm, width of hoop 2.4 cm;
weight 29.3 g
British Museum GR 1917.5-1.94; bequeathed by
Sir A.W. Franks, 1897

This massive, man-sized gold ring has an
oval bezel bearing a chased and engraved
frontal representation of the severed head
of the gorgon Medusa. She is shown with
protruding tongue and snake-infested
coiffure, and below her chin is a small
dolphin. This probably refers to the version of the story in which Medusa's sisters
chased Perseus over the sea after he had
decapitated her.

The ring and the hoop are formed from
a single piece of gold, and fine hammer-
marks are still visible on the hoop. The
gold has occasional platinum-group metal
inclusions.

BIBLIOGRAPHY: *BMCR* 94; Boardman *GGFR*,
colour pl. on p. 217, no. 6, and pl. 731 (shape
VII); *LIMC* IV, pl. 171, no. 96.

59

Dardanelles Tomb Group *(nos 60–61)*

Two interesting pieces of jewellery, an oak wreath and a belt, were bought for the British Museum in 1908. The dealer reported that they both came from the same tomb, somewhere on the Dardanelles.

Nothing more is known of the context of this find, but another gold oak wreath was discovered in a tomb in the same probable area. This tomb, at Çoban Tepe, near Pınarbası on the coast north of Troy, was opened by a group of workmen under the direction of a Turkish village priest on 6/7 March 1887. The Turkish authorities, however, got wind of the discovery, imprisoned the priest and confiscated the finds, which they sent to Istanbul. The tumulus contained a rectangular stone-lined chamber in which were found, in addition to the wreath, three embossed gold strips, gold myrtle sprigs, a bronze mirror, a bronze patera and an alabaster *alabastron*.

BIBLIOGRAPHY: *BMCJ* 1628–9. Çoban Tepe tomb: F. Calvert, *JHS* 17 (1897), pp. 319–20; C. Schuchhardt, *Schliemann's Excavations: An Archaeological and Historical Study* (London 1891), p. 86. These finds do not seem to be listed in A. Joubin, *Musée Imperial Ottoman: Bronzes et Bijoux* (Istanbul 1898).

60 Gold oak wreath with a bee and two cicadas

Said to be from the Dardanelles
350–300 BC
Diameter as restored *c.* 23.0 cm, length of bee 2.1 cm; weight 276 g (including modern rod core)
British Museum GR 1908.4-14.1

This wreath consists of two branches. At the back the stems have obliquely cut end-plates; at the front the two branches are held together with a split pin fastener that has a bee as its cap. The branches are made of sheet-gold tubes, over a modern copper core. Each branch has six sprays with eight leaves and seven or eight acorns, as well as a cicada. In addition, there are about a dozen single leaves set straight into each branch. The leaves are of three different sizes and are made in one piece with their stalks. The acorns are made in left and right die-formed halves; the cups are cross-hatched and there is a point on the top of the fruit. The cicadas (see Fig. 35, p. 41) are constructed from four separate sheets of gold – lower body, upper body, two wings. There is a modern Russian assay mark on the cut ends of one of the stems: it shows a head,

60

the letter G and the number 94 (94 solot-niks, that is about 97.9% gold).

Perhaps the most famous oak wreath is that from the tomb at Vergina identified as that of Philip II. A second comes from the nearby Prince's tomb. A particularly fine example was discovered in a tumulus at Pergamon. The idea of indicating the cut through the stem by means of a decorated plate set at an angle can also be

observed on an olive wreath from the Kekuvatsky kurgan (no. 105) and on one said to be from Asia Minor, now in Berlin.

BIBLIOGRAPHY: *BMCJ* 1628. For the Vergina wreaths see *Vergina*, figs 137 and 184. For Pergamon, tumulus II, see *AM* 33 (1908), pp. 429–35, pl. 25, and Pfrommer, HK 62 with pl. 6, 1–3. For the bee cf. Greifenhagen II, pl.1, olive wreath with cut stem plates. For the cicadas cf. *Brooklyn*, no. 4.

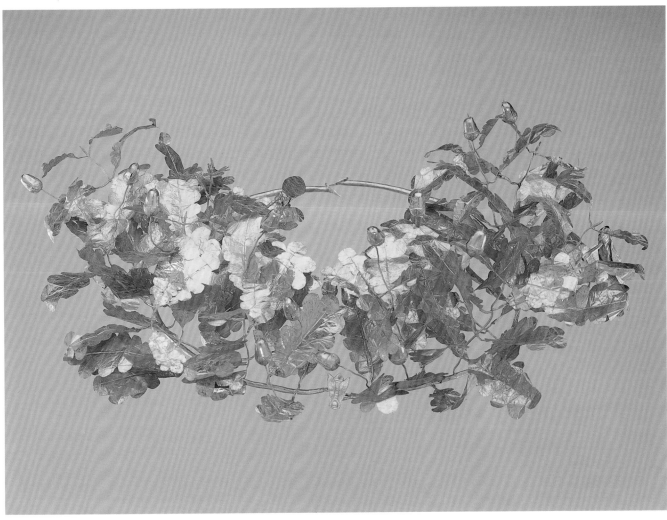

60

61

61 Plain gold funerary band or belt

Said to be from the Dardanelles
350–300 BC
Length 125.8 cm, height 5.0 cm; weight 34.5 g
British Museum GR 1908.4-14.2

This long sheet-gold band is undecorated and the ends are cut to a rough triangle. There are small pin-holes at the top and bottom along the length of the band – a total of thirteen pairs – and a larger hole at either end. These perforations suggest that the band was originally attached to some fabric or leather.

No other object of this form is known, although parts of other examples of belts survive (no. 141). It seems unlikely that it was made to be worn in life.

BIBLIOGRAPHY: *BMCJ* 1629.

The Madytos Jewellery *(nos 62–7)*

This group of jewellery, bought by the Metropolitan Museum in 1906, was said to have been found in a tomb at Madytos on the European side of the Hellespont, opposite Abydos. The pieces consist of a diadem, a pair of earrings, an elaborate necklace, a simpler necklace, a ring and seven flower-heads, probably attachments from a headdress. As such they form a plausible *parure*, although presumably incomplete. Indeed, John Marshall, the Metropolitan Museum's purchasing agent in Europe, wrote on 18 July 1906 that 'other portions of the same find exist, and, as I wrote to you, I tried when in Munich to get them brought to Athens: but in Athens I was told that the owner had gone to Macedonia and for the moment could not be reached.' These other items have never been traced.

It is clear that the flower-heads and the earrings have been subjected to fire, for their surface has been slightly damaged. Furthermore, a tubular loop from the back of one of the rosettes has become fused to the disc of one of the earrings. The earrings and the flowers were, therefore, evidently close together on the corpse as the funeral pyre was lit; owing to the slightness of the damage it seems likely that they were quickly removed or the flames were speedily quenched. The strap necklace has also been damaged by fire, and its style links it closely with the earrings. There are also iconographic links between the diadem and the earrings.

BIBLIOGRAPHY: E. Robinson, *BMetrMus* I (1905–6), pp. 118–20; Becatti, p. 197, no. 391, pl. 103; Segall, pp. 22–4, pl. 40; Higgins in Barr-Sharrar and Borza, p. 142, fig. 4; *Search for Alexander, NY Suppl.*, pp. 6–7, nos s11–23.

62 Pediment-shaped gold diadem

Said to be from Madytos
330–300 BC
Length 36.8 cm, height in centre 5.9 cm; weight 11.03 g
New York 06.1217.1; Rogers Fund, 1906

In the centre of this highly decorative funerary diadem Dionysos and Ariadne sit back to back (Ariadne in *chiton* and *himation* on the left, Dionysos on the right, similarly clad, but with the addition of the soft skin boots called *kothornoi*). Between them is a large acanthus leaf complex, on which they seem to sit, while under its leaves shelter tiny birds. Dionysos and

62

62

Ariadne are faced by five seated women on each side, separated and supported by thick vegetal spirals. These women, presumably Muses, are engaged in a variety of activities: one plays an angular harp, another holds a pair of *auloi* (pipes), a third plays a rectangular lyre, a fourth holds a book roll in her hands, and the last plays a lute. The border consists of a row of dots within an egg and dart pattern. The ends of the diadem are pierced so that it could be fitted with a cord and tied to the forehead.

The diadem was made by pressing a single piece of sheet gold into a design carved in intaglio in a die, most probably of copper alloy. One large die was used to produce the whole design in one process, rather than one or more smaller dies being used sequentially. The outline of the diadem was cut with a sharp knife after the design had been impressed.

This is the finest of a series of such diadems. They are found most commonly in the eastern Mediterranean, with a high concentration on the coast of Asia Minor: other reported find-spots include Abydos and Perinthos, as well as Kyme (no. 44), the Gulf of Elaia, Myrina and Kolophon. The closest iconographical parallel is the diadem found by Frank Calvert at Tagara, just north of Abydos, on the European side of the Hellespont. A related type is also common on Cyprus (nos 168–9).

The Madytos piece is particularly remarkable for the detailed representation of its figures, especially the Muses with their variety of cultural paraphernalia. For example, even the clamps that were set across the tops of the reeds of the *auloi* in order to maintain their shape are clearly delineated.

BIBLIOGRAPHY: See introduction to group; Hoffmann and Davidson, p. 68, fig. 7b; Higgins *GRJ*[2], pl. 45c. Abydos diadem (London, Victoria and Albert Museum 627.1884): *JdI* 82 (1967), pp. 34–5. A modern replica of the V & A diadem, presumably by Castellani, is in Berlin: Greifenhagen II, pl. 82, 1.

63 Pair of gold earrings with elaborate disc and boat-shaped pendant

Said to be from Madytos
330–300 BC
Height 7.6 and 7.4 cm, diameter of discs 2.3 cm;
    weight 15.6 and 15.7 g
New York 06.1217.11–12; Rogers Fund, 1906

Each disc consists of a pan-shaped piece of sheet gold; a corrugated sheet has been attached to the upturned edge of the disc and the junction at the top has been disguised by a row of large grains topped by smaller ones. The inner surface of the disc is decorated with concentric rings of granulation and decorative wires, both plain and twisted, framing a frieze of spiky-leaved palmettes, spirals and quatrefoils. In the centre is a rosette surrounded by two layers of long, thin, drooping leaves.

The boat-shaped pendant is suspended by means of two strap loops attached to the ends of the boat. Concealing both of these connecting elements is an acanthus and a spiky-leaved palmette, while on the outer side stands the elongated figure of a naked winged figure, presumably an Eros. The hollow of the boat is filled with a floral complex consisting of three acanthus leaves and two spirals ending in a quatrefoil, in the centre of which, below a spiky-leaved palmette, sits the tiny figure of a Muse holding a lyre, as on the diadem (no. 62).

The front of the boat is decorated

with very fine granulation arranged in diamond-shaped groups of four grains (the back is plain). Beaded and plain wires border the ends and top of the boat; the bottom contour is bordered with a plain wire and eight two-tiered rosettes which alternate with seven tiny protomes of the winged horse, Pegasos. From each protome hangs a disc and below it a small flat plain seed; on one earring (06.1217.12) the central seed has been replaced with a tiny swaddled woman. From each rosette hangs a plain seed and two loop-in-loop chains which form a festoon that supports five large seeds decorated with ribs and with a spiky calyx at the top (grains at apices).

On the right side of the disc of one earring (06.1217.11) is a corrugated hoop from the back of one of the rosettes, which became attached in the heat of the funeral pyre. The earrings show other traces of fire damage.

These intricate and elaborate earrings belong to a group that have been found on Crete, in northern Greece (Derveni), East Greece (no. 70) and on both the northern (no. 122) and southern shores of the Black Sea (Trebizond).

BIBLIOGRAPHY: See introduction to group; Higgins *GRJ*[2], pl. 25A; Pfrommer, pls 26, 14 and 31, 14 (a chart suggesting the development of the type). Earrings from Crete, *BMCJ* 1655–6; from Derveni, tomb z 8, *Search for Alexander*, no. 138; from Trebizond (Dallas, Schimmel collection), Deppert-Lippitz, fig. 130.

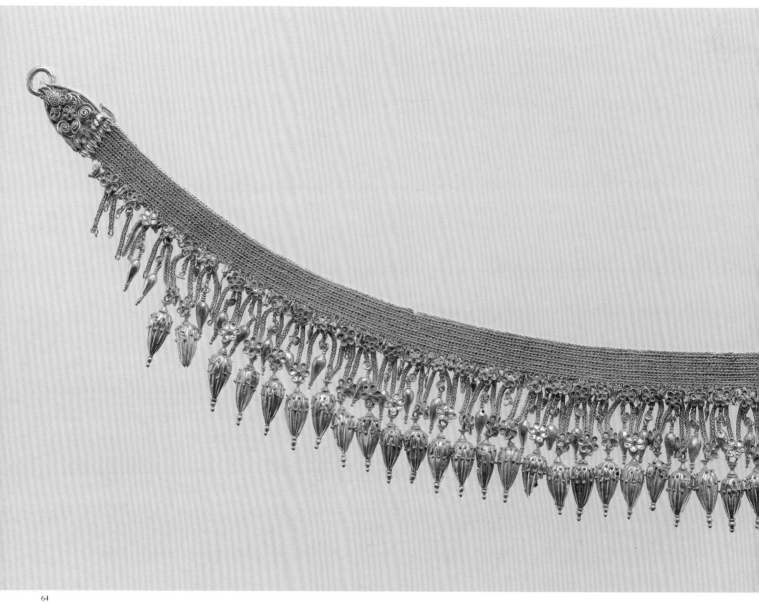

64

64 Gold strap necklace with seed-like pendants

Said to be from Madytos
330–300 BC
Length 32.3 cm, length of terminals 2.0 cm,
    height 3.2 cm, height of strap 0.8 cm; weight
    65.1 g
New York 06.1217.13; Rogers Fund, 1906

The strap is composed of five double loop-in-loop chains with doubled interlinking. Along the lower edge are attached alternating two-tier rosettes and miniature foreparts of the winged horse, Pegasos. As on the earrings, the Pegasos protomes support small plain one-sided seeds, while the rosettes bear plain seeds (forty-six preserved) with discs above and pairs of chains that make up the festoon from which hang rosettes and large, ribbed seed-like pendants (fifty-five preserved of a presumed total of sixty-one). Each pendant is made from two die-formed halves and is decorated with a spiky calyx at the top (apices filled with a grain).

The terminals are attached to the strap by transverse wires, which are bent back along the sides of the terminals. The terminals are bordered with beaded wire and decorated with a floral complex consisting of four plain wire coils, a central rosette

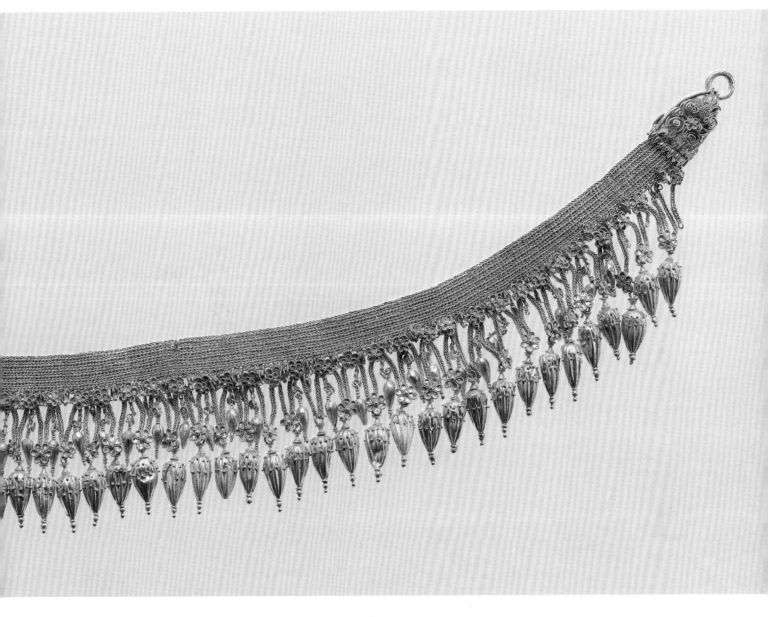

and a spiky palmette, the large central tongue of which is filled with granulation. At the base of the complex is a row of cut-out spiky leaves, turned up at an angle of 45 degrees, and then a row of cut-out darts.

There is fire damage to the strap, parts of which are considerably fused and thus made brittle, thereby supporting the association of the necklace with the earrings and the rosettes.

The festoon and its members match those of the earrings and we may presume that they were made as a set. A very similar necklace, said to be from Trebizond, is in Dallas: with its accompanying earrings (only one preserved), it is probably from the same workshop as the Madytos set. Pegasos protomes also occur on a number of other necklaces, for example one from the Great Bliznitza (no. 123), and on some of the most elaborate earrings, including, of course, the pair from Madytos (no. 63), as well as on some of the Macedonian fibulae (no. 33).

BIBLIOGRAPHY: See introduction to group. For the Dallas necklace (Schimmel collection) see Deppert-Lippitz, pl. 12/13.

65

65 Gold necklace of beads and tubes

Said to be from Madytos
330–320 BC
Present length 20.9 cm, length of columnar beads
  2.3 cm, length of spherical beads 0.9 cm;
  weight 10.1 g
New York 06.1217.3; Rogers Fund, 1906

In this necklace thirteen columnar sheet-gold tubes are combined with five sheet-gold spherical beads with beaded wire collars.

Such simple necklaces have a number of parallels. One of these, from Mount Pangaion in Macedonia and formerly in Berlin, consists of similar tubes and beads, with the addition, however, of biconical pendants. The Herakles knot from Tsagezi, near Amphipolis, was accompanied by columnar and biconical beads. Plain columnar beads have also been found at Gela in Sicily and at Kertch (Hadji Mouschkai).

BIBLIOGRAPHY: See introduction to group.
Berlin necklace: Greifenhagen I, pl. 12, 12.
Tsagezi: Pfrommer, pl. 1, 3–4. Gela: *MonAnt* 17 (1906), pp. 539f., fig. 371; Deppert-Lippitz, fig. 148. Kertch: (Hermitage P.1841/2.1) *ABC*, pl. 9, 3. Cf. also *Stathatos*, no. 227.

66

66 Gold snake ring

Said to be from Madytos
330–300 BC
Diameter 2.2 cm; weight 7.9 g
New York 06.1217.2; Rogers Fund, 1906

This simple ring is formed from one piece of gold hammered into a rod with a D-shaped section and worked into three complete coils. The terminals are in the form of chased snake-heads, with an additional decoration of punched dots on the necks.

Other examples of the type come from the Great Bliznitza and from the Gela hoard. Later examples tend to have more coils.

BIBLIOGRAPHY: See introduction to group.
Great Bliznitza ring: *CR* 1869, pl. 1, 19–20. Gela hoard: *MonAnt* 17 (1907), p. 538, fig. 371.

67 Seven gold rosettes

Said to be from Madytos
330–300 BC
Diameter *c.* 2.0 cm; the three largely complete examples weigh 1.4, 1.8 and 2.0 g
New York 06.1217.4–10; Rogers Fund, 1906

Each of the six-petalled flower-heads is cut from hammered sheet gold. The centre is constructed over a tube which supports wire rings onto which the two tiers of radiating wire stamens are soldered. The tube itself is capped by a spiral dome of spiral-beaded wire with a grain at the top. The stamens end either in discs (which may have been filled with enamel) or anthers. Soldered onto the back of each flower is a double attachment loop formed from corrugated sheet gold.

These flower-heads were originally threaded or sewn onto a fabric or leather

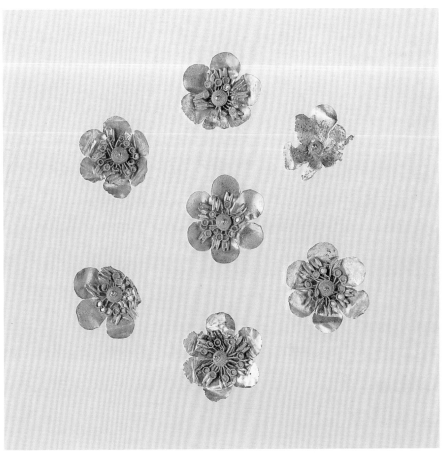

67

backing. Like other objects from the group, they show considerable fire damage; indeed, the loop from one is now fused to one of the earrings (see no. 63). Most of the remaining attachment loops also show distortion and damage, probably the result of being roughly ripped off their backing, after rapid retrieval from the funerary pyre.

Similar flower-heads have been found in a number of burials. The most elaborate are those from the Great Bliznitza (see no. 130). A group of eight with three tiers of down-turned petals were found in a tomb at Nymphaion (see Nymphaion, 1866 tomb, p. 173 below). Six slightly simpler examples than those from Madytos are in Brooklyn. A series of twenty-four flowers without stamens come from the so-called tomb of Ada recently discovered at Halikarnassos, with which may be compared a group said to come from Mylasa, also in Caria. Such flower-heads were probably attached to clothing or a veil.

The Madytos flower-heads resemble most closely the common wild or dog rose. The rose was, of course, much prized in ancient times, as now, for its wonderful scent. The lyric poet Anakreon called it 'the perfume of the gods, the joy of men . . . the favoured flower of Aphrodite'.

BIBLIOGRAPHY: See introduction to group; *Stathatos* III, p. 227, fig. 132. For the Brooklyn flower-heads see *Brooklyn*, nos 29 and 30; for the Mylasa group, *Brooklyn*, no. 30.

68   Gold strap necklace with seed-like pendants

From Asia Minor, perhaps from Mytilene;
  bought by General L.P. di Cesnola, who
  acquired it from O.A. van Lennep, together
  with two other pieces, one of which (99.23)
  was said to have been found in a tomb at
  Mytilene on 9 November 1898
330–300 BC
Length 23.5 cm; weight 47.4 g
New York 99.24; purchase, 1899

The strap consists of two doubled loop-
in-loop chains with doubled interlinking.
Along the full length of the strap are
attached alternate rosettes and die-formed
ivy leaves. The ivy leaves have green
enamel upper sections and blue lower
ones; from them hang very small plain
seeds. From the rosettes hang larger plain
seeds and two chains which make up the
festoon supporting large ribbed seed-like
pendants, each with a spiky calyx at the
top (apices and interstices marked with
grains).

The terminals take the form of a small
cut-out palmette on a volute capital with
a dark enamel fill (probably blue originally). They are fastened to the strap by
means of gold rivets with nail-like heads.

The ivy leaves find parallels on the large
disc pendants from Kul Oba (no. 87) and
the Great Bliznitza (no. 120), as well as
on a number of necklaces, one from Melos
(no. 22) and one from Sardis, now in
Pforzheim.

BIBLIOGRAPHY: Alexander, fig. 15; Segall,
pl. 38. Pforzheim necklace: Segall, pls 4 and 15.

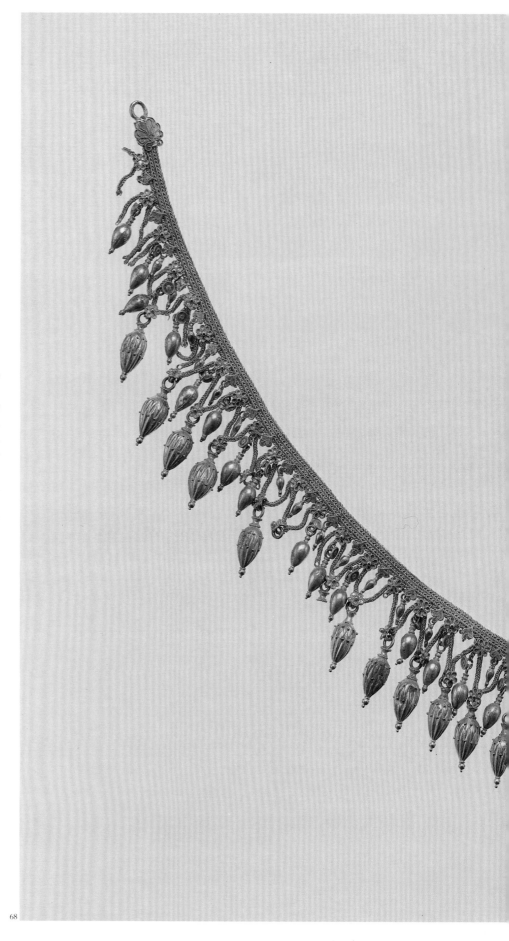

68

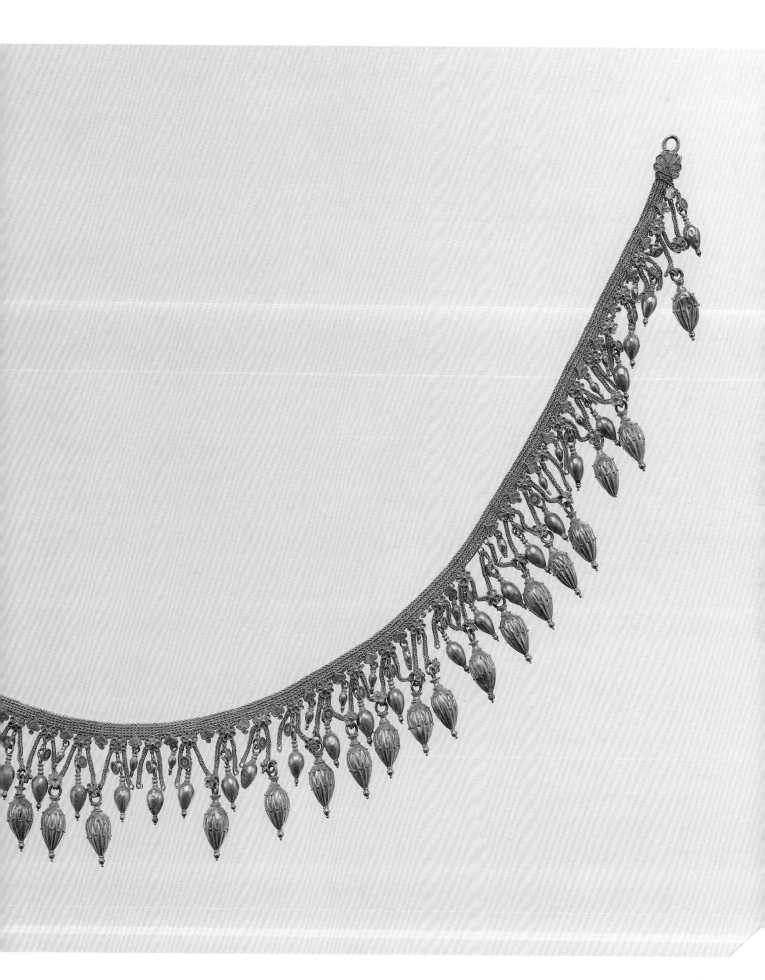

69 Gold slip-knot strap necklace

From Asia Minor, perhaps from Mytilene;
 bought by General L.P. di Cesnola, who
 acquired it from O.A. van Lennep together
 with two other pieces, one of which (99.23)
 was said to have been found in a tomb at
 Mytilene on 9 November 1898
330–300 BC
Length 33.5 cm, largest bead 1.2 cm,
 middle-sized beads 1.5 cm; weight 25.2 g
New York 99.25; purchase, 1899

This ingenious necklace can be lengthened
or shortened at will. It consists of two
straps, each made from four doubled
loop-in-loop chains with doubled interlinking. One end of each strap has a terminal with a spiral-beaded palmette and
acanthus-leaf motif within a beaded wire
border. These terminals are attached to
the straps by long gold wire pins. The
other ends of the straps pass, from opposite directions, through a large biconical
sheet-gold bead and terminate in smaller
biconical beads with a festoon of chains,
beads and seed- or bud-like pendants.

The central, sliding, biconical bead is of
sheet gold and decorated with plain and
beaded wire collars and spiral-beaded
filigree. The filigree on the two symmetrical halves consists of palmettes (the hearts
are tiny applied rhomboidal sheets) on
spirals, which have central grains. The
central leaves of the palmettes retain traces
of deliberate red cinnabar colouring. We
may probably assume that the other leaves
of the palmettes were originally enamelled, probably in blue, green or both.

The smaller biconical beads are fastened
onto the straps by wire rivets and are decorated with filigree spirals and granulation. From the lower end of these beads
emerge four loop-in-loop chains, each
of which passes through a small sheet-
gold spherical bead, plain with plain
wire collars, and then divides into two
thinner-gauge loop-in-loop chains which
cross-link to form a festoon supporting
five pendants, perhaps representing asphodel seed-pods. Above each pendant is a
small disc, and the pendants themselves
are made up of six leaf-like sections.
Within the pointed ends of these sepals is
a domed boss or lid with a filigree five-
pointed star and a circle and grain in the
centre. The arms of the star are filled with
red cinnabar, the outer interstices with
green enamel.

For parallels with this remarkable necklace, which may well have been a particularly favoured local type, see the examples
from Kyme (nos 54–5).

The asphodel grew widely in Greece
and was often associated with Hades,
the land of the dead, where desolate
meadows were said to be overgrown
with asphodels.

BIBLIOGRAPHY: Alexander, fig. 16; Segall,
pl. 39.

Opposite: 69

70 Gold earrings with elaborate disc and boat-shaped pendant

Said to be from western Asia Minor, together with a number of other pieces of jewellery now dispersed
About 300 BC
Height 6.6 and 6.7 cm, diameter of disc 1.6 cm; weight 12.7 and 12.8 g
New York 48.11.2–3; Rogers Fund, 1948

The discs are pan-shaped with turned-up edges. A corrugated sheet is attached to the exterior, with a row of large grains surmounted by small ones masking the joint. On the interior of the discs a row of small grains on large grains and plain wire surrounds an elaborate multi-tiered floral motif. A thin central tube supports spiralling wires ending in rosettes, palmettes with tongue-shaped hearts filled with granulation and curled-up pointed leaves, as well as a many-petalled central rosette.

From loops on the reverse of the discs are suspended gold rods which are soldered into the terminals of the boats. Each boat is constructed from sheet gold, in back and front halves, and is bordered above and below with beaded and plain wires. The front of each boat has an intricate pattern of diamond-shaped clusters of four granules arranged in a precise lattice (cf. Fig. 25); the backs are plain. Above the centre of each boat, on a rectangular base bordered with beaded wire and a small pointed tongue at the two front corners, is a diminutive figure of a winged Nike who has no chariot but controls the reins in the mouths of two rearing horses. These figures are tightly flanked by large palmettes with large, domed tongue-shaped hearts and by smaller palmettes with pointed tongue-shaped hearts infilled with granulation. There are also small discs with infill granulation. The space below the base is filled with acanthus leaves which sprout spirals and a central palmette with a heart infilled with granulation.

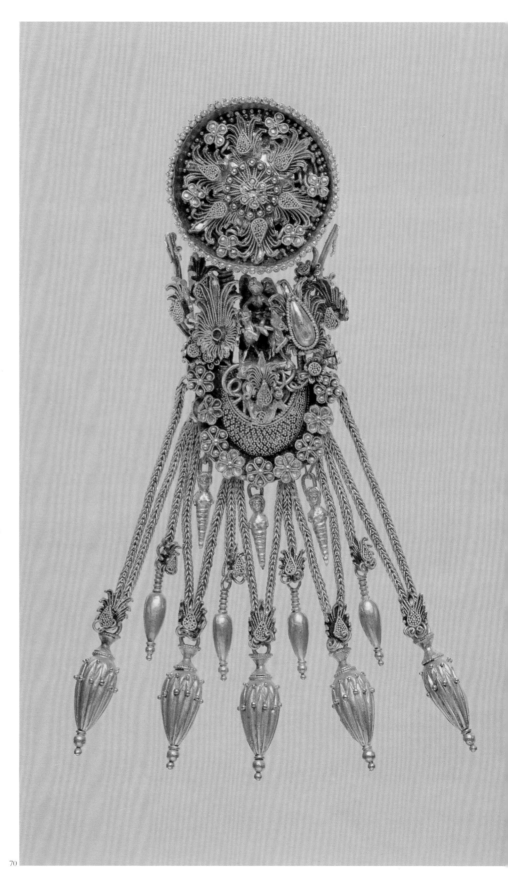

70

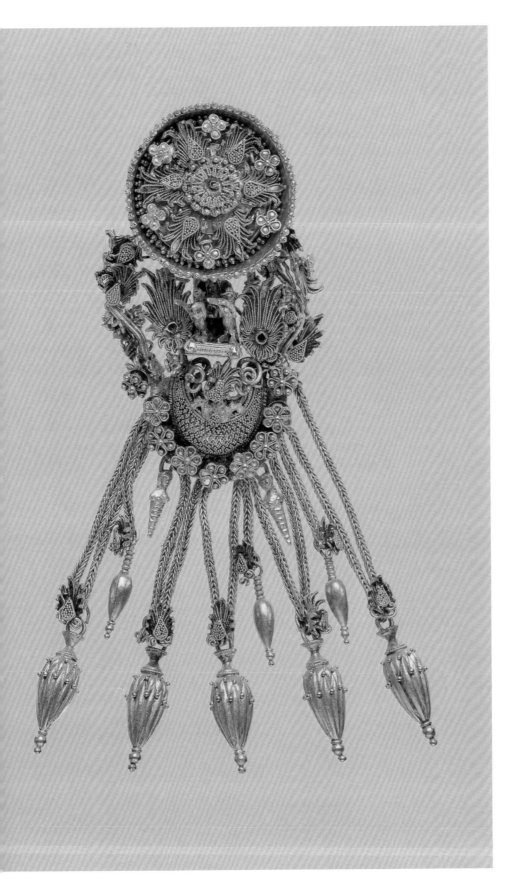

Attached to the lower edge of the boats are nine rosettes, from behind which hangs a system of chains and pendants. Five long pairs of chains each bear a palmette with curled-up spiky leaves and a tongue-shaped heart filled with granulation, and a large ribbed seed-like pendant with a calyx at the top and grains at the apices and interstices. Between these long chains, shorter single chains hold a palmette with curled-up spiky leaves and a tongue-shaped heart filled with granulation, and a plain seed with a long corrugated neck. Three of the rosettes also support a tiny armless female figure, tightly swaddled below the waist.

As in other elaborate Greek goldwork, the intricacy of this piece is almost unbelievable. The dexterity needed to produce and position each component – indeed, the sheer number of separate components – is extraordinary. Even minute parts, such as the horses, are themselves made up of more than one sheet-gold component. The use of infill granulation links these earrings with other Greek necklaces and earrings.

This pair of earrings belongs near the end and apogee of a long series. Comparable pieces include a pair from Chersonesos, a fragmentary pair said to be from Crete and now in London, a damaged pendant in the Istanbul Museum and the famous pair from Theodosia, which are all probably products of a single workshop. There are also close links with no. 70.

BIBLIOGRAPHY: Hoffmann and Davidson, fig. 54i; Oliver, p. 273, figs 8–9; *Search for Alexander, NY Suppl.*, nos s 59–60; Pfrommer, pls 28, 2 and 31, 15 (a chart suggesting the development of the type). Chersonesos earrings: Pfrommer, pl. 27, 5–6. The London fragments are *BMCJ* 1655–6; for the Istanbul fragment see Y. Meriçboyu, *Çaglar boyu anadolu takilari* (Istanbul, n.d.) p. 6; cf. also the sale catalogue, Michael Ward, *Form and Ornament* (New York 1989), no. 25. Theodosia earrings: Pfrommer, pl. 28, 1. On the group of jewellery said to have been found with these earrings see D. Buitron in *Baltimore*, p. 89 on no. 267.

3 The North Pontic Cities

The Greek geographer Strabo tells us that the first Greeks to encounter the Black Sea called it the 'Inhospitable Sea' (Pontos Axeinos or Axenos), but once they had made it theirs they renamed it the 'Euxine' (Hospitable). It was, however, most frequently referred to simply as the Pontos. In contrast to the situation along the shores of Italy and Sicily, there seems to be no real evidence, as yet, that the Greeks ventured this far in the Mycenaean period. The earliest literary evidence for the Greek penetration into the Black Sea is the tale of the Argonauts' adventure to Colchis in search of the Golden Fleece, but this is sometimes dated as late as the middle of the eighth century BC, and the first unequivocal archaeological evidence belongs to the middle of the seventh.

The approach to the Black Sea was lengthy and bedevilled by strong currents and prevailing northerly and north-easterly winds. Upon gaining the Pontos, the sailor was greeted by a wide expanse of dark water, without islands and often shrouded in thick fog. There were also extremely violent and unpredictable storms. The climate was never very attractive, with eight months of cold weather and four months of cool. Nevertheless, various groups of East Greeks began to settle at the entrance and eventually the Milesians came to ring the Pontos around with colonies.

The attractions of the distant northern shore were the abundant sup-

FIGURE 44 Gold stater of Pantikapaion, about 400–300 BC: griffin and ear of corn (British Museum SNG 867).

plies of grain and fish. Both were vital staples for the colonists and proved major exports. The ear of wheat was a symbol of the city of Pantikapaion on its coinage (Fig. 44), and at nearby Tyritake twenty-four reservoirs for salting fish have been discovered, complete with the bones and scales of herrings.

On the north coast, the Greek cities came to be concentrated on the

122

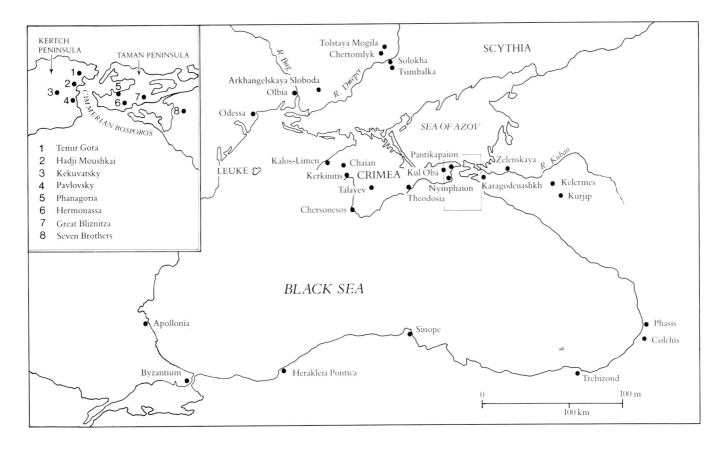

KERTCH
PENINSULA

TAMAN PENINSULA

1 Temir Gora
2 Hadji Moushkai
3 Kekuvatsky
4 Pavlovsky
5 Phanagoria
6 Hermonassa
7 Great Bliznitza
8 Seven Brothers

eastern side of the huge peninsula now called the Crimea, especially around the Cimmerian Bosporos, the passage between the Kertch peninsula and the Taman peninsula. The south and south-eastern parts of the Crimea were occupied by the Tauroi, who, according to Herodotos, sacrificed all shipwrecked sailors and such Greeks as they happened to capture upon their coasts. The south coast of the Crimea – what used to be called the 'Russian Riviera' – is, in fact, the only part of the Black Sea to have a climate resembling the Aegean. The Kertch peninsula in the east is hilly and steppe-like, with limestone outcrops, and the western or European side of the Cimmerian Bosporos is treeless and almost waterless. There is no river system and the climate is quite dry. The Greek settlers seem to have had good relations with the Scythian nomads who dominated this part of the Crimea after the displacement of the Cimmerians.

The first wave of colonies were established in the first half of the sixth century. The key foundation was that of the Milesians at Pantikapaion, but soon all of the European coast of the Bosporos was occupied. On the Asian side, the coast of the Taman peninsula consisted of a group of islands. The River Kuban (ancient Antikeites) has changed its course many times, greatly altering the coastline. The area was part of the territory of sedentary agricultural tribes, the Maeotians and the Sindians.

Here the most important Greek colonies were Phanagoria, founded in about 540 BC by Teians, and Hermonassa, both, it would seem, islands in antiquity.

Colonies were eventually planted elsewhere in the Crimea. Theodosia, a Milesian colony, was probably founded by the middle of the sixth century BC. It is quite close to the main concentration of colonies in the east, but slightly set apart. On the south coast, Chersonesos was probably founded in 422/1 BC by Megarians and people from Herakleia Pontica, although early fifth-century material has been found. The western coast of the Crimea seems always to have remained sparsely populated. The Greek colonies there were Kerkinitis, established in the early fifth century, and Kalos-Limen, probably a late fourth-century foundation.

From about 480 BC the Greek cities around the Bosporos formed themselves into a political unit, usually called the Bosporan kingdom. The early rulers of this kingdom were the Archeanactids. In 438/7 BC there was some sort of a crisis and a new group of rulers, the Spartocids, took power. This dynasty lasted throughout the fourth century and into

FIGURE 45 View of Kertch (ancient Pantikapaion): Mount Mithradates and the Iuz Oba ridge, seen from across the bay, 1857 (MacPherson, frontispiece).

the middle of the third without serious interruption: indeed, its story can be followed until the end of the second century.

From the middle of the fifth century the history of the Bosporan kingdom was closely linked to that of Athens and her maritime empire. For, following the defeat of her fleet in Egypt in 454 BC, Athens began to look elsewhere for its food supplies and in the 430s Perikles made an expedition to the Euxine. It was at this time too that Athens went to the trouble of taking over Sinope and planting a settlement at Amisos (renaming it Peiraeus), both on the south shore of the Euxine, as well as occupying a Megarian colony on the Propontis at Astakos. On the north shore the Athenians seem to have gained possession of Nymphaion and begun a dialogue with the Spartocids. At this time Athens may also have planted military colonies at Athenaion near Theodosia and at Stratokleia near Phanagoria. By the 420s between forty and fifty cities in the Euxine were paying tribute to Athens and all corn bound for Greece had to pass through the city.

This Athenian domination, however, was short-lived, for at the end of the Peloponnesian War the Bosporan rulers were able to reassert their sway over the Greek cities, to unify the Taman peninsula and to add to their domain both Theodosia and Chersonesos. The fourth century was a time of immense prosperity, indeed it was to prove the heyday of the Bosporan kingdom. Demosthenes reveals that the normal annual Athenian import of corn was 800,000 *medimnoi*, half of which came from the Bosporus, and the regular price for one *medimnos* was five *drachmai*, an income of 4 million *drachmai*. The Bosporan kingdom no doubt also sold corn to other parts of the Black Sea and beyond. Leucon I (389/8–349/8 BC) allowed the Athenians many advantages and was in return granted citizenship and immunity from civic burdens and was crowned at the Panathenaia with a golden wreath worth 1000 *drachmai*.

During the reign of Paerisades (349/8–310/9 BC) prosperity reached its peak, although in about 330 BC commerce was interrupted by a war with the Scythian king. After Paerisades' death, however, the Bosporan kingdom was shaken by political disorders and, although stability returned, by the second half of the third century economic and political decay had set in, chiefly brought about by the drop in productivity occasioned by disturbances in the steppes.

The first jewellery from the North Pontic region to show some Greek influence is that from Kelermes, which belongs to the second quarter of the sixth century. Among the very rich finds are a diadem with a three-dimensional griffin-head at the front, a strip diadem with owls and rosettes and a mirror back decorated with animals and figures, all of which seem to have Greek connections. Stylistically they follow on from some of the Rhodian jewellery of the second half of the seventh century, but are not of the same quality as the material from the Sacred Way at Delphi, which is probably a little later.

In the second half of the sixth century and the early fifth century a number of centres of production sprang up around the Black Sea which seem to diverge from the dominant Animal Style of the Scythian world. They are to be found at Olbia, at Nymphaion and at Colchis. The degree of Greek influence is far from clear, since this period is not particularly well attested in terms of jewellery from any of the Greek cities themselves.

In the Bosporan kingdom in the second half of the fifth century there seems to have been a gradual strengthening of Greek influence on jewellery, perhaps, but not necessarily, through the medium of Athens. This is well represented by the burials from the Seven Brothers complex (nos 71–5) and from Nymphaion (nos 76–80), where the gold is still very pale. It is really only in the last decades of the fifth century that we find purely Greek jewellery. Much of this late fifth- and early fourth-century material was clearly imported, often from the East Greek region, but during the first half of the fourth century, probably in its second quarter, high-quality works made specifically for the Scythian market begin to appear, most notably in the Kul Oba burial. There is the possibility that some were imports from Greece, but the detailed knowledge of Scythian dress and physiognomy, which differs greatly from the generalised versions that appear on Athenian vases, and the gradual, but slight divergence of the style point to the presence of immigrant Greek craftsmen. From the second century BC there is positive evidence of local production in the form of a stone mould.

The emigration of goldsmiths from mainland Greece and the East Greek cities to the Bosporan kingdom makes perfect sense, for of all craftsmen goldsmiths were no doubt the most likely to move to the homeland of their possible patrons and clients, rather than subject their products to the vagaries of long-distance trade. It seems probable that such migrant jewellers went to the chief cities of the region, especially Pantikapaion. The great prosperity of the Bosporan kingdom throughout the fourth century ensured goldsmiths a flourishing market, while continued contact with Macedonia and the cities of East Greece provided constant inspiration and competition.

Examination of the material from the great burials in the Bosporan region suggests that, as in South Italy, there were relatively few major goldsmiths or workshops. Two immigrant Greek goldsmiths can be identified, who produced masterpieces before the middle of the fourth century. One is the master who created the Kul Oba sphinx bracelets (no. 83) and who seems also to have been responsible for the Kul Oba touchstone (no. 84). The Kul Oba complex also contains works by a second jeweller, whose masterpiece is the torque with terminals in the form of mounted Scythians (no. 81). The ornamental bands on this torque are closely paralleled on a fragment of a lion-head torque from the same burial. This lion-head, as well as the ornamental band, matches two further lion-head torques, one from the Solokha kurgan, the other from Arkhangelskaya Sloboda. Furthermore, the same ornamental band recurs on a touchstone from the Talayev burial. The lion-heads of the torques are identical to that on a fragment from a torque in Berlin and to those on the lion-head bracelet from Temir Gora.

A further master goldsmith is recognisable amongst the jewellery from the Great Bliznitza. He produced a number of necklaces from this complex (nos 121 and 123), a pair of earrings (no. 122), the Nereid disc pendants (no. 120) and the pectoral with animals. The latter is very close to the pectoral from Tolstaya Mogila, which is also closely connected with the works of the master of the Scythian riders torque, as indeed is the famous Solokha comb. It is possible that the Great Bliznitza master and the master of the Kul Oba torques are one and the same, and that he also produced the Solokha comb, but one cannot be certain.

BIBLIOGRAPHY: In general see Artamonov, *passim*. For the Delphi material see *L'oro dei Greci*, p. 96, 6–9. For the jewellery from Kelermes see Artamonov, pp. 24–9, pls 4–55. For the existence of matrices see M.J. Treister, *Journal of the Walters Art Gallery* 48 (1990), pp. 29–35. Kul Oba lion-head torque: *Scythian Art*, pl. 212. Solokha torque: *Scythian Art*, pls 122–3. Arkhangelskaya Sloboda torque: *Ukraine*, no. 105. Talayev touchstone: *Scythian Art*, pl. 175. Temir Gora bracelet: apparently unpublished (Hoffmann and Davidson, p. 169, fig. 61c does not show the Temir Gora bracelet). Berlin fragment: Greifenhagen I, pl. 19, 1–3. Bliznitza pectoral (Hermitage BB 115): *Scythian Art*, pls 255–6. Tolstaya Mogila pectoral: *Scythian Art*, pls 118–21. Solokha comb: *Scythian Art*, pls 128–9.

Seven Brothers Barrows *(nos 71–5)*

In the lower reaches of the Kuban are a group of seven tumuli which were excavated in 1875–6 by Baron B.G. von Tiesenhausen. The largest of the mounds, the second, was 18 metres high and contained a mud-brick tomb chamber. Much of the chamber was filled with the skeletons of thirteen horses and their bronze trappings, but in one corner a male skeleton was laid out on a platform. He wore a corslet of leather with iron and bronze scales (probably all gilded) and a decorated pectoral. There were three gold ornaments around his neck: a plain tubular torque, a necklace of simple fluted tubes and a necklace with seed-like pendants (no. 71). Over the skeleton were strewn a great number of gold plaques originally sewn onto his clothing or shroud. In addition to the bull's, ram's and gorgon's heads shown here (nos 72–4), there were plaques showing human heads, Acheloos-heads, combined heads of a warrior and a lion, the foreparts of oxen and winged boars, running youths, owls, lions, sphinxes, stags, panthers, hens, and, finally, rosettes.

Lying around the body were a sword, iron spears and bronze arrow-heads. There was also a very impressive series of silver vessels: a large *rhyton* ending in a lion's head, a *phiale* with relief satyr-heads around the central raised *omphalos*, a zone-cup with partially gilded and engraved figures (on the tondo, Bellerophon on Pegasos and the Chimaira; in the zone, warriors). Bronze vessels were also included among the offerings: a cup, a strainer, two dippers and a large tripod vessel with lion-paws for feet. Finally, there was an alabaster footed *pyxis*, an Attic black-glaze 'Pheidian' mug of the third quarter of the fifth century BC, a mortarium, and pieces of gold sheet decorated in relief which probably came from a wooden vessel.

The first barrow was almost empty; the third and fifth had also been plundered. The fourth contained a silver-gilt cup with a figure of Nike seated on a stool and an Achaemenid silver *rhyton*. The sixth had not been opened and contained another silver-gilt cup with a genre scene and fragments of textiles decorated with painted figured scenes taken from Greek mythology and with names in Greek. The seventh had been robbed, but contained a horse tomb and a pair of earrings (no. 75).

BIBLIOGRAPHY: *CR* 1875, pp. iv–xiv; *CR* 1876, pp. 114–58, pl. 2, 15–22 and pls 3–4; Minns, pp. 206–10; Artamonov, p. 39 (plan: App. fig. vii).

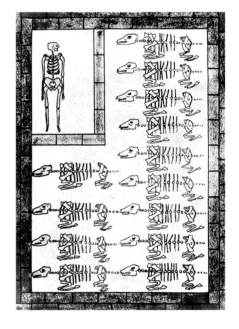

FIGURE 46 Seven Brothers, kurgan II: schematic plan of burial chamber (from Artamonov, plan VII).

71

71 Gold necklace with seed-like pendants

From Seven Brothers, kurgan II
450–425 BC
Length as strung 27.5 cm, height of pendants 3.0 cm, length of spacers 1.0 cm; weight 46.93 g
Hermitage SBR II.27

The necklace, as preserved, consists of nineteen seed-like pendants alternating with eighteen oval beads. The body of each pendant is made from two die-formed halves with added cross-hatched decoration. To each base is attached a single grain with a plain wire spacer. The top of each pendant consists of a spool-like neck in sheet gold and the suspension loop is in the form of a spherical bead. Each of these suspension beads is made of sheet gold in two halves, with the perforation holes punched from the inside so that the raised burr forms a collar. The oval beads are each made in two halves from sheet gold with added cross-hatched chased decoration, and have beaded wire collars.

The colour of the gold suggests relatively high purity and the wear on the elements indicates use in antiquity.

BIBLIOGRAPHY: *CR* 1876, pl. 4, 7; Ruxer, pls E 4c, H 2 and pl. 14a, 1; Artamonov, fig. 41.

72 Gold-sheet appliqués in the form of bulls' heads

From Seven Brothers, kurgan II
450–425 BC
Height 3.7 cm, width 3.5 cm; weight 2.21 and
  2.28 g
Hermitage SBR II.10

The bulls' heads are shown frontally with up-curved horns. These appliqués are die-formed or punched from behind, with some details chased on the front. The gold is of fairly high purity but is still brittle. There are three attachment holes, one in the nose and one in either horn. Twenty-three such appliqués were found in the tomb.

BIBLIOGRAPHY: *CR* 1876, pl. 3, 13; Artamonov, fig. 47; *Scythian Art*, pl. 81.

72

73 Gold-sheet appliqués in the form of rams' heads

From Seven Brothers, kurgan II
450–425 BC
Height 3.3 cm, width 2.9 cm; weight 1.93 and
  2.15 g
Hermitage SBR II.1

The rams' heads are shown frontally with down-curved horns and with a rosette formed of a figure-of-eight scroll in the centre of the forehead. They are manufactured from sheet gold, like no. 72, and the quality of gold is similar. There are attachment holes in the nose and each horn. Thirteen such appliqués were found in the tomb.

BIBLIOGRAPHY: *CR* 1876, pl. 3, 15; Artamonov, fig. 48; *Scythian Art*, pl. 80.

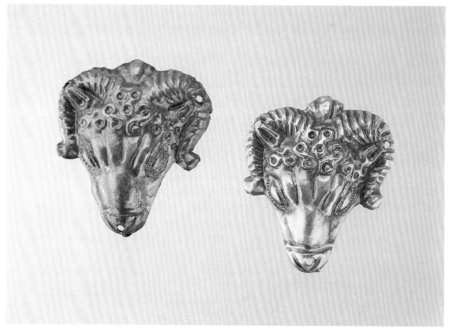

73

74

74 Gold-sheet appliqués in the form of gorgons' heads

From Seven Brothers, kurgan II
450–425 BC
Diameter 2.6 cm; weight 1.69 and 1.69 g
Hermitage SBR II.15

The gorgons' heads are shown frontally, with a row of curls across the forehead and a projecting tongue. There is a beaded border. The appliqués are made of sheet gold like nos 72–3, and in gold of similar quality. The variations in the present surfaces are due to different degrees of modern cleaning. There are attachment holes in ears and chin. Fourteen examples of this type were found in the tomb.

BIBLIOGRAPHY: *CR* 1876, pl. 3, 10; Artamonov, fig. 45.

75

75 Pair of gold boat-shaped earrings

From Seven Brothers, kurgan VII
450–425 BC
Height 3.1 cm, width 1.7 cm; weight 2.41 and 2.48 g
Hermitage SBR VII.13

The boats are made in two die-formed halves with subsequent chased decoration. The decoration on the two sides of each boat differs slightly, and the hooks are positioned to form a true mirror image. Each terminal has a spool-shaped collar with notching to imitate beaded wire. The hook is soldered to one terminal, and a gold sphere to the other. The earrings are made of pale gold.

The patterned decoration on these earrings closely recalls that on the necklace pendants from Seven Brothers II (no. 71). They may well have been made in the same workshop or by the same jeweller, in a local tradition but under some influence from Greek style.

BIBLIOGRAPHY: *CR* 1876, pl. 3, 42; Hadaczek, fig. 40.

Nymphaion, Kurgan 17 *(nos 76–80)*

In 1876 A.E. Lutsenko excavated a series of ten tumuli just to the north of Nymphaion, near the shore of the salt lake Kamysh-Burun. The seventh of this series, a medium-sized tumulus, had in the very centre, under a stone layer, a stone chamber (length 2.5 m, width 1.2 m, depth 1.25 m) containing fragments of a wooden sarcophagus and a male skeleton. On the breast of the skeleton were found a short necklace (no. 76), four pairs of identical earrings (no. 77) and a series of appliqués. In addition to those shown below (nos 78–80), there were appliqués decorated with gorgoneia, lion-heads, griffins, sphinxes and birds. On the body's left hand was a gold ring with a pointed oval bezel engraved with a flying Nike. Near the skeleton were also found fragments of a bronze helmet, a bronze greave, a scale corslet with fragments of its leather backing, arrow- and spear-heads, an iron sword and an iron dagger. At its feet were a bronze dipper with a swan's head, a bronze strainer, two Attic black-glaze cups of the last quarter of the fifth century BC, a plain bronze mirror, an alabaster *alabastron*, a bone spindle, a sponge and numerous pieces of horse trappings.

Although, as can be seen from other burials in the North Pontic area, men did wear jewellery, the four pairs of earrings are rather unexpected. Were they gifts for the dead man from his wife, laid on the corpse perhaps as surrogates for her own life? It seems very unlikely, however, that either a woman or a man would have had four pairs of identical earrings. The possibility, therefore, that these earrings were in fact used as clothes-fasteners deserves consideration.

Dug into the virgin soil was also a pit with horse skeletons, and in the fill of the tumulus another tomb was found. It was small and had been robbed.

BIBLIOGRAPHY: A.E. Lutsenko, *CR* 1876, pp. viii–xxx (esp. xiv–xv); *CR* 1877, pp. 220–40, pl. 3; Minns, pp. 210 and 215; Artamonov, p. 39; Silantyeva, pp. 71–8 and 105–6, no. 114, fig. 38.

76

76 Gold necklace with box-beads decorated with scrolls and rosettes with seed pendants

From Nymphaion, kurgan 17
425–400 BC
Length as strung 18.5 cm; weight 25.33 g
Hermitage GK/N.16

This short necklace is made up from ten hollow die-formed box-beads, with the top sheets bent over to form the sides and with separate back sheets. Each bead has two string holes. The lines of grains forming the scroll decoration are aligned along shallow grooves to facilitate their pos-

itioning, a practice occasionally employed by goldsmiths from the Mycenaean period onwards. In the centre of each bead is a rosette with petals bordered in plain wire and filled alternately with blue and green enamel. To the lower edge of each box-bead are attached three loops from which hang identical ribbed seed pendants, perhaps fennel seeds. Each seed is of sheet gold and formed in two halves. The terminals are of similar construction to the main units, but are decorated with a simple addorsed palmette and lotus in relief.

The contents of a burial at Nymphaion,

now in Oxford (grave 1) seem to have included another similar necklace of eight units, now lost. Two identical scroll and rosette units complete with seed pendants passed into the de Massoneau collection and were offered for sale in Europe in 1921: their origin, like their present whereabouts, is unknown.

BIBLIOGRAPHY: *CR* 1877, pl. 3, 34; Ruxer, pl. 32, 10; Artamonov, pl. 90; Silantyeva, fig. 38, 1 (should be 2); Pfrommer, p. 12, fig. 1a. Oxford tomb: Vickers, p. 9. De Massoneau pieces: photograph in the Department of Greek and Roman Antiquities, British Museum.

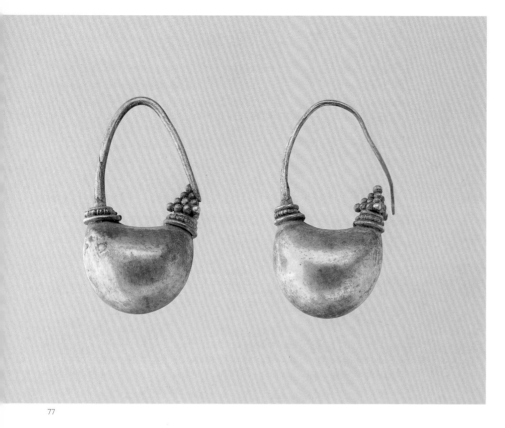

77

78

77 Gold boat-shaped earrings

From Nymphaion, kurgan 17
425–400 BC
Height 2.4 cm, width 1.2 cm; combined weight 2.94 g
Hermitage GK/N.17

The sturdy plain boats of these pale gold earrings are made in two halves. The terminals are decorated with poorly formed beaded wire, one surmounted by a three-sided pyramid formed from granules (four grains to each baseline). Each pyramid was made as a unit and then soldered in place. The tapered wire hoop is soldered into the other terminal.

This pair of earrings is only one of four identical pairs from the grave. They were found on the chest of the skeleton and so cannot have been worn in the ears. Their function is uncertain, but they may well have been used as clothes-fasteners.

BIBLIOGRAPHY: *CR* 1877, pl. 3, 33; Hadaczek, fig. 41; Artamonov, pl. 98; Silantyeva, fig. 38, 2 (should be 1). The objects in Oxford from Nymphaion identified by Vickers as clothes-fasteners (Vickers, pl. 6d) are really earrings, cf. *Sardis*, no. 69, pl. 7, fig. 8.

78 Gold-sheet appliqués with a triple form (human head, lion's head and fish)

From Nymphaion, kurgan 17
425–400 BC
Height 2.4 cm, length 3.0 cm; weight 1.18 and 1.57 g
Hermitage GK/N.20

These appliqués combine in one design a female head wearing a *sakkos* to the left with a lion's head to the right and a fish to the left below. They are die- or punch-formed from the back, and have three crudely pierced attachment holes (in the snout of the lion and in the tail and nose of the fish). The gold is of a pale colour and is brittle. There is a reddish patina on the inside surfaces.

These plaques show definite signs of wear, indicating that they were not made solely for the funeral. Indeed, damage to one of the fish-tails had necessitated an ancient reperforation. There were five appliqués of this design in the tomb.

BIBLIOGRAPHY: *CR* 1877, pl. 3, 19; Artamonov, pl. 94; Silantyeva, fig. 38, 13.

79 Gold-sheet appliqués in the form of stags

From Nymphaion, kurgan 17
425–400 BC
Height 1.8 cm, length 2.3 cm; weight 0.89 and
    1.00 g
Hermitage GK/N.23

A stag with bent-up legs and multiple branched, curling antlers faces to the right. The appliqués are die-formed or punched from the back, but one of the examples also has a minimal amount of chasing from the front. They have three crudely pierced attachment holes (in the nose, between the hooves and in the last antler or in the rump). The gold is pale and brittle. Three such appliqués were found in the tomb.

The representation of the stags on these plaques is typical of the Scythian animal style, and, like the other appliqués from this tomb, they were no doubt the work of local craftsmen. The designs on other plaques from the burial include griffins; these may be thematically linked to the stags, since the theme of griffins fighting stags was particularly popular in the North Pontic region.

BIBLIOGRAPHY: *CR* 1877, pl. 3, 24; Artamonov, pl. 100; Silantyeva, fig. 38, 7.

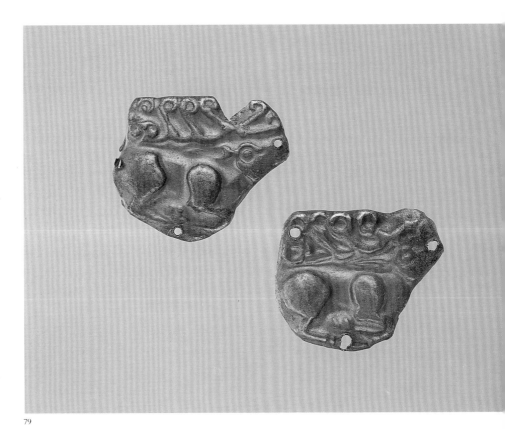

79

80 Gold-sheet appliqués in the form of cockerels

From Nymphaion, kurgan 17
425–400 BC
Height 2.5 cm, length 2.6 cm; weight 1.08 and
    1.35 g
Hermitage GK/N.30

These appliqués show a cockerel standing to the left. Like nos 78–9, they are die-formed or punched from behind, but in this case with many more chased details added from the front. The crudely pierced attachment holes appear between the feet, in the tail-feathers and in the crest. The gold is pale and brittle, and there is a reddish patina on the back surfaces. Five such appliqués were found in the tomb.

BIBLIOGRAPHY: *CR* 1877, pl. 3, 29; Artamonov, pl. 106; Silantyeva, fig. 38, 14.

80

Kul Oba *(nos 81–92)*

The great stone chamber with a stepped roof in the kurgan of Kul Oba near Kertch was discovered accidentally by Russian soldiers on 19 September 1830: it was cleared by P. Dubrux. Subsequent investigations were carried out by A.E. Lutsenko in 1875.

Much of the chamber (*c.* 4 m square and *c.* 12 m high) was taken up by a large painted wooden sarcophagus, which was divided into two parts. In one part was a male skeleton of large stature with the remains of a *bashlyk*, or felt hat, decorated with gold strips and small plaquettes. Round his neck was a torque with terminals in the form of Scythian horsemen (no. 81); on his right upper arm was a bracelet decorated with reliefs showing Peleus and Thetis and Eos and Kephalos (no. 82); at his elbows were armbands in a local style; and around both wrists were bracelets with sphinx terminals (no. 83). In the other compartment were the dead man's weapons and other accoutrements – iron sword with gold hilt and scabbard cover (inscribed PORNACHO, but of mixed Scythian and local style), greaves, whip handle, *phiale* and touchstone (no. 84).

Alongside the sarcophagus was a female skeleton arranged on a couch. She had an elaborate headdress on her head (no. 85) and a torque and a necklace round her neck. Also on the body were two large discs decorated with the head of Athena (no. 87) and a pair of earrings (no. 88), as well as a single earring (no. 89). Between her knees was the famous vase decorated with Scythians, which bears a Greek weight inscription, 35, under its base (representing a modern weight of 328.12 g). The woman may have been holding it in her hands. At her sides were also armbands decorated in relief with griffins and stags (no. 86). Around her head were disposed a silver spindle and a bronze mirror with a gold sheet over the handle, crudely decorated in relief.

Above the heads of these skeletons, and at right angles, was the skeleton of a servant. Beside him were six knives, one of them with a hilt covered with a gold sheet, crudely decorated in relief in Scythian style. In a special pit in the floor were horse bones, a helmet and a pair of greaves. Vessels were placed around the walls of the chamber, five of silver (one inscribed ERMEO), four of bronze, as well as four Thasian wine amphorae. All over the floor of the tomb were numerous gold plaques (nos 90–92) and buttons, perhaps originally sewn onto textiles which hung on the walls. There were also fragments of ivory plaques, delicately engraved and painted with figures. These ivory inlays may have come from an elaborate couch or from the sarcophagus.

BIBLIOGRAPHY: Ashik, pp. 29–33; *ABC* I, pp. ix–li; MacPherson, pp. 61–6; *CR* 1875, pp. xxx–xxxii; Newton, pp. 377–80; Minns, pp. 195–206; Rostovtzeff *SuB*, pp. 334–41; Artamonov, pp. 67–72; Pfrommer, FK 153.

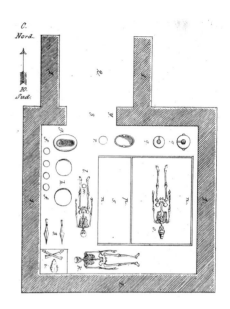

FIGURE 47 Kul Oba: schematic plan of burial-chamber (from *ABC*, plan A).

FIGURE 48 Detail from the ivory inlays for a couch: Hera wearing a wreath, earrings, necklace and bracelet (Hermitage KO 116/2).

81 Gold torque ending in Scythian riders

From Kul Oba
400–350 BC
Width 26.6 cm, height 24.0 cm, height of
   horsemen 3.0 cm; weight 460.00 g
Hermitage KO 17

The torque is not a normal item of Greek jewellery, for the form, which could be worn by both men and women, was distinctly barbarian in Greek eyes. In the hands of a Greek jeweller the terminals of this piece, although Scythian in subject, are imbued with all the subtlety of Greek design and craftsmanship.

The hoop consists of six gold rods of circular section twisted together. It terminates in superbly modelled Scythian riders and the foreparts of their mounts. The Scythians and their horses are slightly turned outwards, away from the chest of the wearer, to add life and a sense of depth. The decorative collars, which are attached to the hoop by plain gold pegs, are elaborately decorated in filigree and enamel. There are two friezes of palmettes, half-palmettes and lotus leaves, the leaves alternately filled with blue and green enamel, together with blue ivy leaves floating in the field; three rows of ovolos similarly picked out with enamel; and a frieze of plain wire double spirals. These friezes are bordered by decorative wires – beaded, plain and rope.

The Scythians have long hair (tied at neck level, with a bunch below) and are bearded. They wear long belted jackets, baggy trousers and soft shoes. The right hand of the horseman on the left hangs down, holding something: this is now lost, but the presence of two wires down the inside of the right leg, next to the horse, suggests that the object was a whip. His left hand is drilled for reins, now also missing. The other horseman has his left hand outstretched, holding the reins, which are tied together; his right hand is

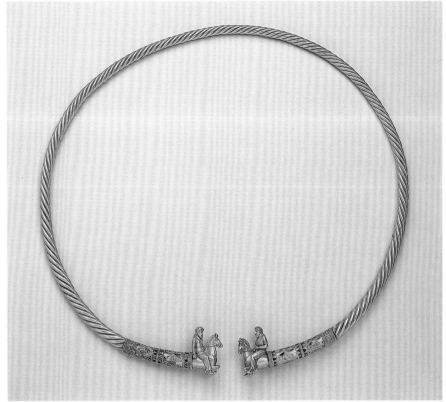

81

empty. The forelegs of the horses are tucked up and their cropped manes are arranged in separate tufts.

The horses and riders appear solid, but may be of thick sheet gold. Their entire surfaces show fine hammer marks, burnishing and chasing, which have concealed the exact nature of their construction. It is possible that the riders were made separately from the horses and soldered in place, and even that the terminals were wholly or partly cast, although they show no indications of this.

The whole object, including the enamel, is in a remarkable state of preservation and shows little, if any, evidence of ancient wear, in contrast to some of the other objects in the tomb.

The style of the decoration on the collar suggests that it was made in the same workshop as the fragment of a lion-head torque also from Kul Oba, a number of other such torques and the touchstone from the Talayev kurgan near Simferopol. These pieces are in turn closely related to the great necklace (no. 121) from the Great Bliznitza and the great pectoral from Tolstaya Mogila (see p. 127 above, where other related pieces are also noted).

BIBLIOGRAPHY: *ABC*, pl. 8, 1; T&K I, fig. 80; Artamonov, pls 201–2; *Or des Scythes*, no. 93; *Scythian Art*, pls 126–7; *Zürich*, no. 39. Kul Oba lion-head torque: *Scythian Art*, pl. 212. Talayev touchstone: *Scythian Art*, pl. 175. Tolstaya Mogila pectoral: *Scythian Art*, pls 118–21.

Overleaf: 81

82

of the reliefs point to the second quarter of the fifth century BC. The armlet also shows considerable signs of wear.

BIBLIOGRAPHY: *ABC*, pl. 13, 3; T&K II, fig. 71; A. Manzewitsch, *AA* 1931, pp. 106–15; Artamonov, pl. 206; *LIMC* III, *sv* Eos, no. 279; *Scythian Art*, pl. 180; *Zürich*, no. 35. On winged women carrying off boys see also S. Kaempf-Dimitriadou, *Die Liebe der Götter in der attischen Kunst des 5. Jahrhunderts v. Chr.* (Bern 1979).

82 Gold armlet with mythological scenes in relief

From Kul Oba
475–450 BC
Outer diameter 10.3 cm, width 2.5 cm, height of Peleus and Thetis reliefs 4.0 cm, height of Eos reliefs 2.0–2.5 cm; weight 108.61 g
Hermitage KO 18

This armlet is a singleton. It is formed from a sheet-gold band with up-turned longitudinal edges and beaded wire borders. Two types of cut-out sheet reliefs, each repeated five times, are soldered in place.

One set of reliefs shows Peleus wrestling with Thetis. It had been foretold that the goddess Thetis' son would be more powerful than his father, so despite her beauty all the other gods decided she should be married off to a mortal. Peleus was chosen, but Thetis proved reluctant and he had to withstand a variety of her transmutations to win her. On these reliefs Thetis stands to the right, her head back to the left, wearing a *chiton* with vertically hatched border and overfold, and her hair loose. Her hands are on top of Peleus' head, her elbows out. Peleus stoops to the right (only his head, arms and shoulders appear) as he grasps Thetis round the waist. A lion, one of Thetis' mutations, rears up on the right.

The other set of reliefs shows a winged woman in a *chiton* moving rapidly to the right and holding a naked boy by his legs and under his arm; the boy's right hand is extended to the woman's chin. This is probably the goddess Eos (Dawn) abducting a beautiful youth, either Kephalos or Tithonos.

These plaques were die-formed, with some detailing added from the front. The joints between them are partly concealed by two rosettes of sheet gold with plain wire outlines. Several of the rosettes contain a brown resinous substance which may or may not have been an intentional filler.·

This armlet was found on the man's upper arm and was no doubt an heirloom of considerable family or even tribal importance. The pale gold from which it is made suggests an early date and the style

83 Gold bracelet with sphinx protomes (one of a pair)

From Kul Oba
400–350 BC
Width 10.0 cm, height 11.0 cm; weight 176.22 g (KO 19: 174.92 g)
Hermitage KO 20 (the pair is KO 19)

These are the most majestic of all Greek bracelets. The combination of powerful modelling and exquisite detailing places them among the masterpieces of ancient art.

The sphinx terminals are made from several sheet-gold components, including separate wings and limbs. Minuscule details have been added in wire and moulded sheet gold. These include a filigree diadem with a rosette in the centre and spirals either side hidden in the hair, droplet earrings hung from the ears, and a choker necklace with seed-like pendants surrounding the neck. Other meticulous details, such as the horse's veins under the bellies of the sphinxes, are in repoussé. The feathers of the wings are particularly carefully delineated. Between them are two types of support, a strap behind the head and a rod at the back. The paws of the sphinx protomes are linked together: there is a pair of loop straps under both pairs of paws, through which a wire with snake-heads was threaded. This fastening was damaged in antiquity.

The sheet collars are decorated with a frieze of palmettes (pale green above) and lotus (white or pale blue above); one collar has the palmettes and lotus buds facing in the same direction, the other has them alternating up and down. The borders are formed from plain wires, rows of large grains, beaded wire and spool-beaded wire, as well as a frieze of egg and dart

83

(alternately pale green and white or pale blue). It is remarkable that all the beaded wires, even the tiniest (*c.* 0.2 mm in diameter), are properly beaded and not spiral-beaded. The use of a row of large grains instead of a beaded wire at one point, and of spool-beaded wire is also unusual at this period.

The twisted hoop is of sheet gold of substantial thickness, spirally fluted to imitate three gold rods twisted together. Lengths of beaded wire follow the valleys. A bronze fastening pin secures the hoop

to the collars. The core of the hoop appears to be a brown resinous substance mixed with a white material, probably the resin with crushed calcite filler that has been noted in other Greek goldwork; this filling is also visible inside the sphinxes.

There are substantial signs of ancient wear (and damage) on the bracelet. It and its pair were clearly worn by the male in the centre of the tomb in life as well as in death.

Sphinx protome terminals are also found on a bracelet of the first half of the

third century BC from the Tuch el-Karamus temple treasure. Later still, they recur as terminals for hoop earrings. The style of the bracelets suggests that they may be from the same workshop as the touchstone (no. 84).

BIBLIOGRAPHY: Ashik, fig. 123; *ABC*, pl. 13, 1; Artamonov, pls 200 and 205; Higgins *GRJ*², pl. 30b; Ogden *JAW*, p. 40, fig. 4:11; Deppert-Lippitz, fig. 138; *Scythian Art*, pl. 182; *Zürich*, no. 40. For the brown core cf. the Loeb diadem, Hoffmann and Davidson no. 1, and see Ogden *JAW*, pp. 40–43. Tuch el-Karamus group: Pfrommer, FK 6; bracelets, pl. 21, 3 and 5.

84

84 Gold-capped touchstone(?)

From Kul Oba
400–350 BC
Length 17.0 cm, height of gold cap 5.8 cm;
    weight 102.57 g
Hermitage KO 36

This intriguing object, one of several similar known, consists of a slightly tapering rod of smooth black stone set in an ornate sheet-gold handle. On top of the handle is a nine-petal rosette with a grain between the ends of the petals. The decoration of the cylindrical sides consists of two main friezes, one of rosettes and double lotus blossoms with tiny gold-sheet frontal faces inserted at the bottoms of the lotuses, the other of pairs of addorsed palmettes and lotus buds on spiral bases. These are separated by bands of beaded wire, rope and lines of grains, as well as narrow friezes of ovolos. The handle decoration terminates in triangular tongues overlaid with granulation. A suspension hole is pierced laterally through the object near its upper end.

The stone has been repaired in recent times. The handle shows extensive wear and there is no longer any indication as to whether it was originally enamelled. Apart from rings (nos 17, 29, 58–9, 97, 156–8 and 190) and beads (no. 95), this is the only object in this catalogue to show abundant platinum-group metal inclusions.

The identification of such objects as touchstones is tentative. They are usually described as whetstones, but the hard fine-grained nature of the black stone has more in common with the 'Lydian stone' famed in antiquity for testing gold than with a functional sharpener. Moreover, they would not appear to have much practical use for sharpening iron or copper alloy weapons. In a society in which the display of gold was so important, a touchstone would have formed a vital piece of equipment for the ruling élite.

The style of the border patterns suggests a link with the master craftsman who designed and produced the sphinx bracelets (no. 83).

BIBLIOGRAPHY: *ABC*, pl. 30, 7; Artamonov, pl. 212; *Scythian Art*, pl. 176. For other touchstones see *Scythian Art*, pls 175 (Talayev kurgan, near Simferopol) and 177 (Malaya Bliznitza). There are also touchstones from the Chertomlyk, Salgir and Zubov burials; those from Karagodeuashkh and Vettersfelde have plain gold hilts.

85 Gold diadem with winged vegetation gods and palmettes

From Kul Oba
400–350 BC
Height 4.0 cm, flat length 37.5 cm; weight
    61.66 g
Hermitage KO 1

This spectacular gold diadem consists of a broad band of gold with a repoussé design and a series of rosettes attached along the top edge. The design was produced by pressing the sheet gold into an intaglio die. It depicts four palmettes with dotted hearts and thistle-like fruits which alternate with three bearded and winged figures wearing *poloi*. The curling tendrils that grow from the waists of these demons end in *kete* (sea-monsters) and sprout pomegranate-like fruits, which are being eaten by birds. Above and below the scene is a border of ovolos.

Twenty-eight rosettes are attached to a plain zone above the frieze. The rosettes are formed from slightly concave circular discs to which are soldered plain wires delineating six petals, with a central grain. The petals are enamelled alternately blue and green. The rosettes appear to show more wear than the rest of the diadem and were perhaps transferred from another object.

The design starts about 2.5 centimetres from the left end of the diadem, while at the right end an equal margin has been produced by flattening out the repoussé design. There are attachment holes at either end and three perforations along the bottom, at the base of each vegetation god. A further series of holes, slightly above the pairs of holes that hold the rosettes in place, were perhaps for attachment to a backing.

This diadem probably formed part of an elaborate *polos*, built up from a number of elements. A similar arrangement was discovered in the Chertomlyk and Tolstaya Mogila kurgans. The most spectacular surviving *polos* is the large, one-piece band from the Great Bliznitza.

The vegetation god is a counterpart to the similar, but female, figure encountered on objects such as the Tsimbalka nose-piece or on some of the Kul Oba cut-out plaques. This goddess may be related to the snake-legged woman with whom the Greeks thought Herakles had coupled to create the first of the Scythians.

BIBLIOGRAPHY: *ABC*, pl. 2, 3; Artamonov, pl. 199 (part). Chertomlyk *polos: Scythian Art*, pl. 233; Tolstaya Mogila: *Ukraine*, fig. 54 (?). Great Bliznitza: *Scythian Art*, pls 226–8. Tsimbalka: *Scythian Art*, pl. 144. Kul Oba cut-outs: *Scythian Art*, pls 203 and 208.

85

86 Gold bracelet with stags and griffins (one of a pair)

From Kul Oba
400–350 BC
Diameter *c.* 8.0 cm; height 5.5 cm; weight 83.12 g
Hermitage KO 3

This armlet consists of a broad band of pale gold with turned-up edges and a central longitudinal ridge. The ridge separates the two friezes of griffins and stags and serves as the ground line for both. The reliefs are separate die-formed cut-outs (only two complete dies used), with some additional chased detail from the front, and are soldered onto the background. The sequence, from left to right, is a griffin leaping to the right and a griffin biting into the back of a fallen stag facing

86

left, both repeated, and ending with a griffin leaping to the right. At either end of each frieze are two die-formed lion-skin heads, also with chased details. Each end of the armlet is marked by a thick beaded wire.

Ten examples of this form of bracelet, but with no added reliefs, were found in the same burial. Others have been found in the Solokha, Tolstaya Mogila and Chertomlyk kurgans. It seems to be a Scythian type, here considerably enriched in the hands of a Greek jeweller.

BIBLIOGRAPHY: *ABC*, pl. 13, 2; T&K II, fig. 72; Artamonov, pls 237–8; A.P. Manzewitsch, *TrudyErmit* 7 (1962), p. 112, fig. 9. Plain examples: (Kul Oba) *ABC*, pl. 26, 3–4; (Solokha) Artamonov, fig. 82.

87 Gold pendant disc with head of Athena (one of a pair)

From Kul Oba
400–350 BC
Height 18.0 cm, diameter of disc 7.0 cm; weight
85.34 g
Hermitage KO 5

The large, slightly convex disc of this remarkable pendant shows the head of the famous statue of Athena Parthenos by Pheidias in three-quarter view. She wears an elaborate helmet with a triple crest (sphinx between Pegasoi) and deer- and griffin-heads attached to the top of the diadem-like peak, which is itself decorated with dotted spirals. The turned-up cheek flaps are decorated with griffins and the neck-piece with spirals. Athena wears earrings of the disc and pyramid type and a three-tier necklace. A coiled snake appears at either shoulder, presumably emanating from her *aegis*, while up on the left is her symbol, the owl. The flat rim of the disc bears a frieze of ivy leaves, alternately dark blue and green, and spiral tendrils in spiral-beaded wire, between borders of beaded and plain wires.

Along the lower circumference rosettes alternate with ivy leaves (one retains its green enamel fill). From the rosettes hang a complex festoon of doubled loop-in-loop chains, heavy wire spirals, discs (green with inner blue alternating with blue with inner green), rosettes and four varieties of seed-like pendants. The uppermost two rows of seeds are ribbed and have a zigzag of grains at the apices of the calyx, the next row have tongues alternately filled with blue and green enamel, and the lowest are ribbed and have three rows of feathers, with grains at the apices and cross-hatched panels.

At the top of the back of the disc is a suspension hoop. The pendants were found on the middle of the body of the woman, rather than beside her head, so one might guess that they were attached to her garments, perhaps over her breasts. The Hellenised wearer of these pendants must have been particularly proud to have the image of the greatest statue of Athena on her jewellery.

BIBLIOGRAPHY: Ashik, fig. 121; *ABC*, pl. 19, 1; *AM* 8 (1883), pp. 291–315 and pl. 15; T&K II, fig. 65; Artamonov, pls 214–15; Gorbunova and Saverkina, no. 61; Higgins *GRJ*², p. 130, pl. 29.

Opposite: 87

88 Pair of gold earrings with disc and boat-shaped pendant

From Kul Oba
About 350 BC
Height 10.0 cm, diameter of disc 3.5 cm; weight 53.26 g
Hermitage KO 6

The pan-shaped disc of each earring has a corrugated sheet outside the up-turned edge, which is topped by a row of grains. Within this rim are a series of decorative wires (thick beaded wire, ropes, spiral-beaded wire) and a ring of ovolos filled alternately with green and blue enamel. Within these is a frieze of spirals with groups of three grains on stems and acanthus leaves covering the joins. In the centre is a multi-level flower-head built up on a tube. The lowest level has stamens ending alternately in a rosette (four rosettes, petals filled alternately with blue and green enamel) and a cut-out sheet Nereid riding a dolphin (four Nereids, each holding an item of the new armour made for Achilles by Hephaistos at Thetis' request: a shield, a helmet, greaves and a cuirass). The upper level of the flower-head consists of a long-petal rosette. The central, capping element is missing. The whole of the depression under this flower-head was filled with a green substance which has the appearance of a copper compound, perhaps ground malachite, with a resin or glue binder. This is undoubtedly original to the earring and was presumably intended to provide a coloured background.

The 'hull' of the boat is decorated with two friezes of spirals and omegas, bordered by rows of decorative wires (beaded and plain) and rows of ovolos alternately filled with green and blue enamel. There is a large four-level rosette on each terminal of the boat: the petals of the innermost rosette are filled alternately with blue and green enamel. In the centre of the boat is a two-level palmette with pointed petals and three acanthus leaves at the heart: the leaves of the front palmette are again filled alternately with blue and green. Attached to the back of each terminal are two thick wires with discs near the ends (once filled with enamel) and with six spiky leaves with central ribs. The backs of the boats are more simply decorated, omitting the rows of ovolos with enamel filling.

Along the lower contour of the front of the boat are eleven rosettes, alternately single-level and double-level. The single-level rosettes have alternate green and blue enamel petals. Below hangs a festoon of chains and pendants. From each of the single-level rosettes hangs a single small plain seed. From each of the double-level rosettes hangs a disc (inner disc blue, outer band green) and a seed decorated with a long pointed calyx, alternately filled with blue and green enamel. To either side of these extends a chain supporting a two-level rosette and a large seed-like pendant with a calyx consisting of three rows of feathered leaves and four rows of grains, and a ribbed seed with cross-hatching on alternate panels. There were originally five small, four middle-sized and five large seeds. On one earring three of the large pendants are later replacements.

It is interesting to note that the decorative wires on the discs are all plain or spiral-beaded, even the borders. The only beaded wire is a circle underlying the central rosette on just one of the earrings. On the pendants the wires are all plain or beaded: there is no spiral-beaded wire. This suggests one of the following possibilities: that the discs and pendants were made by different goldsmiths within the same workshop; that the goldsmith used his stock-in-trade of wire; or that the discs do not belong with the pendants, the whole being an adaptation motivated by wear, loss or fashion.

In their original state these earrings must have been truly remarkable, with the rich green background to the central flower-head, the smaller points of blue and green and the minuscule figures of Nereids on dolphin-back.

BIBLIOGRAPHY: Ashik, fig. 122b; *ABC*, pl. 19, 5; T&K II, fig. 66; Artamonov, pls 221–3; Gorbunova and Saverkina, no. 60; Ogden *JAW*, pl. 28; Deppert-Lippitz, fig. 129; *Scythian Art*, pl. 133; Pfrommer, pl. 27, 1; *Zürich*, no. 53.

Opposite: 88

89 Single gold earring with disc and boat-shaped pendant

From Kul Oba
About 350 BC
Height 9.0 cm, diameter of disc 2.8 cm; weight 22.35 g
Hermitage KO 7

The pan-shaped disc has an up-turned edge, on the outside of which is attached a plain sheet and a corrugated sheet, while on top is a row of small grains above large grains. Within the edge are a series of decorative wires (plain and rope wires) and a frieze of spirals with buds between (joints covered with corrugated bent sheets). In the centre is a multi-level flower-head built up on a central tube. Two levels of down-turned narrow leaves are preserved, but the central cap is missing. The whole of the central depression was filled with red cinnabar. The hook on the back of the disc ends in a snake's head.

The 'hull' of the boat is decorated with granules in groups of four on either side of a central division made up of a beaded wire flanked by plain wires. The grains probably moved slightly during soldering, thus producing the small irregularities. There is no granulation on the back. The central floral motif takes the form of a circumscribed downward-facing palmette, with a pair of additional spirals above (another element may be lost here). On each terminal, above plain and beaded wires, is mounted a three-level spiky-leaved palmette with an ovoid heart filled with red cinnabar. Additional cut-out sheet figures of Nikai are attached to the top of the backs of the terminals. The Nikai sit adjusting a sandal, their hair tied up in a top-knot. One wing of each is integral to the figure, the other is separate and soldered to the back.

Along the lower contour of the boat are attached eight two-level rosettes which support a festoon of chains and pendants. From each rosette hangs a plain seed with

89

a disc above (inner disc green, outer band blue, alternating with inner blue and outer green; this is the only enamel on the earrings) and two chains that spread out on either side to help support a rosette and a large seed with a calyx made from three rows of zigzags with granulation at the apices and rows of dots down the ribs to the base. Between each rosette a small

ribbed seed is suspended on a short chain.

As in no. 88, the minute detail and the colouristic effect of these earrings must have been particularly spectacular. The pair to this earring appears not to have been discovered in the tomb.

BIBLIOGRAPHY: Ashik, fig. 122a; *ABC*, pl. 19, 4; Artamonov, pl. 304; *Scythian Art*, pl. 130; *Zürich*, no. 52.

Opposite: 89

90

90 Square gold appliqués with dancers

From Kul Oba
About 350 BC
Width 4.7 cm; weight 4.79 and 4.88 g
Hermitage KO 50

Within a bead and reel border are two heavily draped female dancers. That on the left moves to the right, head back, kicking up her right heel behind her, her right hand up to her neck. The other dancer moves to the left, *krotala* (castanet-like clappers) in either hand, her left foot only touching the ground with the toes. These appliqués were die-formed or punched from the back, with no additional chasing. There is an attachment hole in each corner. Five such plaques were found in the tomb.

The identity of these two dancers cannot be determined precisely. They may be Muses, Horai (Seasons) or Charites (Graces) who accompanied divine processions, or maenads associated with Dionysiac revels.

BIBLIOGRAPHY: Ashik, fig. 141; *ABC*, pl. 20, 5; T&K II, fig. 38; Becatti, fig. 464; Artamonov, pl. 234; *AT*, p. 149, fig. 5.

91 Round gold appliqués with a human head

From Kul Oba
About 350 BC
Diameter 5.5 cm; weight 5.26 and 5.51 g
Hermitage KO 53

Within a dotted border is a head with wavy hair, almost in three-quarter view to the left. It is difficult to be sure of the sex of the figure: if female, it is perhaps Aphrodite or a maenad; if male, perhaps Dionysos, Apollo or even Orpheus. These appliqués were die-formed or punched from the back, with no additional chasing. There are four attachment holes. Five such plaques were found in the tomb.

BIBLIOGRAPHY: *ABC*, pl. 21, 11; Artamonov, pl. 219; *AT*, p. 149, fig. 8.

91

92 Gold cut-out appliqués of a human head

From Kul Oba
About 350 BC
Width 3.7 cm; weight 2.97 and 3.16 g
Hermitage KO 54

In the curly hair of these frontal heads is an ivy wreath with a central group of berries, suggesting that they may be intended to represent a maenad, or even a young Dionysos. These appliqués were die-formed or punched from behind, with no chasing from the front, apart from the eyes of one example (KO 54.16). There are four attachment holes. Fifty-four such appliqués were found in the tomb.

BIBLIOGRAPHY: *ABC*, pl. 21, 10; Artamonov, pl. 216; *AT*, p. 150, fig. 9.

92

Pantikapaion, 1854 Stone Tomb *(nos 93–8)*

In November 1854 Lutsenko excavated a tumulus on a rocky hill on the northern slope of Mount Mithridates. In the centre was a slab-grave cut into virgin soil at a depth of 3.20 metres from the top of the tumulus. Almost the whole of the space within the tomb (length 2.31 m, width 1.42 m, height 1.42 m) was occupied by a wooden sarcophagus made of planks of cypress wood and with a ridged roof. The sarcophagus, which rested on a stone support (cf. Kekuvatsky kurgan, p. 164 below), contained a woman's skeleton. This lay on a textile with a layer of oak bark beneath. The body had been covered by a woollen textile, dyed purple, and the report lists a number of items around it, including a wooden comb, a spindle, a copper make-up stick, an alabaster *alabastron*, a box woven from hemp and a wooden box painted blue, inside which were ten copper-wire pins in the shape of snakes, perhaps hair coils.

On the body itself were found several items of jewellery. At the level of the ears was a pair of earrings (no. 93), and still in place on the neck itself was a necklace with Acheloos-head pendants (no. 94), while the remains of a second necklace with spherical beads (no. 95) lay scattered nearby. On the arms, at the level of the elbows, was discovered a pair of silver bracelets with gold lion-heads (no. 96). On the left hand there were two gold rings (nos 97–8), while nearby lay a rock-crystal scaraboid decorated with a griffin.

The jewellery provides the only evidence for dating this burial. It seems that the two rings may have been heirlooms. [Y.K.]

BIBLIOGRAPHY: Unpublished report by A. E. Lutsenko in the Archive of the Hermitage Museum; partial description, *ABC* II, pp. 338–9, with explanation of vignettes at beginning of volume (=Reinach, pp. 137); Pfrommer, FK 152.

93

93 Pair of spiral gold earrings with copper core

From Pantikapaion
About 400 BC
Height 3.2 cm, width 3.1 cm; weight 13.49 and
17.01 g
Hermitage P.1854.24

These spiral earrings terminate in carefully built-up pyramids of grains, below which are cylindrical sheets decorated with figure-of-eight spirals of plain wire between borders of beaded and plain wires, and triangles of grains. The copper-rod core must have been first overlaid with a sheet of gold, the longitudinal seam of which has been almost completely obscured by fine burnishing.

Similar earrings have been found at Nymphaion, as well as in other burials at Pantikapaion, and there are many parallels from Asia Minor (no. 47) and northern Greece, as well as Thrace. This type of earring is known in gold, silver and bronze.

BIBLIOGRAPHY: P.F. Silantyeva, *TrudyErmit* 17 (1976), p. 126, fig. 3b (variant II). Nymphaion earrings (Oxford 1885.483): Vickers, pl. 11c.

94 Gold necklace with rosettes, lotus-rosettes and Acheloos-heads

From Pantikapaion
400–380 BC
Length as strung 26.5 cm; weight 46.63 g
Hermitage P.1854.22

This delicate necklace with its pastel blue enamel epitomises the finest late fifth- and early fourth-century Greek jewellery. It is made up of two basic elements. The first is a series of lotus-rosettes (twenty-four preserved, one perhaps missing) from which are suspended die-stamped Acheloos-heads (eighteen preserved). There is pale blue enamel in the petals of alternate rosettes: the other rosettes also probably contained enamel, but they have been scraped clean. This series alternates with the second, which takes the form of large two-level rosettes (complete total of twenty-four), from which are suspended twenty-two (of twenty-four) vertically

 Overleaf: 94

ribbed seeds, perhaps fennel seeds, constructed from front and back halves. The borders of the upper level of rosettes are of plain wire; those of the lower level and those of the borders of the lotus-rosettes are of fine beaded wire.

The terminals are oval in shape and are each decorated with a palmette, the leaves of which are all filled with pale blue enamel. The leaves are bordered with plain wire, and the outer contour of the terminal with fine beaded wire. To the back of each unit are soldered two corrugated tubes to hold the suspension threads.

Acheloos was a river god. His name was synonymous with water and he was thought of as the father of many springs and their associated nymphs throughout the Greek world. He was also connected with the cult of the wine-god, Dionysos, for the Greeks drank their wine mixed with water. He was subdued by Herakles, an important hero to the Scythians through their contact with the Greeks. Acheloos was particularly popular in Italy, and Acheloos masks occur in both Etruscan and South Italian jewellery.

The combination of rosettes and lotus-rosettes is found on a number of necklaces. From the North Pontic region come two examples with acorn pendants, one in Oxford from Nymphaion, the other in the Hermitage from Temir Gora. The Nymphaion piece has been dated by its context to about 400 BC. The Temir Gora necklace, which has beech-nut pendants, belongs to the first quarter of the fourth century, as is indicated by the other jewellery found with it and the Athenian red-figured *pelike* found in the fill of the tumulus. The necklace from Taranto (no. 135) is of mid-fourth-century date, while an example from Homolion in northern Greece belongs to the second half of that century.

BIBLIOGRAPHY: *ABC* II, p. 338; Reinach p. 137, no. 2; Miller, pl. 5c; M. Pfrommer, *IstMitt* 36 (1986), pp. 65–6, and p. 61, fig. 1, 5. Acheloos masks on a necklace (Cumae, tomb 126): *MonAnt* 22 (1913), p. 596; Breglia, pl. 9. Nymphaion necklace: Vickers, pl. 11, a–b. Temir Gora: Miller, pl. 5a. Homolion: Miller, pl. 4. For comments on rosette and palmette necklaces see Pfrommer, *IstMitt* 36 (1986), pp. 59–76.

There are a number of late fifth-century parallels from tombs at Eretria for the beads with rings of granules.

BIBLIOGRAPHY: Unpublished. Eretria necklaces: (Athens National Museum) *AM* 38 (1913), pl. 15, 3 (two beads); (Berlin) Greifenhagen II, pls 4, 2 and 5, 1–2.

96   Pair of silver bracelets with gold lion-heads

From Pantikapaion
400–380 BC
Width 8.3 cm, height 7.8 cm; weight 120.11 and 124.08 g
Hermitage P.1854.28–9

These magnificent bracelets have solid silver hoops, which are gilded in a dog-tooth pattern near the lion-head terminals (the gilding is discoloured by silver corrosion). The lion-heads are powerfully modelled and the details in the sheet gold very finely chased. Their manes are arranged in three levels and there is stippling under their chins. The tongues (with a long ridge in the centre) and incisors have been added separately (the rest of the teeth are represented with beaded wire). The eyeballs are modelled in relief. The collars are formed from a cylinder of sheet gold decorated with a frieze of double spirals in plain wire, bordered by fine and thick beaded wires.

The lions' heads do not face each other directly, but are slightly turned away, thus giving the bracelets still more vitality. The dog-tooth border to the band of gilding can be found on a number of fine examples of metalwork, for example the lantern from the tomb of Philip II at Vergina.

BIBLIOGRAPHY: *ABC* II, p. 339; T&K I, fig. 85; Deppert-Lippitz, fig. 111; Pfrommer, pl. 17, 3 (TA 73).

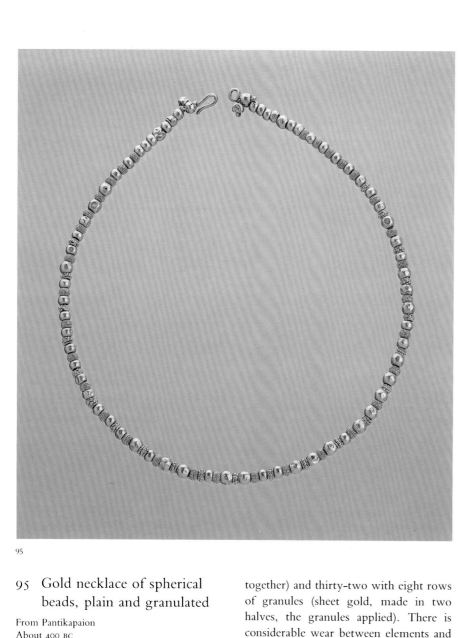

95

95   Gold necklace of spherical beads, plain and granulated

From Pantikapaion
About 400 BC
Length 30.8 cm; weight 29.84 g
Hermitage P.1854.23

This necklace consists of some seventy plain beads (made in two halves), twenty-two with three rows of granulation (made from three rings of granules soldered together) and thirty-two with eight rows of granules (sheet gold, made in two halves, the granules applied). There is considerable wear between elements and the first two types of bead show platinum-group inclusions (the third type does not).

The simple, twisted loop terminals are modern and the bead with spiral-beaded wire collars attached to one of these may also be intrusive.

Opposite: 96

97

98

98

The dress of the figure clearly distinguishes him from the Scythians, with their long, lank hair, looser garments and simpler headgear (no. 81). From the later sixth century BC the Persians had become a threat to both the Greeks and the Scythians, both of whom resisted Persian expansionism in the fifth century. It was only in the later fourth century that Alexander the Great finally broke the Persians' power.

The hoop is faceted both inside and outside, and has been soldered to the ends of the bezel. The hoop and bezel are worn, and platinum-group inclusions are visible, and tangible, on both.

BIBLIOGRAPHY: *ABC* II, p. 338; Reinach, p. 137, no. 1; T&K I, fig. 88, and II, fig. 36; Furtwängler *AG*, pl. 10, 27 (mid-fifth century BC); Boardman *GGFR*, pl. 681 (shape III); *AT*, p. 145, fig. 4; *Zürich*, no. 119. Xenophantos vase: *ARV²*, 1407, no. 1.

98 Gold ring with a seated figure of Penelope in relief

From Pantikapaion
About 450 BC
Length of bezel 2.0 cm; height 2.2 cm; weight 8.59 g
Hermitage P.1854.25

The pointed oval bezel consists of a sheet of gold with the die-struck design of a seated woman on the upper surface. She is seated on a plain stool facing left, her head turned towards the front but resting on her right hand. She wears a *chiton* and a *himation* around her legs. There is a double ground line below. The bezel is bordered by a plain wire and a beaded wire; the underside is decorated with an unusual design of four spirals and two crescents in plain wire, while the edge has pairs of spirals in plain wire.

The hoop thickens at the base and is made of three gold rods twisted together with a thin beaded wire laid in the valleys. The joint between hoop and bezel is decorated with a beaded wire flanked by plain wires. There are slight traces of wear.

The thickening hoop and its decoration may be paralleled on three rings from late fifth-century graves at Eretria. The identity of the seated woman as Penelope on the top of the bezel is determined by comparison with other representations, where she sits in a similar pose, her face turned towards the viewer to demand sympathy. The figure recurs on two other rings from Pantikapaion, one in intaglio and one similarly in relief, in which her husband's famous bow is also shown. On a ring formerly in a New York collection the figure is both named and accompanied by Odysseus' bow.

BIBLIOGRAPHY: Furtwängler *AG*, pl. 10, 20 ('Severe Style'). Eretria rings: *AM* 38 (1917), pl. 16, 6–9; cf. also *Stathatos*, no. 214. For Penelope see most recently W. Gauer, *JdI* 105 (1990), pp. 31–65: this ring is his no. 20. For the other relief ring in the Hermitage see *ABC*, pl. 18, 9. New York ring: Boardman *GGFR*, pl. 656.

97 Gold ring with the figure of a seated Persian in intaglio

From Pantikapaion
About 420–400 BC
Length of bezel 2.3 cm, width 1.4 cm; weight 6.89 g
Hermitage P.1854.26

The pointed oval bezel of this superb ring depicts, in shallow-groove engraving, the figure of a bearded Persian seated on a folding stool, testing an arrow. His left knee and foot are fully frontal and foreshortened; his right leg is in profile to the left, and his bow, which is hooked over his right wrist, is visible beyond. In his left hand he holds the feathered haft, his right hand holds the tip. He wears a flat-topped soft hat with long flaps and trousers decorated with dotted cross-hatching. His jacket is decorated with stippling, but his shoes are plain. His face is shown in three-quarter frontal view. There is a plain ground line.

In the top right corner is neatly engraved ATHENADES, the artist's signature. The name proudly suggests an Athenian heritage and recalls a fine Athenian vase from Pantikapaion which bears the signature of the artist, Xenophantos, followed by his ethnic, Athenaios.

The conception of the composition and its execution are of the highest quality.

Pantikapaion, 1845 'Wooden Tomb' *(nos 99–100)*

In 1845 D.V. Kareisha excavated a tumulus on the Quarantine Road along the north shore of Kertch bay (his third barrow in the area during this campaign). It contained a robbed central vault and six other burials, including a 'wooden tomb'. This wooden tomb either consisted of a pit cut into the earth covered with a wooden roof or an earth grave with a wooden coffin. Beside the head of the skeleton was a pair of earrings (no. 99), at the neck a bull's head pendant (no. 100), and on a finger a plain silver ring. By the feet were a clay lamp and a terracotta figurine of a winged demon, probably Thanatos. The jewellery was sent to the Hermitage, and the other objects placed in the Kertch Museum.

From one of the other burials in the tumulus came a small red-figured squat *lekythos* decorated with a griffin and an Arimasp, as well as six other small vessels, probably net-pattern *lekythoi* and palmette *lekythoi*.

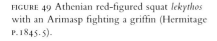

FIGURE 49 Athenian red-figured squat *lekythos* with an Arimasp fighting a griffin (Hermitage P.1845.5).

Since all the burials are probably fairly close in date, the red-figured squat *lekythos*, which may be placed in the second quarter of the fourth century, is the only indication of the date of the jewellery.   [Y.K.]

BIBLIOGRAPHY: D.V. Kareisha, *Zhurnal Ministerstva vnutrennikh dêl* 1846, part 16, pp. 387–9. For the squat *lekythos* (P.1845.5, St 2258) see *ABC*, pl. 58, 6–7.

99 Pair of gold boat-shaped earrings decorated with filigree palmettes

From Pantikapaion
375–350 BC
Height 2.5 cm, width 1.9 cm; weight 2.63 and
    2.84 g
Hermitage P.1845.6

The boats are, as usual, made in two halves from sheet gold. There is a central vertical division marked by a beaded wire flanked on either side by a plain wire. On either side of this is a palmette motif in plain wire, consisting of a large palmette below and a small one above (in the centre of the supporting spirals is a grain). The terminals of the boats are decorated with a plain wire flanked on either side by a beaded wire. The tapered hoop is soldered into one terminal and locates into the other.

The surface of these earrings is badly fused: this may well have occurred at the time of manufacture, rather than in a funeral pyre.

This type of earring is well known in southern Italy, especially in Tarentine tombs of the first and second quarters of the fourth century BC (cf. no. 144). Examples also occur in East Greece (no. 38) and Greece itself (nos 9, 11 and 13).

BIBLIOGRAPHY: Unpublished. For the Tarentine earrings see *Taranto*, nos 56–68. For the filigree decoration cf. the last of these and two pairs from the Metaponto area: *AA* 1966, p. 325, fig. 96; J.C. Carter, *Ancient Crossroads: The Rural Population of Classical Italy* (n.d.), fig. 31a.

100 Gold pendant in the form of a bull's head

From Pantikapaion
375–350 BC
Height *c*. 2.0 cm; weight 2.46 g
Hermitage P.1845.7

This pendant is made in left and right halves of pale, brittle sheet gold, with separate sheet-gold ears and horns and chased details. The eyes are recessed for enamel. Tied around the bull's horns is a garland made of twisted wires to represent an ivy or vine stem. At the front are ivy leaves, which were once filled with enamel, and

99

in the centre two little clusters of granules to represent grapes or ivy berries. In the centre of the forehead, between the eyes, is an incised star-whorl, and at the base of the neck a border consisting of a plain wire and ropes.

There is no hole in the back-plate: instead, it has a flange which locates with a push-fit into the back of the head. The ears, however, are open, and this pendant could therefore have been used as a pomander. The suspension loop is decorated with three spiral-beaded and two plain wires.

The bull's head pendant is a particularly common form and is known from both the fifth and fourth centuries BC. It could, of course, be worn with a string of beads or other pendants (cf. the necklace depicted on the earrings in no. 103), but it is also found in isolation, as here.

100

BIBLIOGRAPHY: Unpublished. There are many other examples in the Hermitage: e.g. *AA* 1912, p. 347, fig. 35 (Pantikapaion), *ABC*, pl. 32, 12 (Hadji Moushkai). In Berlin there are three: Greifenhagen I, pl. 19, 6–7, from Pantikapaion; Greifenhagen II, pls 15, 1 and 16, 5, from the Taman; Greifenhagen II, pls 15, 2 and 16, 3.

Pantikapaion, 1840 Tile Grave *(no. 101)*

In 1839 D.V. Kareisha investigated a barrow on the Quarantine Road side of Kertch. Within the barrow was an earth grave with a richly decorated stone slab top that contained nothing more than bones, and three graves with tile walls and tops. In each of the first two of these there was only a broken vase, but in the third were found a plain pot, a plain cup, seven glass beads, a gold amulet in the form of an arm, an oval plaque and a single gold earring.

Such tile graves seem to have been built in the Greek necropoleis of Pantikapaion from the fourth century BC.   [Y.K.]

BIBLIOGRAPHY: *ABC*, pls 7, 2; 24, 3; 23, 2 (=Reinach, p. 47).

101

101 Single gold earring with rosette and Pegasos

From Pantikapaion
400–350 BC
Height 3.0 cm, width 2.0 cm, diameter of disc
    1.2 cm; weight 4.41 g
Hermitage P.1840.2

The rosette is made up from two tiers of petals, all convex and bordered in spiral-beaded wire. The Pegasos pendant below is constructed from left and right halves with a chased wire tail and legs pushed into the body and with separate sheet wings. Between the wings is a long, vertical, beaded wire with a loop at the end for suspension.

Horses of one form or another appear as earring pendants on two other pieces, a simple piece in Baltimore and the famous Nike driving a chariot in Boston.

BIBLIOGRAPHY: *ABC*, pl. 7, 2. Baltimore earring (WAG 57.1728): *Baltimore*, no. 256. Nike chariot: Hoffmann and Davidson, no. 12.

Pantikapaion, 1840 Stone Tomb *(nos 102–3)*

In 1840 D.V. Kareisha excavated a small tumulus on the road to Hadji Moushkai, north-east of Pantikapaion. It contained a stone grave cut into the virgin soil (length *c.* 2 m, width and depth 1.60 m), the stone lid supported by three wooden beams. In the fill above was a layer of stone slabs.

The wooden sarcophagus was elaborately decorated and contained the skeleton of a young woman. On either side of her head was a pair of earrings (no. 103) and at her throat was a necklace (no. 102). Nearby lay three alabaster *alabastra*. On the fingers were two rings: a plain silver ring of D section and a gold ring engraved with a dolphin, a bird and a fish. Next to the hand was a second gold ring. Arranged around the feet were a bronze mirror with a gilded centre, a large alabaster *alabastron* and two Attic red-figured vases. One of the vases was a *pelike* decorated with Greeks fighting barbarians, the other a *lekanis* with wedding preparations on the lid, both dated by Schefold to 360–350 BC. [Y.K.]

BIBLIOGRAPHY: *ABC*, pp. 52–5 on pl. 7, 11 (=Reinach, p. 48); Rostovtzeff *SuB*, p. 258 (noted only). For the red-figured *pelike* (P.1840.45, St 1863) see Schefold *UKV*, no. 374; for the *lekanis* (P.1840.44, St 1809) see Schefold *UKV*, no. 11.

102

102 Gold necklace of beads alternately plain and decorated with spiral filigree

From Pantikapaion
About 350 BC
Length as strung 23.0 cm; weight 16.30 g
Hermitage P.1840.36

This string of beads includes twenty-three plain beads, made in left and right halves, and twenty-three decorated with plain wire spiral filigree and grains. The seams are hidden by a beaded wire flanked on either side by a plain wire. The beads have all worn heavily into each other, and there is no indication that any stones were included in the necklace. No terminals are preserved.

This sort of bead is well represented in the North Pontic region, but it is also known in the East Greek cities of Asia Minor (no. 48).

BIBLIOGRAPHY: P.F. Silantyeva in K.S. Gorbunova (ed.), *Iz Istorii Severnogo Prichernomorya v Antichnuyu Epohu* (Leningrad 1979), p. 51, no. 6 (not illustrated).

103

103 Pair of gold earrings with pendants in the form of female heads

From Pantikapaion
About 350 BC
Height 4.0 cm; height of head and diadem 2.9 cm;
    weight 8.31 and 8.55 g
Hermitage P.1840.37

These exquisite pendants are made in front and back halves (the fill is still inside) with a sheet base in which there is a round expansion hole. The details are finely chased and the eyes are enamelled, white for the white of the eye and black for the pupil. On the ears are rosette earrings, with petals filled alternately with green and blue enamel and a grooved seed pendant (the front in relief, the back sheet flat) suspended below. A necklace of two rows of grains (one large and one small) with a central bull's head pendant is tied round the neck and fastened at the back in a Herakles knot. The hair is brushed up from the brow, and the multi-peaked diadem of sheet gold is decorated with a plain wire filigree palmette and lotuses, their leaves filled alternately with blue and green enamel. On top of the head is a ring through which passes a tapered wire hoop, one end of which is pointed to locate into the hollow at the other end.

A number of similar head-pendant earrings have been found in South Russia: the Pantikapaion pair are perhaps the finest, the enamel inlay of the eyes being particularly striking. Pieces like these and the lion-head torque from the Solokha kurgan, the fifth-century gold horse-head *phiale* from the Bratoliubovsky kurgan and even the sixth-century panther from Kelermes show the naturalistic effects that were attempted with enamel, perhaps more often than is commonly realised.

BIBLIOGRAPHY: *ABC*, pl. 7, 11; T&K I, fig. 79. Other head-pendant earrings: (British Museum GR 1934.11-15.2–3, ex de Massoneau collection) *BMQ* 9, 1 (1934–5), p. 6 with facing pl.; (Victoria and Albert Museum) MacPherson, pl. 1, and Coarelli, fig. 37; Ukraine National Museum DM 6327 (head with a high, rounded diadem); (Hermitage) *ABC*, pl. 7, 10. Solokha torque: *Scythian Art*, pl. 122. Bratoliubovsky *phiale*: *Zürich*, no. 45. Kelermes panther: *Scythian Art*, pl. 17. For an example of such eyes in Cypriot jewellery see no. 165. Cf. also Fig. 39.

Kekuvatsky Kurgan *(nos 104–5)*

In January 1839 A. Ashik excavated a tumulus at the western end of the Iuz Oba ridge. It contained a stone vault with a stepped roof and inside was a wooden sarcophagus resting on a stone support. The sarcophagus was elaborately decorated with reliefs showing griffins fighting animals: these reliefs were located over Greek letters cut on the backing boards.

On the skull of the skeleton was found a gold olive wreath (no. 105) and on the index finger of his right hand a massive gold ring (no. 104). In each hand he held a bunch of arrows: 215 bronze arrow-heads are preserved in the Hermitage, some with parts of the wooden shaft still in place. At his feet were an iron sword with a gold covering decorated with a stag in Scythian style, similar to a piece from Kul Oba, a bronze Attic helmet, a pair of bronze greaves and a flat whetstone. There was also a magnificent Athenian red-figured *pelike* with figures of Apollo and Marsyas, the name piece of the Marsyas Painter, which was dated by Schefold to 340–330 BC but has more recently been put around 360 BC. From the fill come fragments of Thasian amphorae with stamped handles.

BIBLIOGRAPHY: *ABC* I, pp. lxix–lxxi; Artamonov, p. 72. For the *pelike* (St 1795) see Schefold *UKV*, no. 370; *ARV*², p. 1475, no. 3; Valavanis, p. 269, no. 3. On the Marsyas Painter see also Robertson, pp. 280–83.

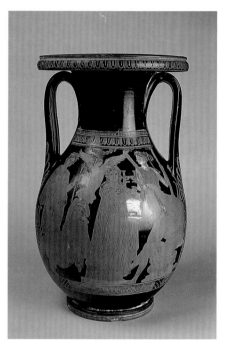

FIGURE 50 Athenian red-figured *pelike* showing Apollo and Marsyas (Hermitage Kek 8).

104 Gold ring with four lions

From the Kekuvatsky kurgan
About 350 BC
Inner diameter 2.2 cm, length of lions 1.7 cm;
    weight 27.46 g
Hermitage Kek.2

This massive solid gold ring is of unusual form. The shank forks at each end into pairs of lions, which lie flat with their front paws out before them. The lions appear to have been formed by hammering the gold into a bronze die. The tails are chased separately.

There are traces of considerable wear. The ring is not soldered closed and therefore could be adjusted to fit fingers of different sizes. Adjustable rings of various types are known from both Pontic and Greek finds.

BIBLIOGRAPHY: *ABC*, pl. 18, 6; Artamonov, fig. 141; *AT*, p. 146, fig 5.

104

105

105 Gold olive wreath

From the Kekuvatsky kurgan
About 350 BC
Diameter *c.* 17.5 cm; weight 264.35 g
Hermitage Kek.1

The stems that form the hoop of the wreath are made from slightly tapering tubes of sturdy sheet gold. Some leaves and olives are attached directly into the main stem, others to short subsidiary branches which are located over square-sectioned spikes. The leaves are pointed and have central ribs. They have integral stalks and are of three sizes, the largest being fixed into the main stem. Eighteen olives are attached: they are of two sizes.

Each olive is made in two halves – top and bottom – to which are soldered sheet tubes into which the ends of the wire stalks are located. At the back of the wreath the stems have oblique sheets with concentric circles, representing the cut ends of the stems. The stems are held together with plain wire bindings, at both front and back.

Many fragments of this wreath are not shown here, some damaged by fire; a further thirteen olives are preserved separately.

BIBLIOGRAPHY: *ABC*, pl. 4, 2; Artamonov, pls 268–9. For comments on the wreath see Reinach, p. 49.

Pavlovsky Kurgan *(nos 106–8)*

This huge kurgan, nearly 13 metres high and 64 metres in diameter, was excavated in 1858 by Lutsenko. It lies at the eastern end of the Iuz Oba ridge. At its base was a kerb wall, which on one side was of finely dressed blocks.

Within the mound were three burials, two cremations with poor offerings and, in the centre of the mound, an unplundered stone-lined rectangular chamber with a long *dromos*. The chamber is 4.33 metres long, 2.20 metres wide and 2.60 metres high: it is cut into the bedrock, which rises at the centre of the mound. Most of the chamber was filled with a wooden sarcophagus (*c.* 2.49 m long and 1.42 m wide) with a ridged roof, fluted columns with Ionic capitals and inlaid, painted and gilded panels on the sides. It contained the skeleton of a young girl or a particularly petite woman. She was covered with a shroud and over her bones

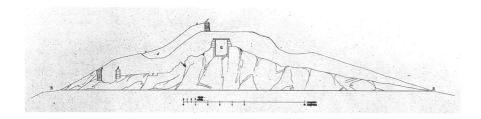

FIGURE 51 Pavlovsky kurgan: section drawing (from *CR* 1859, pl. 5, top).

were also fragments of her clothes, richly decorated with floral motifs, ducks and an Amazon on horseback, while under her head was a pillow filled with wood-shavings.

On her head was a *stlengis* of the same shape as that from the Great Bliznitza (no. 119), but without figured decoration, and at her neck were earrings in the form of Nikai (no. 107) and a beech-nut pendant necklace (no. 106). On the fingers of her left hand were three rings: one with gold foils laid on blue glass (no. 108), the second of gold engraved with an eagle, and the third a scarab engraved with a crouching woman. Nearby was a bronze mirror with gold foil over the spirals at the base, which seems to have been made in the same workshop as the mirror from Kul Oba, dated to the middle of the fifth century BC. On her feet were thin leather boots (19 cm long and *c.* 26 cm high).

Above her head was a basket made from hemp, a painted wooden box and three *alabastra*. At her feet were two sponges, one at either foot, and, nearby, two more *alabastra*. There were also five walnut shells, a bronze ointment stick and a silver coin of Pantikapaion, probably datable to the last decades of the fourth century BC. Outside the sarcophagus were two sponges, nine *alabastra* (eight of alabaster, one of glass) and three Athenian vases. These were a black-glaze ribbed trefoil *oinochoe*, a large and particularly remarkable red-figured *pelike* attributed to the Eleusinian Painter and dated by Schefold to 340–330 BC, although recent research tends to suggest a date of 360–350 BC, and a *lekythos* in the form of a figure of an Amazon, with a great deal of painted decoration.

From the fill of the barrow came many fragments of wine amphorae with stamped handles (Thasos and Sinope) and near the top a huge pottery *krater* with a diameter of 63 centimetres (whereabouts unknown, *pace* Rostovtzeff). Some of the Sinope stamps are the same as examples from the Zelenskaya kurgan and may be dated to the last decades of the fourth century BC. These amphora stamps seem to date from the final use of the kurgan.

The jewellery displays an unusual variety of styles, the necklace and glass ring possibly having northern Greek connections, while the *stlengis* is seemingly very North Pontic. The ring and earrings may be heir-looms.

BIBLIOGRAPHY: A.E. Lutsenko, *CR* 1859, pp. 6–15, pl. 5, 1–4 (plans); Newton, pp. 380–81; Rostovtzeff *SuB*, pp. 178–9; Artamonov, p. 73. For the *pelike* attributed to the Eleusinian Painter see Schefold *UKV*, no. 368, pl. 35; *ARV*², p. 1476, no. 1; Robertson, pp. 283–4.

FIGURE 52 Detail from an Athenian red-figured *pelike* showing Eleusinian deities (Hermitage Pav 8).

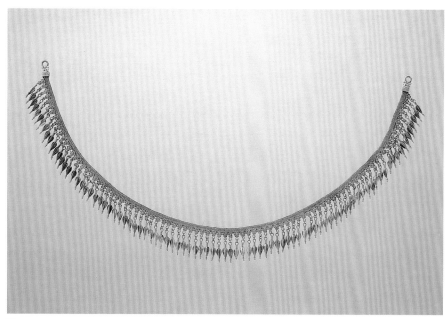

106

106 Gold strap necklace with beech-nut pendants

From the Pavlovsky kurgan
330–300 BC
Length 33.5 cm; total height 2.0 cm; weight 42.18 g
Hermitage Pav.2

This wonderful necklace with its beech-nut pendants is of a type that first appears in the second half of the fourth century. It is in truly remarkable condition: only three tiny grains of gold have been lost from one of the pendants.

The strap consists of two doubled loop-in-loop chains interlinked side by side. Attached to the lower edge of the strap are eighty-nine rosettes with slightly concave petals bordered with spiral-beaded wire: originally the petals were probably enamelled (modern cleaning has removed all traces). From each rosette hangs a three-lobed beech-nut pendant ending in a small circle of plain wire and three grains (eighty-nine beech nuts preserved). The box-like terminals are held onto the strap

by lateral rivets, both ends of which are neatly flattened. To the top of each box terminal is attached a die-struck sheet decorated with the foreparts of a lion-skin. A plain loop is attached to each terminal.

A very similar necklace has been found at Corinth in association with coins of about 330–320 BC and a pottery dish dated 325–315 BC. The Corinth necklace has two levels of beech nuts and the lion-skin heads are from a different die, but the two necklaces were very probably made in the same workshop. In addition, a necklace in Pforzheim, which combines beech nuts and ribbed seeds and is part of a group said to be from Sardis, is probably from the same workshop: the lion-head terminals are extremely close to those on the Corinth piece.

BIBLIOGRAPHY: Ruxer, pls 27, 3 and K, 3; Artamonov, pl. 277; Segall, pl. 44. For the Corinth necklace see *Corinth* XII, pl. 109, and for the context *AJA* 74 (1970), pp. 343–50; for the Pforzheim piece see Segall, pls 4 and 14–15.

106

107

107 Pair of gold earrings in the form of Nikai

From the Pavlovsky kurgan
About 350 BC
Height 4.8 cm, width 3.2 cm; weight 16.35 and
    18.00 g
Hermitage Pav.3

Each earring consisted of a figure of a winged Nike with a small rosette above, partially disguising the hook for attachment to the ear; one is damaged.

The Nikai wear a *polos*, a belted *chiton* and shoes (even the minute details of stitching and the soles are shown). One Nike turns her head to her right and holds a fillet up in her right hand as she clutches the edge of her *chiton* in her lowered left

hand. The more damaged Nike has her head to her left, holds the fillet in her raised left hand and has her right hand on her hip. The figures are hollow-backed but of substantial thickness. They were probably produced by hammering gold into a copper alloy die, but it is just possible that they were cast and then extensively worked by hand from the front and back. Both up-raised arms were separately made and soldered on. The lowered arms are possibly integral to the bodies. The wings were separately made in sturdy sheet gold with chased feather patterns and were soldered to the backs of the figures.

The ear-hook is D-shaped in section and one earring still retains a two-tiered flower-head (concave petals bordered in fine beaded wire), which may once have held coloured enamel. The hook on the other earring has broken off just above the figure's head: it was repaired in antiquity with a single gold rivet. An attachment ring has been set into the back of the figure at about knee height and it is possible that the ear-hooks once extended this far. The earrings were probably heirlooms.

The combination of a single figure with a smallish rosette above recurs on another pair of earrings from Pantikapaion (summit of Iuz Oba) which have a maenad as the pendant: this tomb also contained another vase by the Eleusinian Painter, the companion piece to the Pavlovsky *pelike*. One should also compare an earring in Berlin with a naked Nike or Psyche pendant and a pair, with larger rosettes and Erotes playing the kithara, now in Munich.

BIBLIOGRAPHY: *CR* 1859, pl. 3, 3; Hadaczek, fig. 66; Artamonov, pl. 273; Hoffmann and Davidson, p. 83, fig. 12h; Segall, pl. 44; Deppert-Lippitz, fig. 162. Maenad earrings: *CR* 1860, pl. 4, 4–5. Berlin earring: Greifenhagen II, pl. 41, 6. Munich earrings: *MüJb* 40 (1989), pp. 245–6.

108 Gold ring with a clear and blue glass bezel

From the Pavlovsky kurgan
About 350 BC
Length of bezel 1.8 cm; weight 7.61 g
Hermitage Pav.4

This special ring is unusually colourful. The bezel consists of an oval piece of blue glass with die-formed gold-foil motifs set on either side, over which has been fused a layer of clear glass. The top side, which is slightly convex, depicts two dancing barbarians. They both have their hands clasped over their heads and their faces are turned so as to be almost frontal: it is the so-called *oklasma*, an oriental, perhaps Persian, dance. They both wear peaked hats and their *chitones* hitched up with an overfold. The figure on the left bends slightly; that on the right stands more upright and on her toes. Below is a ground line decorated with a guilloche pattern. The underside, which is flat, has foil motifs of a *ketos* facing left in the centre, with a spiky-backed fish, perhaps bream, above and below, and at either end a pair of dolphins swimming to the left.

The gold frame around the glass has a panel with a frieze of double spirals (spiral-beaded wire) with grain centres between borders of beaded wire. The hoop is rectangular in section, widening slightly towards the back, and has cup-shaped terminals through which a pin passes to hold the oval scaraboid bezel and allow it to rotate freely.

The gold mount is very worn, although the glass insert is in good condition. The hoop may be an ancient replacement, for the gold seems slightly paler. The ring may well, therefore, be an heirloom.

A similar ring was found at Homolion in northern Greece, but there the clear casing is said to be of rock crystal. The Homolion reliefs show a Nereid carrying new arms for Achilles and riding on the back of a *ketos* on one side and Eros on a dolphin on the other. A third example of the type was recently on the London market. On one side the glass cover had been lost but the gold foil showing a flying Nike was still in place; on the other side the glass cover was still preserved, but it was too decayed for the gold foil to be visible.

The *ketos* with dolphins on the Pavlovsky ring and the Nereid on the Homolion ring find close parallels on an ivory bezel with gold foils attached, said to be from Taranto and now in Berlin. Boardman has suggested that the Pavlovsky and Homolion rings may be from the same workshop.

BIBLIOGRAPHY: *CR* 1859, pl. 3, 4–5; Artamonov, pls 274–5; Boardman *GGFR*, p. 233, pl. 822; Miller, p. 20, pl. 11e–f; Higgins *GRJ*[2], pl. 31b; *L'oro dei Greci*, no. 127. Homolion ring: Deppert-Lippitz, pl. 16. London market ring: Sotheby's, 10 July 1992, lot 318. Berlin bezel: Greifenhagen II, pl. 56, 13–15.

108

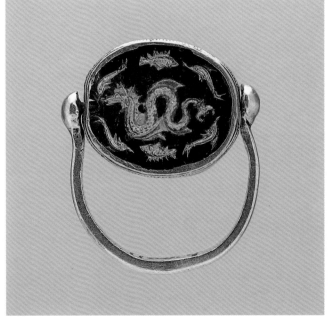

108

Taman Peninsula, 1855 'Pyre' Grave *(no. 109)*

In 1855 K.R. Beguitchev excavated a tumulus near the Semenyaka estate on the Taman peninsula, in the area between the post road to Sennaya village and two barrows excavated in 1852.

It contained a cremation grave not more than 0.35 metres deep. A number of clay figurines, damaged by fire, and a broken red-figured vase with two handles, probably a *pelike*, were found, together with a pair of gold ear studs. The latter were immediately sent to St Petersburg, but the other finds were not. [Y.K.]

BIBLIOGRAPHY: K.K. Goertz, *Archeologicheskaja Topographia Tamanskago Poluostrova* (2nd edn, St Petersburg 1898), pp. 141–2.

109

109 Pair of gold ear studs with floral decoration

From the Taman peninsula
350–300 BC
Diameter of disc 2.4 cm, diameter of stud 1.6 cm;
    weight 8.70 and 8.71 g
Hermitage T.1855.4

The disc is concave with down-turned sides to which is soldered a corrugated outer wall with a row of large grains around the top. The field of the disc bears concentric bands of beaded, plain and rope filigree with a frieze of plain wire double spirals with central grains. In the centre of each disc is attached a vertical tube over which are located two tiers of floral motifs (rosettes and quatrefoils) on wire stamens and an upper sheet-gold flower-head with pointed petals. The tiers are retained by a large grain held into the tube by means of a gold wire.

The back of each disc has a large tube which passed through a hole in the earlobe and was held in place by a tight-fitting stud. The back-plate of the stud has a grooved ring and central depression.

This type of ear stud is particularly common in burials from the Greek cities of Asia Minor (nos 51–2) and from Cyprus. Representations of the type may be found in northern Greece and in southern Italy, where a pair was found in a small sanctuary near Herakleia. A singleton in Edinburgh is from Egypt.

BIBLIOGRAPHY: Unpublished. Cypriot examples: Pierides, pl. 20, 1–2 and 3–4. Pair from S. Maria d'Anglona (near Herakleia): *NSc* 23 (1969), p. 178, fig. 12. Egyptian example in Edinburgh: Ogden, forthcoming.

Nymphaion, 1866 Tomb *(no. 110)*

In December 1866 some peasants opened up a stone grave in a tumulus near ancient Nymphaion. Unfortunately, no further details of the find are known, but a number of items of gold jewellery were swiftly sent to the Hermitage. There were eight fine rosettes with three levels of down-turned petals, a ring with a flat hoop and running filigree spirals on the edge of the setting (the stone was missing), eleven gold buttons, part of a necklace with filigree spiral beads and plain beads hanging from stalks, and a magnificent pair of earrings showing Artemis riding on a stag (no. 110). In addition, there was a cornelian cylinder seal showing Herakles and Apollo struggling over the Delphic tripod.

BIBLIOGRAPHY: *CR* 1868, pp. 5–51; Silantyeva, p. 7 with fig. 2.

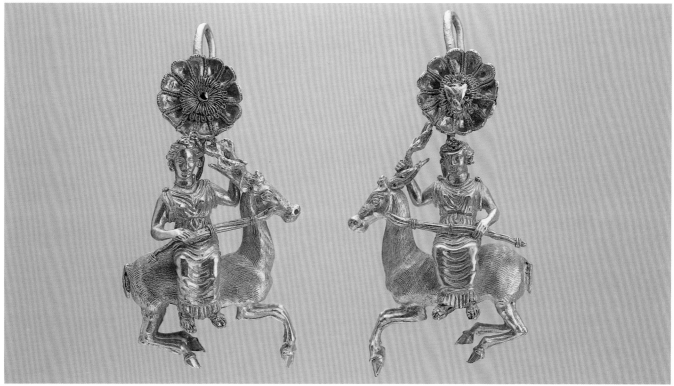

110

110 Pair of gold earrings with a rosette and Artemis riding a stag

From Nymphaion
325–300 BC
Height 4.4 and 4.6 cm; length 2.5 cm; weight 8.55 and 8.57 g
Hermitage GK/N.2

The wonderful pendants of this pair of earrings take the form of the goddess Artemis riding side-saddle on the back of her sacred stag. She wears a belted *peplos* buttoned at the shoulders (a ring of wire), a *himation* over her legs, square-toed sandals (a wire for the thong), a twisted wire necklace and disc earrings with inverted pyramids (some missing). Her hair is wavy and has a tiny Herakles knot at the top. She holds a burning torch (consisting of seven or five rods of plain wire, bound in three places with three wires) in one hand, while her other hand clutches the stag's antlers. She is constructed in sheet metal from several components, including separate head and feet. The torch may originally have been held in a more upright fashion.

The stag is similarly made up from sheet gold in several components, with separate legs, ears, antlers and tail. Its coat and fine facial details are rendered by very carefully chased wavy lines.

The rosettes above are made from concave sheet gold, the petals bordered with spiral-beaded wire. In the centre, set on a central tube, are two levels of convex tiny petals (lined with plain wire) and above them stamens ending in discs, each disc filled with coloured enamel (perhaps originally blue). The tube is capped by a tiny sheet-gold bee (only one preserved). The hook on the back of the rosette ends in a snake-head; one hook has been reattached.

The rosettes show ancient wear and repair or adaptation, whereas the pendants are in almost pristine condition and the workmanship is of outstanding quality, from the stags' faces to Artemis' sandals. This suggests that the pendants are ancient replacements.

Artemis riding a stag and holding a torch recurs on a gold ring once in the Harari collection, where stars have been added in the field, suggesting a syncretism with the moon goddess, Selene. There were also close connections between Selene and Iphigenia, who had particular significance in the Crimea, land of the Tauroi. An Orphic fragment preserves the tradition that Zeus sent Artemis to help look for Persephone, and this may be the subject of such scenes.

Little birds and insects are sometimes found amongst the flora of Greek jewellery. Tiny bees, for example, are also seen feeding on the rosettes and palmettes of the diadem from the antechamber of the so-called tomb of Philip II at Vergina.

BIBLIOGRAPHY: *CR* 1868, pl. 1, 2–3; Hadaczek, fig. 74; Silantyeva, p. 7 with fig. 2, 2; Hoffmann and Davidson, p. 82, fig. 12f. Harari ring: J. Boardman, *The Ralph Harari Collection* (London 1976), no. 7. Vergina diadem: *Vergina*, figs 158–9.

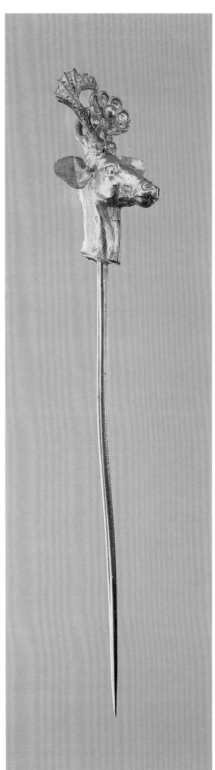

111

111 Gold pendant with a stag's head, turned into a pin

From Pantikapaion, without context (sent by Peroffsky)
350–300 BC
Height 8.1 cm, width 2.0 cm, height of stag's head 2.5 cm; weight 3.54 g
Hermitage P.1851.2

The stag's head is made in left and right halves from sheet gold: the ears and antlers have been added separately. There is a patch repair under the chin. Above the head is a rosette (plain wire borders, concave petals). On top of the head, and hidden by the antlers and the rosette, there is a spool-shaped tube supporting a wire ring. The base of the neck is closed with a circular sheet with an expansion hole in the centre. Into this hole has been driven a straight, pointed pin, which may well be a nineteenth-century addition.

Among animal-head pendants the stag's head is an extremely rare variety. The stag is, however, a frequent motif in the art of the North Pontic region and often shown being attacked by griffins (no. 86). The stag's head also appears on a series of attachments from a grave on the Taman peninsula.

BIBLIOGRAPHY: *ABC*, pl. 24, 7. The Taman pieces are Hermitage T.1880.2 (seven examples).

THE NORTH PONTIC CITIES

Chaian Kurgan *(no. 112)*

A group of objects said to have been found in a kurgan in the neighbour-
hood of Chaian, in the north-western Crimea, in the 1880s included a
sheet-gold decoration for a sword scabbard, fragments from the gold
sheet that covered the sword hilt, and a fragmentary rectangular gold
appliqué, together with a gold torque and a band or diadem, both once
on the Munich market. During their travels on the antiquities market a
modern gold bowl, with decoration based on one of the Kul Oba bracelets, became associated with the group: its present location is unknown.

BIBLIOGRAPHY: A.N. Shcheglov and V.I. Katz, *MetrMusJ* 26 (1991), pp. 97–122. The hilt
fragments are New York 30.11.12 a–g; the appliqué, New York 30.11.12 h; the band is
Hoffmann and Davidson, no. 82. Kul Oba bracelet: Artamonov, pl. 254.

112

112 Sheet-gold decoration for a sword scabbard

Said to be from near Chaian
340–320 BC
Length 54.5 cm
New York 30.11.12; Rogers Fund, 1930

This gold relief is not conventional jewellery. Greek goldsmiths were commissioned to produce display armour and
vessels as well as jewellery for the wealthy
martial aristocracy of the North Pontic
region.

In the main horizontal frieze of the scabbard sheet, within a border of short
oblique-angled lines (perhaps imitating a
stitch pattern), are scenes of combat
between Greeks and Scythians. At the left
end, a bearded warrior moves to the right
but looks back, seeming to encourage
more comrades to come to his assistance.
He wears a Corinthian helmet, cuirass and
short *chiton*, with a sword in a scabbard
at his left hip, suspended from a baldric
over his right shoulder; he has a spear in
his left hand and over his left arm is a
shield with a dotted wave-pattern on the
inside edge of the rim and a strap (*porpax*)
ending in dotted spirals. Behind him is a
bearded Scythian in a short *chiton*, a
trouser suit and a soft skin hat with tails.
He holds a bow in his lowered left hand
and his right arm is raised, wielding a

machaira. He seems about to deliver a blow to the first Greek warrior.

The next group consists of three figures. On the left a bearded Greek warrior pulls a fallen comrade by the upper right arm; the latter's *chlamys* is draped over his left arm and thighs, and the rim of his shield is visible behind his left arm. From the right a bearded Scythian in local garb directs his spear at the fallen Greek in a back-handed thrust. The spear shaft is held in both hands, the right elbow covering part of the shaft. Roughly in the centre of the frieze a beardless Greek warrior strides to the right. He is about to finish off a Scythian who has fallen to his knees, vainly trying to defend himself with an axe.

The subsequent groups are specially designed to fit the tapering form of the scabbard. First there is a bearded Scythian who seems to have made his horse kneel so that he can mount or dismount, unless his horse is simply stumbling; in his left hand he holds the reins short, in his right a spear. Next comes a pair of Greeks. The one on the left kneels, holding the leg of his wounded comrade as he pulls a bandage tight with his teeth. At the far right of the frieze, a Scythian has fallen off his horse, but still grips the reins in his left hand. It is not clear whether the steed has also fallen or is rushing away. The frieze terminates in a Corinthian helmet.

At the left end of this zone are two confronted griffins, with a palmette above and below. In the triangular area above, a lion has leapt onto the back of a stag and, to the right, a second lion tears at the throat of a doe.

The design was produced by pressing the sheet gold into an intaglio die. The main frieze recurs on the scabbard from the Chertomlyk kurgan and that from kurgan 8 of the Five Brothers complex: all three are from the same die. The triangular panel above, however, is from a different, otherwise unknown, die. The scabbard from the Tolstaya Mogila barrow is decorated only with animal scenes, but was probably a product of the same workshop. There are a number of other scabbards which are much more Scythian in style.

112

These elaborately decorated scabbards (*akinakai*) seem to have formed part of a ceremonial set of Scythian weapons: Scythians even swore oaths by their swords. Such sets would also include bow-cases (*gorytoi*), and both Scythian and Greek styles of relief decoration may be discerned on both scabbard sheets and bow-cases. In the case of the latter, two Greek dies have been identified: the first is represented by two examples (Karagodeuashkh and Vergina), the second by four examples (Chertomlyk, Ilyintsy, Melitopol and Five Brothers, kurgan 8). The subjects of the friezes seem to centre around the life of Achilles and the Trojan War. They were very probably produced in the same workshop as the Greek scabbard sheets and all may be dated to the third quarter of the fourth century.

BIBLIOGRAPHY: R. Zahn, *Mitteilungen der Bachstitz Galerie* 1 (1929), p. 36; G.M.A. Richter, *BMetrMus* 26 (1931), pp. 44–8; G.M.A. Richter, *MetrMusStudies* 4 (1932), pp. 109–30; D. von Bothmer, *BMetrMus* 42, 1 (Summer 1984), p. 53, no. 91; *MMA Greece and Rome*, pp. 78–9; A.N. Shcheglov and V.I. Katz, *MetrMusJ* 26 (1991), pp. 97–122 (earlier bibl. p. 119, n. 4). See also W. Rätzel, *BJb* 178 (1978), pp. 163–80 (on *gorytoi*); and for the scabbard from the Tolstaya Mogila barrow, *Scythian Art*, pls 150–54.

Zelenskaya Gora *(nos 113–14)*

In 1911–12 V.V. Shkorpil explored a tumulus on the Zelenskaya hill, 7.5 kilometres south-west of the settlement of Taman and 3.2 kilometres north-east of Cape Panagia. The tumulus was about 53 metres in diameter and 4.45 metres high.

The tumulus had already been rifled in 1866 by robbers who uncovered a vault with a stepped roof. Further robbers returned in 1911 and came upon a cremation tomb and banqueting area in the centre of the barrow. Here they found a large Attic red-figured amphora of Panathenaic shape and an Attic ribbed black-glaze amphora, also of Panathenaic shape, with a gilded olive wreath on the neck. They also found a fragment of a gold oak wreath (no. 113), a gold stater of Alexander the Great, and, reportedly, just over two-thirds of a kilo of gold. Shkorpil bought a fragment of the wreath and the vases from the robbers for the Hermitage, but nothing more is said of the rest of the gold.

In 1912 Shkorpil excavated a grave cut into the virgin soil, with a short *dromos* and pit in front. The chamber (1.98 by 1.80 m) had a roof of round wooden logs. Against the centre of the back wall was a black-glaze *hydria* with a gilded wreath on the neck. It contained not only ashes and bones, but also a gold stater of Alexander the Great, part of a gold laurel wreath, fragments of a necklace (four doubled loop-in-loop interlinked chains, simple rosettes and beech-nut pendants), four pomegranate pendants, a gold-plated copper ring, and an earring pendant in the form of a siren (no. 114). All the pieces of jewellery were damaged by fire. Along one side wall were arranged a splendid series of silver vessels; along the other a bronze jug, a fragmentary bronze bowl and an alabaster *alabastron*. Scattered about the tomb there were also weapons and horse trappings and many fragments of alabaster *alabastra*.

Shkorpil also excavated a stone chamber in which were found part of a wreath, a disc-fibula with a satyr-head carved from garnet in the centre, and a ribbed black-glaze *pelike*, as well as a collection of iron weapons. In addition, there was a horse burial.

In the fill of the tumulus were found, besides fragments of amphorae and tiles, two fragments of an Attic Panathenaic prize-amphora with part of the name of an archon (perhaps Neaichmos, 320/19 BC; Demogenes, 317/16 BC; or Demokleides, 316/15 BC).

BIBLIOGRAPHY: *AA* 1912, p. 334, no. 5; B. Pharmakovsky, *AA* 1913, pp. 178–82; V.V. Shkorpil, *Izvestia Imperatorskoi Archeologjicheskoi Kommissii* 60 (1916), pp. 22–33 (figs 11–12 show the disposition of the tombs and the finds); Rostovtzeff *SuB*, pp. 260–62; Pfrommer, FK 161–3. For the red-figured amphora of Panathenaic shape see Schefold *UKV*, no. 1 and pp. 63–4, no. 2, and Valavanis, p. 294, no. 7, pls 149–51 (Painter of the Wedding Procession, 335–330 BC); for the Panathenaic prize-amphora, M. Maximova, *KraSoobInstA* 83 (1961), p. 17, and N. Eschbach, *Statuen auf panathenäischen Preisamphoren des 4. Jhs. v. Chr.* (Mainz 1986), p. 153, no. 81, pl. 40, 1–2.

FIGURE 53 Silver vessels: a juglet of the Talcott Class (Hermitage Zel. 8) and a *phormiskos* with added gilding on the decorative bands (Hermitage Zel 33).

FIGURE 54 Fragment of gold wreath (National Museum of American Art, Smithsonian Institution 1929.8.185.1, gift of John Gellatly).

113

114

113 Fragment of a gold oak wreath

From Zelenskaya Gora
320–300 BC
Length as preserved 14.0 cm, length of tube
   11.0 cm, width 11.0 cm; weight 19.25 g
Hermitage Sel.1

The stem of the wreath is made from a hollow, slightly tapering tube of substantial sheet gold. Five acorns and seven leaves remain in place, located into the tube; two further small leaves have been stuck in one end. The leaves are of four sizes and have integral hammered stalks. They have been precisely chiselled to a characteristic oak-leaf outline. The intricate veining is lightly incised.

The acorns are made up from a large number of separate sheet-gold components. The nut is of sheet gold with a grain forming the apex. The cup is made from a hemispherical sheet of gold around which are soldered several tiers of pointed sheet-gold scales. Inserted into a gold tube on the base of each acorn is the plain wire stalk.

A larger piece of this same wreath passed into the de Massoneau collection: it must have been sold by the robbers before the intervention of Shkorpil. It was being offered for sale in the early 1920s (photograph in the archive of the Department of Greek and Roman Antiquities, British Museum) and was eventually sold in Paris in 1922. It was bought by John Gellatly, who gave it to the Smithsonian Institution, Washington.

BIBLIOGRAPHY: *AA* 1912, pp. 335–6, fig. 19. The unpublished de Massoneau part: Paris sale, Hôtel Drouot, 5 July 1922, lot 63, with parts of a different wreath; now National Museum of American Art, Smithsonian Institution, 1929.8.185.1. The alien leaves on the Washington piece come from a myrtle wreath and perhaps belong to *Brooklyn*, no. 33, which also came from de Massoneau's collection.

114 Single gold earring pendant in the form of a siren playing the pipes

From Zelenskaya Gora
320–300 BC
Height 3.4 cm, width 2.5 cm; weight 11.97 g
Hermitage Sel.28

The siren is composed from several sheet-gold components, but the present fused surface obscures any evidence of the seams. Her hair is tied up on top of her head, and she wears an armlet (spiral-beaded wire) on her upper right arm and a snake bracelet on her left wrist. The pipes have a mouth-piece and are separated into a small section and a larger section. The siren's navel and pubic hair are indicated and she has feathers from the tops of her thighs to the knee joints, below which her legs turn into those of a cockerel, with claw feet with three toes and a spur at the back. The wings are of substantial sheet gold with a chased feather design on the fronts, while the backs are flat; they are soldered into slots in the shoulder-blades of the siren. The fanned tail is in two layers: the upper surface is chased, while on the lower surfaces spiral-beaded wire filigree delineates the feathers. Two tapering wires emanate from under the tail: they may be part of a cockerel's plumage, or perhaps had some supporting function. There are remains or traces of attachments for suspension on the back of each wing.

Despite the condition of this pendant, the figure of the siren has great presence. The modelling and the conception of the pose are particularly fine. Hoffmann has suggested that a Nike in Paris may be by the same hand.

BIBLIOGRAPHY: *AA* 1913, p. 184, fig. 9; Hoffmann and Davidson, p. 90, fig. 15c; Pfrommer, pl. 6, 5. For the method of attachment to an upper unit cf. the pair of earrings from Kalymnos: Greifenhagen II, pl. 40, 4. For the Paris Nike see Hoffmann and Davidson, no. 98.

Great Bliznitza *(nos 115–30)*

On the Taman peninsula, near Phanagoria, is a vast mound (340 m in circumference, 15 m high) that was excavated over many seasons (1864–85). The tombs within it all belong to roughly the same period and have similar contents, and so may well have been the last resting places of people from the same aristocratic family or kinship group. There were at least three separate female burials, a male burial and a robbed chamber that had in all probability also held a female.

BIBLIOGRAPHY: Rostovtzeff *AD*, pp. 10–29; Artamonov, pp. 73–9.

THIRD WOMAN'S BURIAL *(nos 115–18)*

This burial was on the south-east side of the mound and was excavated in 1883 by S.I. Verebrjusov. It consisted of a stone chamber with a flat wooden roof. Inside was a wooden sarcophagus with ivory inlays that contained, in addition to the jewellery shown here, a gold ring, seven terracottas, a bone spindle, a bronze mirror and a number of vases. These were a local black-glaze *oinochoe* with rough decoration in added colour depicting a woman seated on the end of a couch, a miniature Attic black-glaze cup-*skyphos*, an Attic black-glaze *lekanis* and a miniature Attic red-figured squat *lekythos* with two Amazon heads (the latter was at the skeleton's feet).

BIBLIOGRAPHY: *CR* 1882–8, pp. xliii–xliv; Artamonov, p. 77; Pfrommer, FK 133.

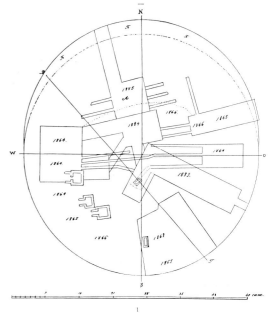

FIGURE 55 Great Bliznitza: schematic plan of the tumulus, showing the dates of the various excavations (from Rostovtzeff *AD*, pl. 11, left).

115

115 Gold olive wreath

From the Great Bliznitza
330–300 BC
Diameter *c.* 18.0 cm; weight 167.47 g
Hermitage BB 191

The stems take the form of two tapering gold tubes. At the front the ends overlap and are twisted round each other. At the back they are similarly overlapped, but are bound together with two wires. The long pointed leaves have a central spine and integral stalks. The longer leaves are individually set into the tube, the shorter ones arranged in sprays (three or four pairs of leaves per spray), which are fitted over square-sectioned spikes, as on the Keku-vatsky wreath (no. 105). There are some repairs holding on broken sprays; these are almost all ancient.

No fruit are included in this wreath. Wreaths of other varieties also occur without fruit, for example an oak wreath from Amphipolis.

BIBLIOGRAPHY: Unpublished. Amphipolis wreath: *L'oro dei Greci*, pl. 146.

116 Pair of gold earrings with disc and pyramid

From the Great Bliznitza
330–300 BC
Height 5.0 cm; diameter of disc 1.8 cm; height of pyramid 1.7 cm; weight 6.89 and 7.06 g
Hermitage BB 192

The up-turned edge of each pan-shaped disc is decorated with beaded wire. Within the pan a frieze of spirals with loops between and loose curls (spiral-beaded wires; single wire ties) is bordered by beaded and plain wires. The central flower-head consists of a two-level rosette (concave petals bordered with spiral-beaded wire). From five rings on the back of each disc hang a series of pendants. The outer pair hold double loop-in-loop chains each ending in a small disc with a ribbed seed-like pendant below (the calyx in two rows with grains at apices). Each of the inner pair holds a plain seed with pointed wire tongues. In the very centre is a relief figure of a barbarian crouching down on one knee. He wears a pointed cap with long ear flaps, a short *chiton* and trousers, and holds his hands up above

116

his head: he is performing the so-called *oklasma* dance, as on no. 108.

Beneath each barbarian is an oval sheet platform, bordered with spiral-beaded wire and fine beaded wire; attached to the platform by a split pin through two pairs of ring hoops, all hidden by a disc, is an inverted pyramid pendant. This has a rosette on each top corner and a border of cut-out darts. On each face of the pyramid is attached a cut-out relief sheet of a dancing figure. On one side a satyr dances to the left but turns back to the right; on another a maenad dances to the right, head

back, toes pointed, dress flaring at the ankles, right breast bare; on the third a satyr dances to the right but turns back to the left. Beneath each figure is a tiny spiky acanthus leaf. The edges of the pyramid are bordered with poorly formed fine beaded wire. At the base is a plain wire ring, a ball and a granule.

This type of earring is much more common in other parts of the Greek world, especially in Asia Minor (nos 49–50) and South Italy (no. 147).

BIBLIOGRAPHY: Artamonov, pl. 309 (centre).

117

117 Gold necklace of spherical beads (part only preserved)

From the Great Bliznitza
330–300 BC
Length as strung 28.0 cm; weight with
   aluminium wire on which it is strung 45.73 g
Hermitage BB 193

Only one club-shaped terminal is pre-served (strung back to front). The conical section is decorated with double spirals in plain wire, the hemispherical part with tongues in spiral-beaded wire. The beads are alternately plain and decorated: both are made in two halves. The decorated beads have tongues in spiral-beaded wire and below each is suspended a two-level rosette (concave petals) and a ribbed seed-like pendant. The calyx of these pendants is decorated with a feather-like pattern (granules at apices), and alternate panels between the ribs are cross-hatched. From each plain bead is suspended a two-level rosette (all petals concave) and a small ver-tically ribbed seed-like pendant.

All the pendants are neatly pierced on the shoulder and filled with brown resin. Their chased details were added after the halves of the pendants were soldered together (cf. nos 121–2). All the rosettes have a U-shaped strap behind, the ends of which go up into the bead above.

The style and technique of this necklace match that of one from the tomb of Demeter's priestess (see below), which must be a product of the same workshop. A somewhat similar necklace is in the Indiana University Art Museum.

BIBLIOGRAPHY: Artamonov, pl. 309 (lower). Demeter's priestess necklace (Hermitage BB 117): *CR* 1869, pl. I, 14. Indiana necklace: *Search for Alexander*, no. 56.

118 Pair of gold bracelets with copper cores and terminals in the form of leaping rams

From the Great Bliznitza
330–300 BC
Width 6.9 cm, height 6.5 cm, length of rams
   3.6 cm; weight 41.98 and 45.02 g
Hermitage BB 194–5

The large terminals are in the form of rear-ing ithyphallic rams. They are made from sheet gold with some pieces added separ-ately (phalli, tongues, forelimbs). The fleece is rendered by shaped tufts which are stippled all over. The eyes are hol-lowed out and were probably filled with enamel. The collars are rectangular in sec-tion and are decorated with running spirals in spiral-beaded wire. The filigree work, both running spirals and palmettes, continues up beside the rams' legs. The collars are bordered above and below with beaded and plain wires, and end in cut-out darts.

The bands consist of two hoops spiral-ling in opposite directions, with spiral-beaded wire in the valleys. Each hoop is in fact made up of three copper rods twisted together, with the sheet gold burnished over the top. Copper corrosion stains the gold sheet in a number of places. There are no signs of wear.

The style and technique of these brace-lets clearly indicate that they are from the same workshop as the lioness bracelets from the tomb of Demeter's priestess (no. 124).

BIBLIOGRAPHY: Artamonov, pl. 313; Pfrommer, pl. 21, 2.

118

118

TOMB OF THE 'PRIESTESS OF DEMETER' *(nos 119–30)*

This tomb was excavated in 1864 by I.E. Zabêlin and A.E. Lutsenko. It is the most important tomb in the kurgan and is usually, but probably wrongly, known as the tomb of the priestess of Demeter because of connections between the offerings and the cult of that goddess. It was

FIGURE 56 Great Bliznitza: view of the tumulus during excavation in 1864, with the stone burial-chamber of the Priestess of Demeter on the right (after Gross; from Rostovtzeff *AD*, pl. 5, 1).

in the western part of the kurgan and consisted of a stone-lined chamber with a stepped stone roof and a short walled *dromos*. The burial was virtually intact and contained the remains of a very richly adorned female.

Only a selection of the jewellery is included here. Other pieces included a wonderful gold *polos* decorated with barbarians fighting griffins (sadly, too fragile to travel), two more rings (one engraved with Aphrodite and Eros, the other with a creature – part woman, part grasshopper – playing the kithara) and a great many small plaques for attachment to clothing. As well as jewellery, there was a very fine bronze mirror, a handle from a bronze vessel, a bronze cosmetics spatula like that from the Pavlovsky kurgan, fragments of a pair of very small leather shoes, a bone spindle, and an Attic red-figured *pelike* with figures of Herakles and a centaur on the front and Dionysos with a satyr and a maenad on the back, dated by Schefold to 350–340 BC. There were also parts of four sets of horse-trappings, including bronze *phalerae* and bronze bells with iron clappers.

FIGURE 57 Athenian red-figured *pelike* showing Herakles and the centaur Nessos carrying off Deineira (Hermitage BB 67).

BIBLIOGRAPHY: L. Stephani, *CR* 1865, pp. 5–11, pls 1–6; Newton, pp. 382–4; Minns, pp. 423–9; Rostovtzeff *SuB*, pp. 330–31; Artamonov, pp. 74–6; Pfrommer, FK 127. For the *pelike* (BB 67, St 2016) see Schefold *UKV*, no. 396, pl. 4, 1–2, and Valavanis, p. 294, no. 6, pl. 148 (Painter of the Wedding Procession).

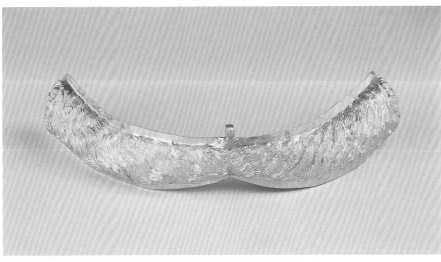

119

119

119 Gold *stlengis* in the form of forehead hair

From the Great Bliznitza
330–300 BC
Length 17.2 cm, height 3.0 cm, present depth
    front to back 9.2 cm; weight 49.36 g
Hermitage BB 30

This ornament is made from sheet gold in repoussé with very fine chasing. It takes the form of multi-strand waves of hair, but at either end is a beautiful relief of a Nike seated on a fleece (?), her hair tied up in a top-knot, wearing a *peplos* and bracelets. There is a strap loop at the top in the centre and a similar loop at either end.

Dark brown resin remains in the depression in the back. It may have been intended as a support when being worn or when being chased (or both). A good number of small sheets have been added to the back to consolidate cracks caused by the strain incurred as a result of the sheer depth of the relief: two large patches are to be found behind one of the Nikai and at the weakest point in the centre of the *stlengis*.

Another similar *stlengis*, but lacking figural decoration, was found in the Pavlovsky kurgan. Both ornaments are of sturdy construction and would seem to have been made to be worn in life, not just in death. From the Great Bliznitza (second woman's burial, 1868) comes another *stlengis*, this time with separate triangular side pieces for the hair in front of the ears. Such *stlengides* in the form of hair appear to have been particularly fashionable in the North Pontic region.

BIBLIOGRAPHY: *CR* 1865, pl. 1, 4–5; Artamonov, pl. 307. Second woman's *stlengis*: Artamonov, pl. 315. On the *stlengis* etc. see F. Hauser, *ÖJh* 9 (1906), pp. 75–130.

120 Gold disc pendant with a Nereid on a hippocamp (one of a pair)

From the Great Bliznitza
330–300 BC
Height 14.5 cm, diameter of disc 7.2 cm; weight
78.38 g
Hermitage BB 31

The large repoussé shield-like disc is strongly convex and shows a Nereid riding on a hippocamp. She wears a *chiton*, a *chlamys* decorated with stippling over her legs, a *polos* with floral decoration and with a veil over the top (stippled), and shoes. She holds a breastplate on her right arm; the fingers of her left hand appear low on the neck of the hippocamp. In the field are two dolphins. The hippocamp has powerful equine foreparts and a scaly fish-tail. (The matching pendant has the hippocamp moving in the other direction and the Nereid holding a greave). Around the rim (the edge is turned down) is a border of palmettes (linked, facing up and down) in spiral-beaded wire, framed by beaded and plain wires.

To the lower segment of the circumference are attached nine two-level rosettes and eight tiny shield bosses. From these is suspended a complex festoon of chains and pendants. From each of the single attachment rings obscured by the shield bosses hang an ivy leaf filled with green enamel and a small ribbed seed. From the double attachment rings behind the rosettes hang, vertically, a short chain with an ivy leaf filled with green enamel and a seed-like pendant with pointed tongues, alternately filled with green and blue enamel, and, spreading out to either side, two long chains that support a two-level rosette. From this rosette in turn hangs, vertically, a short chain with a tiny shield boss above a small ribbed seed-like pendant with a calyx of two rows of feathers (with grains at apices) and cross-hatched panels on alternate ribs, and, spreading out to either side, two long chains that support a further two-level rosette. From this second row of rosettes hangs, vertically, a short chain with a shield boss and a seed-like pendant with alternately blue and green tongues and, spreading out to either side, two long chains that support yet another two-level rosette from which hangs a large ribbed seed-like pendant with a calyx made up of three rows of feathers (grains at apices) and panels of cross-hatching on alternate ribs.

Both series of feathered seed-like pendants have holes in the back for the insertion of a filler (as in the large necklace), but none is preserved: as in nos 121 and 122, the chasing was done after the joining of the two halves of the pendants. On the back of the disc are a number of repair patches to strengthen the gold where it cracked during the raising of the design. At the top of the back of the disc is soldered a gold suspension ring.

This pair of extremely elaborate pendants seems to have been found beside the head of the deceased, for they are described by Stephani as ear pendants. Others call them temple pendants. They should be compared with the pair from Kul Oba (no. 87). The motif of Thetis or one of her sisters carrying the new armour made for her son, Achilles, by Hephaistos is particularly common in the North Pontic region, perhaps because of its close association with Achilles, not least in the tradition that after his death he lived as an immortal on the island of Leuke in the north-west Black Sea. The motif is also favoured by East Greek jewellers (nos 42–3).

BIBLIOGRAPHY: *CR* 1865, pl. 2, 1; T&K I, fig. 75; Artamonov, pls 296 and 300; Ogden *JAW*, p. 166, fig. 10:26; *Scythian Art*, pl. 251.

Opposite: 120

121

121 Gold strap necklace with three rows of pendants and lion-head terminals

From the Great Bliznitza
330–300 BC
Length 37.8 cm, height 6.0 cm; weight 241.67 g
Hermitage BB 34

The scale and detail of this necklace combine to make it one of the most spectacular to have survived from antiquity.

The lion-head terminals are box-like and made of raised sheet gold with a second, plain sheet underneath. The lion-heads are particularly finely chased, and the eyes are carefully modelled. A ring is soldered into the mouth and a lateral rivet, both ends flattened, holds the strap in place. The collar is decorated with a frieze of palmettes surrounded by spirals (all in spiral-beaded wire) and bordered with various decorative wires (large-beaded, plain, spiral-beaded and rope). The substantial strap consists of five rows of doubled loop-in-loop chain interlinked with pairs of links. Along the lower edge are attached twenty-two rosettes (spiral-beaded wire; concave petals) and twenty-one shield bosses (some bordered in fine beaded wire, some in spiral-beaded). From each shield boss hangs a seed-like pendant with tongues filled alternately with blue and white (probably originally green) enamel. From the two-level rosettes (concave petals) hang, vertically, a rosette (as above) and a seed-like pendant with two rows of feathers (granules

121

at apices) and, out to either side, a chain that helps to support a rosette (as above) and a very large seed-like pendant. These large pendants have two sorts of decoration: one has six levels of feathers; the other has three levels of feathers, a frieze of spirals with buds between – the upper buds are filled with blue enamel, the lower with white – bordered by spiral-beaded wires, and, at the bottom, ribbing with vertical cross-hatching in alternate panels. All the pendants are filled with a brown

resinous material and all have a hole in the shoulder. Unlike in simpler pendants of this type, all the chasing was done after the two halves were soldered together.

Style and technique link this piece with a number of other items from the Great Bliznitsa: the Nereid pendants (no. 120), two other necklaces (no. 117 and Hermitage BB 117, also from this burial), and a pair of disc and boat earrings (no. 122). They are all products of the same workshop. There are also clear links between

all these pieces and a number of torques and pectorals from elsewhere in the region (see p. 126). Such large, elaborate necklaces with lion-head terminals are very rare. A fragmentary but virtually identical piece was found at Kul Oba; another, with beech-nut pendants, is in London.

BIBLIOGRAPHY: *CR* 1865, pl. 2, 4; Ruxer, pls 29, 1 and J; Artamonov, pl. 305; Segall, pl. 5 (upper); Sokolov, no. 50; *Scythian Art*, pl. 230. Kul Oba necklace: Ruxer, pl. 26. London (British Museum) necklace: *BMCJ* 1943.

122 Pair of gold earrings with disc and boat-shaped pendant

From the Great Bliznitza
330–300 BC
Height 5.8 cm, diameter of disc 1.8 cm; weight 9.96 and 10.03 g
Hermitage BB 32

The discs are flat; to the outer, up-turned edge are attached a plain sheet and a corrugated sheet, topped by a two-tier row of grains. Inside the edge is a further two-tier row of granules and a series of decorative wires (plain and ropes), which surround a frieze of spirals with omega fillers. In the centre is a flower-head made up of two tiers of down-turned, long thin petals (spiral-beaded wire). The missing central element has been replaced with a modern wooden peg.

The boat-shaped pendant is decorated with granulation in groups of four grains, bordered by beaded wire flanked by plain wire; the backs are undecorated except for a beaded wire flanked by plain wires across the centre. The terminals have similar borders and three acanthus leaves and a palmette with thin pointed leaves. The central floral motif consists of pairs of spirals with a rosette in the centre, a palmette with pointed leaves above and three acanthus leaves at the bottom. Along the lower contour of the boat are attached eight rosettes (concave petals), from which hangs a system of chains and pendants. From alternate rosettes are suspended two chains which meet to support a large seed-like pendant with a rosette above; the pendant has two rows of feathers (grains at apices) and cross-

122

hatched panels on alternate ribs. In addition, from the third, fifth and seventh rosettes hang plain seeds with discs above, while from three of the rosettes hang only tiny die-struck horn shells.

On the back of the disc are two attachment rings from which hang short lengths of loop-in-loop chain which hold the boat-shaped pendant. The large seed-like pendants have tiny holes in the shoulder, but the fillings are lost. The chased details were added after the two halves of the pendants were soldered together (as in nos 120–21). The method of attaching the pendants to double rings is also found on the Nereid pendants (no. 120) and the strap necklace (no. 123), suggesting a workshop connection.

BIBLIOGRAPHY: *CR* 1865, pl. 2, 3; Pfrommer, pl. 27, 4.

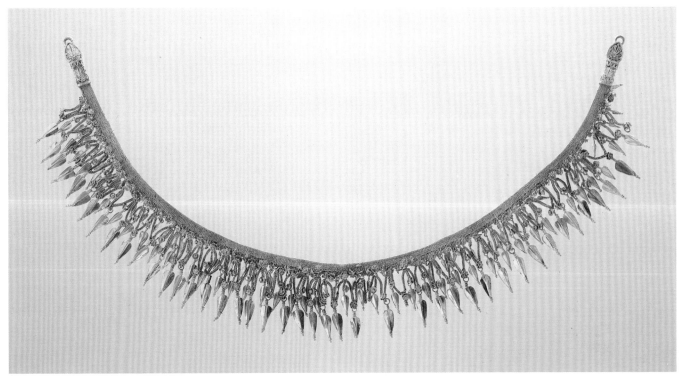

123

123 Gold strap necklace with beech-nut pendants

From the Great Bliznitza
330–300 BC
Length 33.0 cm, height 3.4 cm; weight 63.64 g
Hermitage BB 33

The box-like terminals have attachment rings at either end and are held to the strap by a lateral rivet, flattened at each end. On top of the box is mounted an oval-shaped plate bearing a palmette with a rosette at its base, the petals of which were possibly once filled with blue enamel. The collar is decorated with a row of ovolos and a palmette with a pointed central leaf and a rosette at the base (all in spiral-beaded wire), bordered above and below with beaded wire flanked with plain wire.

The strap is made up from five doubled loop-in-loop chains interlinked. Along the bottom are attached forty-seven two-level rosettes delineated in spiral-beaded wire, the tiers separated by a beaded rod, alternating with tiny Pegasos protomes made of sheet gold with separate wings. From the Pegasos protomes hang tiny three-lobed beech nuts, while from the

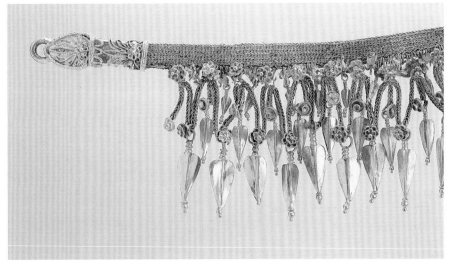

123

rosettes hang, on a short chain, a medium-sized three-lobed beech nut with two-level discs above (traces of green enamel in the centre and blue enamel in the outer band) and, to either side, a longer chain which helps to support a two-level rosette and a large three-lobed beech nut.

The necklace pendants are very delicate and have suffered some damage and loss.

The method of attachment of the backs of the rosettes to the strap compares with that on the earrings, no. 122.

BIBLIOGRAPHY: *CR* 1865, pl. 2, 5; Ruxer, pl. 29, 2; Artamonov, pl. 306; Segall, pl. 5 (lower).

124

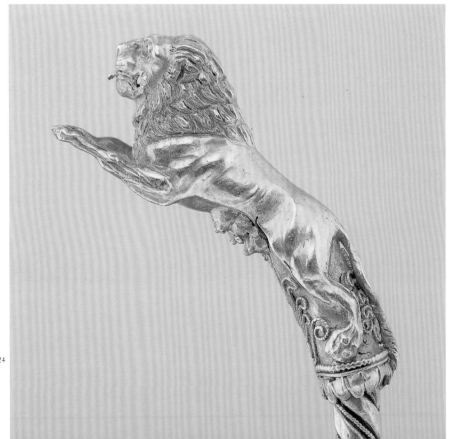

124

THE NORTH PONTIC CITIES

124 Pair of gold bracelets with copper cores and terminals in the form of leaping lionesses

From the Great Bliznitza
330–300 BC
Width 7.3 cm, height 6.5 cm; weight 46.54 and 48.61 g
Hermitage BB 35–6

The lions that form the terminals have male heads and female dugs. This unnatural combination, however, is most probably due to the fact that the artist, like many other Greeks, thought that female lions also had manes.

Each lioness is constructed of sheet gold with separate teeth, tongues, dugs and tails. There are holes at the corners of the mouths, and the eyes were filled with enamel. The hindquarters of the lionesses merge into the collars, which are decorated with spiral-beaded wire filigree palmettes under the tail and between the legs (some blue enamel left in the leaves of the palmette on one bracelet), with cut-out ovolos below.

The hoops are of hollow gold, imitating three rods twisted together. They have metal cores, which appear to be copper.

Lengths of spiral-beaded wire coil along the valleys.

These bracelets were clearly made in the same workshop and at the same date as the bracelets with ram terminals found in a separate burial within the same complex (no. 118).

BIBLIOGRAPHY: *CR* 1865, pl. 2, 6; Artamonov, pl. 279; Deppert-Lippitz, fig. 139; *Scythian Art*, pl. 234; *Zürich*, no. 38. For the misunderstanding about lionesses compare an Athenian red-figured *pelike* by the Berlin Painter of about 490 BC, where on one side of the neck is a male, on the other a female with dugs and mane: *ARV²*, p. 205, no. 114; S. Aurigemma, *Scavi di Spina* (Rome 1960), pl. 193.

125 Gold ring with couchant lion on oval bezel

From the Great Bliznitza
330–300 BC
Width 2.4 cm, length of base 1.8 cm; weight 10.56 g
Hermitage BB 37

The lion, which is turned to the right, is made of sheet gold, probably in one piece, but possibly with the face added separately. The eyes were inlaid, the tongue was added separately and the tail, in front

of the rear right leg, consists of a pair of wires twisted together. The edge of the base has a beaded wire above and below a groove which might have held an inlay.

The underside of the elongated oval bezel is decorated in shallow-groove engraving with a figure of Artemis. She stands on a raised base, facing left and holding a straight bow in her right hand; her left hand clutches at her drapery. She wears a *polos* over her long hair and a belted *chiton*. There is a simple line border.

The hoop is made up of two ropes, each of three gold wires coiled together round a central tapered wire, and a beaded wire laid in the central valley. The bezel rotates on a simple pin that is located in a hemispherical cap at either end.

A similar lion ring was found in the Denisova Mogila near Ordzonikidze: the underside of the bezel depicts in intaglio a griffin attacking a horse. The construction of the hoop is also found on rings (no. 34) and bracelets from northern Greece.

BIBLIOGRAPHY: *CR* 1865, pl. 3, 23; Artamonov, figs 142–3; Segall, pl. 37, 4. Denisova Mogila ring: *Gold der Steppe*, no. 114.

125

125

126

126

127

128

126 Gold scarab ring

From the Great Bliznitza
330–300 BC
Length 2.3 cm, width 1.7 cm, present height 1.3 cm; weight 21.36 g
Hermitage BB 40

The scarab is hollow and slightly crushed. It seems to have been made in two halves, upper and lower, with the legs added separately. Details and areas of stippling are very finely chased; the eyes were probably inlaid. The scarab was fixed to the top of the base with a vertical rod of beaded wire (visible under the front section) and with solder under the legs. The edge of the bezel has a row of cut-out darts, bordered above and below with beaded and plain wires.

The underside of the oval bezel is decorated in shallow-groove engraving, possibly with some chasing, and shows Aphrodite standing to the right, her right elbow on top of a plain pillar, a *chlamys* round her waist and legs and her upper torso bare. On the right Eros crouches to adjust her sandal. His long upper wings bear a tremolo pattern, as does the border. There is a plain ground line.

The hoop is made up of two ropes, each of three gold wires coiled together round a central tapered wire, and a beaded wire laid in the central valley (as in no. 125). A wire passes through the bezel and the hemispherical caps at either end and coils round the hoop.

A number of scarab rings are known. Usually the scarab is rather cursorily rendered, but on a few, all probably produced in the east, the scarab is made as a separate unit.

BIBLIOGRAPHY: *CR* 1865, pl. 3, 24; Artamonov, pl. 280 and fig. 144; Segall, pl. 37, 1; *AT*, p. 146, figs 6–7. On scarab rings see most recently Williams, pp. 89–90.

127 Square gold appliqué with the head of Demeter

From the Great Bliznitza
330–300 BC
Width and height 5.8 cm; weight 4.55 g
Hermitage BB 46

This appliqué shows the head of Demeter in three-quarter view, slightly bent down to the right, perhaps in mourning. She wears a wreath, disc and pyramid earrings and a necklace, and holds a flaming torch to light her path as she searches for her daughter, Persephone (see no. 128). The head is framed by an egg and dart border. There are eight attachment holes. Thirteen examples of this appliqué were found in the tumulus.

The plaque is made from brittle pale gold. It was worked with a die or punch from the back, and the contours of the face and the eyes have been slightly incised. There are traces of a red patina on the back.

129

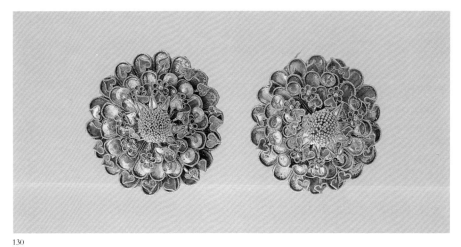

130

These appliqués, together with those in nos 128–9, form a complex of forty-two plaques whose subjects are centred on the Eleusinian Mysteries. As such they stand apart from the many other types of clothing appliqués found in tombs, a fact which, together with their remarkable detail and workmanship, has led to suggestions that the deceased may have been a priestess in Demeter's cult. However, interest in Demeter's Mysteries can be seen in a number of Pontic burials and it is probably best to consider this a sign of Hellenisation.

BIBLIOGRAPHY: *CR* 1865, pl. 2, 8; Rostovtzeff *AD*, pl. 9, 1; Artamonov, fig. 146.

128 Square gold appliqué with the head of Persephone

From the Great Bliznitza
330–300 BC
Width and height 5.8 cm; weight 4.32 g
Hermitage BB 45

The head of Persephone, sometimes known as Kore, the Maiden, is shown fully frontal. Her hair is tied up in a top-knot and she wears disc and pyramid earrings and a necklace. An ear of corn is stuck in her hair on either side, and a veil frames her head. The plaque has an egg and dart border. Fifteen examples of this type were found.

Like no. 127, the plaque is made from

brittle pale gold, and it was worked in the same manner.

Persephone, the daughter of Demeter, was carried off by Hades to the Underworld. After searching far and wide for her, Demeter eventually secured her return, but because Persephone had tasted of the pomegranate while she was in the Underworld, she was bound to spend a third of each year there. This is usually understood as a nature allegory – Persephone being the seed of corn descending into the earth and her ascent the seasonal return of the corn – but there are many complex layers to the myth.

BIBLIOGRAPHY: *CR* 1865, pl. 2, 7; Rostovtzeff *AD*, pl. 9, 2; Artamonov, fig. 145.

129 Square gold appliqué with the head of Herakles

From the Great Bliznitza
330–300 BC
Width and height 5.8 cm; weight 4.87 g
Hermitage BB 44

This plaque shows the head (in almost three-quarter view) and naked shoulders of Herakles. He has a wreath in his hair and his club appears on the left. There is an egg and dart border. Fourteen such appliqués were found.

The plaque is made from brittle pale gold and was produced in the same manner as nos 127–8.

Herakles was the first foreigner, in

other words non-Athenian, to be initiated into the Eleusinian Mysteries. He therefore played an important part in the spread of the cult abroad and is frequently included in scenes associated with the preparatory rites for the Mysteries.

BIBLIOGRAPHY: *CR* 1865, pl. 2, 9; Artamonov, fig. 147.

130 Gold multi-level rosettes

From the Great Bliznitza
330–300 BC
Diameter 2.0 cm; weight 4.02 and 4.06 g
Hermitage BB 41

On a central tube are mounted seven levels of ornament, capped by a dome covered in rings of granulation. The lowest level takes the form of a rosette, the next of a ring with stamens ending in ivy leaves (filled alternately with blue and green enamel); then comes a rosette, followed by stamens ending in concave discs (these are mounted upside-down on one rosette), then stamens ending in ivy leaves (alternately blue and green), and finally a star. On the back are three strips bent up for attachment to a textile or leather garment.

Seven such rosettes were preserved. They are the most complex of a whole series from Greece, Asia Minor and the North Pontic area (see further under no. 67, the Madytos rosettes).

BIBLIOGRAPHY: *CR* 1865, pl.3 , 21; *Stathatos* III, p. 227, fig. 133 (left).

Chersonesos *(nos 131–3)*

In 1899, during research on the city wall of Chersonesos, constructed at the end of the fourth century BC or the beginning of the third, K.K. Kosciuszko-Waluzynicz discovered a hypogeum. Its location under the wall and its unusually rich contents have led to suggestions that it might have been the tomb of a family somehow connected with the construction of that wall. There was a cremation at the very entrance of the tomb and, inside, four burials to the left of the entrance and one to the right. On the left side a group of jewellery was found in a black-glaze *hydria* with white decoration (a painted beech-nut necklace round the neck, a painted ribbon across the vase at handle level) and covered with a lid made of lead. This vase (not sent to the Hermitage) may be dated to the late fourth century or early third century BC. In addition to the jewellery shown here, there was also a plain gold ring.

BIBLIOGRAPHY: Manzewitsch, pl. 1, 1–3 and 8, and pl. 4, 1–2; Pfrommer, FK 125b.

131

131 Gold strap diadem with a central Herakles knot flanked by lion-heads

From Chersonesos
300–280 BC
Length 30.4 cm, height of strap 0.95 cm, height
of siren 1.2 cm; weight 67.94 g
Hermitage X.1899.7

The strap of this superbly elegant diadem is formed from seven strands of doubled loop-in-loop chain attached side by side by interweaving. It is attached to the terminals by a gold wire staple. The outer terminals are D-shaped in section and box-like in construction. They have decorative borders of beaded, twisted and plain wires and two rows of double spiral-beaded wire tongues; cut-out darts project over the strap. There is a strap loop at the extreme end.

The lion-heads are made of sheet gold (possibly in one piece, since the seam can only be traced under the muzzle) and the eyes are recessed, presumably for enamel. The punched recesses on either side of each head may have been for separately attached ears (now missing). The collars are decorated with a frieze of palmettes (a central palmette flanked by two half-palmettes, in spiral-beaded wire with a central leaf of sheet gold) between plain, beaded and twisted wire borders. The rings in the lions' mouths attach to snake-headed hooks on the back of the centrepiece.

The Herakles knot in the centre is made from sheet-gold tubes with applied filigree and other decoration. The tiny central figure of a siren playing the lyre is formed in two parts (front and back). She wears a headdress with rays on top. An unused strap attachment on the back of the siren suggests that the figure might have been intended for a different ornament. The main tube of the knot is decorated with beaded and plain wire edging and spiral-beaded wire tongues in the centre. A coil of wire is soldered into the ends of the tube and the joint is masked by a convex disc or boss. The floral complex on either side of the siren (one side damaged) consists of a palmette on a spiral base, with acanthus leaves on top and a central oval with granulation infill; on each side of the palmette is a rosette (convex petals) with a central disc, also with granulation infill.

Central figures or heads occur in a number of Herakles knots. This is the only preserved example with a siren.

BIBLIOGRAPHY: Manzewitsch, pl. 1, 1; Pfrommer, HK 114, pl. 4, 4. On Herakles knots see Pfrommer, pp. 4–80 (esp. pp. 52–4).

131

132 Pair of gold earrings with lion-head terminals

From Chersonesos
300–280 BC
Height 2.5 cm, width 2.1 cm; weight 6.40 and
    6.92 g
Hermitage X.1899.8

The lions' heads are made in left and right halves. There is an expansion hole in each lion's mouth. The collars are decorated with a frieze of double spiral-beaded wire spirals (single wire doubled back on itself) with grains in the centres of the spirals and at the sides; they end in sheet-gold darts. The hoop is formed from five plain wires coiling round a tapering inner gold tube; all are hammered into a single wire at the point.

The lions' manes and teeth are cursorily rendered, unlike those on the diadem found with them. It seems unlikely that they are products of the same workshop. Lion-head earrings are the earliest type in the long series of animal-head hoop earrings, and seem to have been first developed in Etruria. South Italian jewellers created a number of particularly large examples (no. 148).

BIBLIOGRAPHY: Manzewitsch, pl. 1, 2; Pfrommer, OR 239, pl. 23, 6. On lion-head earrings see Pfrommer, pp. 146–57.

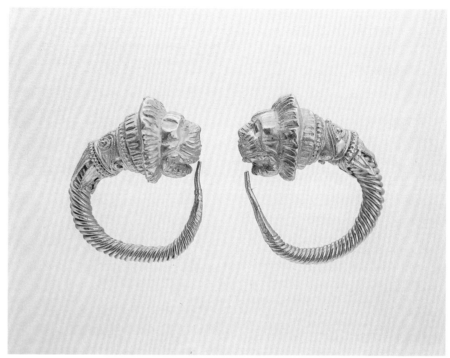

132

133 Gold ring with a seated figure of Athena in intaglio

From Chersonesos
300–280 BC
Diameter of bezel 2.3 cm, height 1.9 cm; weight
    9.9 g
Hermitage X.1899.9

The flat circular bezel bears a figure of Athena seated on a lion-pawed stool, one elbow resting on the rim of her shield (which has a lion-head device), the other arm outstretched and holding a winged Nike who in turn holds out a wreath. Athena wears a high-waisted *chiton* and a *himation*; she has a Corinthian helmet on her head. A spear rests at an angle against the circle of the bezel. There is a plain ground line.

The design is largely, if not entirely,

133

produced by shallow-groove engraving. The top flat surface appears to have been polished or burnished after the design was cut. The massive hoop is D-shaped in section, flaring slightly towards the back.

The figure of Athena may be compared with the design on the coins of Lysimachus, ruler of Macedon and much of Asia Minor from 288 to 281 BC.

BIBLIOGRAPHY: Manzewitsch, pl. 1, 3; Boardman *GGFR*, pl. 744 (type IX).

4 The Greek Cities of South Italy and Sicily

The earliest Greek contact with South Italy and Sicily dates from the sixteenth century BC, but it is only in the fourteenth and thirteenth centuries BC that there is any evidence of possible Greek settlers. This evidence, however, is almost exclusively ceramic. Towards 1100 BC, the Greek world suffered a series of disasters, and contacts with Italy were severed. It was not until the beginning of the eighth century that Greeks, specifically Euboeans, once again began to call there. By 750 BC there was a thriving trading post on the beautiful island of Ischia (ancient Pithekoussai), near Naples. Several Greek cities from the mainland, the islands and the coast of Asia Minor soon followed this lead and established colonies along the coasts of southern Italy and Sicily. This great colonial venture took place mainly in the late eighth and seventh centuries BC.

The Greeks in southern Italy brought with them their language, their religion and their customs, all of which had an immense impact on the indigenous population. Each of the Greek city-states followed its own course in the sixth century. Almost all flourished, but prosperity inevitably brought problems, and some cities clashed with their neighbours, whether native or Greek. Sybaris, proverbial for its luxury, fell to the aggression of its Greek neighbour, Kroton (modern Crotone); Taras (modern Taranto) suffered a heavy defeat at the hands of the neighbouring Italians, the Iapygians.

Syracuse on Sicily was to emerge as perhaps the greatest Greek city in the west, ruled by a succession of vigorous tyrants. Under Gelon it defeated the Carthaginians, the other great foreign power with interests on the island, in 480 BC. In 474 BC Gelon's successor, Hieron I, led the Syracusans to the help of the Greeks in Italy and defeated the powerful Etruscans at sea off Cumae, the northernmost Greek colony, which was settled from Pithekoussai. In the early fourth century Syracuse gained control of most of Sicily and much of southern Italy, with the exception of Taras, which was particularly powerful in the fourth century and a flourishing artistic centre, producing both fine jewellery and pottery. The power of Rome, however, was beginning to be felt, and by 272 BC all of Greek Italy was in Roman hands. Sicily held out longer, but by the end of the third century it too had been absorbed into the centralised culture and economy of the Roman world.

Although, as has been noted, the Greeks' association with South Italy and Sicily can be traced back to the Mycenaean period, it is only really at the end of the sixth century BC that one finds Greek gold jewellery with a distinctive South Italian style. Such sixth-century pieces are, however, particularly rare and few pieces are to be found outside the museums of South Italy and Sicily. The same is true of the fifth and early fourth centuries. In the case of Taranto, the fifth-century tombs may all have

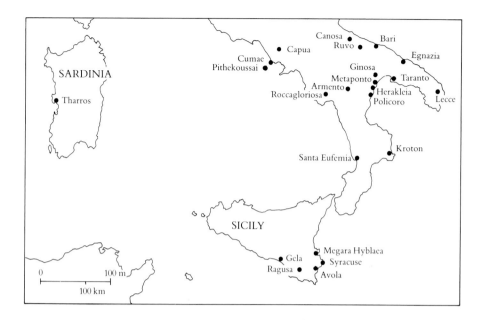

been destroyed by the expansion of the city at the beginning of the fourth, but this would not explain the similar dearth in other cities and one must suppose that there was not yet sufficient surplus of wealth to allow a great display of gold jewellery.

By the second quarter of the fourth century, however, a number of Greek cities had clearly grown in wealth and we begin to find gold jewellery in places such as Taranto, Metaponto, Herakleia and Policoro, as well as at native sites such as Armento, Ruvo, Roccanova, Roccagloriosa, Canosa and Egnazia. In Sicily, too, some gold jewellery has been found in places such as Megara Hyblaea, Gela and Ragusa. Of all these cities it seems that Taranto was the richest and the most artistically innovative.

At Taranto the series of tombs containing Greek jewellery seems to begin in the second quarter of the fourth century and run into the second century. Study of the material from these and from neighbouring sites reveals a remarkable homogeneity of style which suggests a small number of related workshops. Indeed, by employing a combination of stylistic and technical criteria it is possible to identify three main workshops, which we may call the Santa Eufemia workshop, the Crispiano workshop and the Ginosa workshop.

The Santa Eufemia workshop is well represented in this catalogue: five items, from three different contexts, may be attributed to it. First there is the splendid diadem from Santa Eufemia itself (no. 137) with its elaborate filigree tendrils and trumpet-shaped flowers. This concentration on filigree florals is typical of South Italian work, but what is particularly unusual is the corkscrew curl of wire, laid flat, at the ends of these tendrils near the corners of the pediment. This very same corkscrew curl can be found on both the oval box-shaped pendant (no. 138) and, badly worn, on the scarab ring (no. 140). On the box-bezel ring from Avola in Sicily (no. 143) the corkscrew curl appears both on the bezel, framing the dancing maenad, and on the sides of the box. Furthermore, on a circular dress ornament (no. 150), in amongst the filigree decoration are yet more of the same corkscrew curls laid flat on the surface of the disc. This workshop seems to have been active in the last decades of the fourth century, as was the second, the Ginosa workshop, named after a pair of earrings and a Herakles knot from a tomb at Ginosa, around which can be grouped some half a dozen other pieces.

The third workshop, the Crispiano workshop, may have been active slightly earlier, perhaps from nearer the middle of the century. To it may be attributed – besides its name pieces, the wonderful pair of earrings from Crispiano (near Taranto) – the necklace from Taranto (no. 135) and the box-bezel ring said to have been found with it (no. 136). Other associated items include some five pairs of boat-shaped earrings from Taranto and the setting for a cornelian cylinder-seal in the Victoria and Albert Museum, as well as the spiral earrings (no. 145).

With these workshops may be more loosely associated a series of other pieces that span roughly the second half of the fourth century and the beginning of the third, the heyday of Tarentine jewellery. This Tarentine style was highly linear, relying heavily on filigree work. It recalls in many ways the contemporary work on red-figured vases.

One particular predilection of Tarentine jewellers in the last quarter of the fourth century and in the first quarter of the third was large lion-head terminals, both for earrings and for necklaces. This type seems to have been popular not only at Taranto, but also in Sicily (Gela) and Campania (Capua and Cumae).

Local varieties of other late Classical and early Hellenistic earrings can also be distinguished. These include the disc earring with pyramidal or conical pendant, elaborate box-bezel rings, and spiral earrings with human or animal terminals (Fig. 58).

Finally, this material raises some more general questions. Why was there an upsurge in jewellery production at Taranto in the fourth century? Were the jewellers all locally trained or might there have been an influx of immigrant craftsmen? On the first question, we can only suppose that an increase in wealth led to the desire to display it. The second question cannot be answered with any degree of certainty, but a number of factors suggest that immigrant craftsmen might well have given new impetus to the local Greek tradition. These include the appearance of new forms such as the boat-shaped earring.

BIBLIOGRAPHY: Becatti, pp. 61–2; N. Degrassi in S. Finocchi (ed.), *Ori e argenti dell'Italia antica* (Turin 1961), pp. 77–127; *Taranto, passim*; Williams, pp. 75–95; *L'oro dei Greci*, pls 108–9, 116–17, 119–24.

FIGURE 58 Silver tetradrachm of Syracuse, *c.* 420–400 BC, showing the nymph Arethusa wearing a necklace of beads and a spiral earring ending in rams' heads (British Museum, BMC 64).

Tomb of the Taranto Priestess *(nos 134–6)*

A particularly fine and interesting group of jewellery was bought for the British Museum from Alessandro Castellani in 1872. In an Appendix to his Report to the Trustees of the British Museum of 19 July 1871, urging the purchase of the whole of the Castellani collection of jewellery, Charles Newton, Keeper of the Greek and Roman Department, listed and described the pieces, noting that they were all said to come from a single tomb, which 'was probably that of a priestess buried with the insignia of her sacerdotal office'. The group consists of three items, sceptre, necklace and ring. Nothing is known of anything else that might have been found with the group.

The sceptre is a truly remarkable find, for no other certain example is known, now that the famous 'sceptre' from the Tomba degli Ori at Canosa has been ingeniously reinterpreted by Bernard van den Driessche as the top of the handle of an elaborate fan. Sceptres are symbols of authority, either royal or religious. Since any monarchy at Taranto seems to have ended around 473 BC, if not before, it seems most probable that the present example belonged to a priestess, as a symbol of the power of the deity whom she served. The presence in the same tomb of a ring with the depiction of a seated female holding a very similar sceptre suggests that the jewellery worn by this priestess may well have been specially made. As a result, when one notices that two of the female heads on the necklace have horns and therefore represent Io, once the priestess of Hera, it is very tempting to wonder if the owner of this set of jewellery might have been a priestess of Hera at Taranto.

However, since this group of jewellery was bought from Alessandro Castellani, a consummate jeweller and dealer, there must remain the possibility that he was responsible for grouping the pieces together.

BIBLIOGRAPHY: Williams, pp. 76–8. Canosa fan: B. van den Driessche, *BInstHistBelgRom* 43 (1973), pp. 5ff.

134

134 Gold sceptre

Said to be from Taranto
350–320 BC
Height as restored 51.4 cm, diameter of shaft
1.2 cm
British Museum GR 1872.6-4.842

The core of the shaft of this sceptre is not preserved: a modern white resin tube has been inserted for support. The original core may have been of wood and covered with a fabric which not only hid the end of the gold sleeve that supports the capital (see below) but also set off the gold net casing to the greatest effect. This net casing is made up of twelve units of equal size, one slightly longer and one that has been cut down. As a result, it is impossible to be sure of the original length of the sceptre. Each of these units is made up of circles of undulating plain wire, soldered together at the crests and troughs, each junction being hidden by a tiny circle of wire filled with enamel. At the top of each unit is a plain circle of spiral-beaded wire. The enamel fillings are of two colours: one is now white, but was most probably green, and the other is blue. They were so arranged that the colours spiralled down the shaft.

The base consists of a gold disc decorated with concentric rings of beaded, plain and rope wires and, in the centre, a rosette with concave petals with spiral-beaded wire borders. At the centre of the rosette is a large solid gold ball.

The capital consists of a sleeve of gold onto which the various ornaments have been attached. The base of the capital consists of rings of plain and beaded wire, a collar of small tongues which were once filled with enamel (now virtually white), and a ring of acanthus leaves of three different heights. The capital itself has double spiral supports reaching up to the abacus at each of the four corners. Each face is decorated with two spirals of plain wire, with a flower at the point where they meet. The petals of these flowers are filled with blue enamel and at the centre is a corkscrew of wire. The top of the plain abacus is lined with a beaded wire.

The terminal above consists of a six-lobed fruit of pale green glass set within a nest of carefully veined acanthus leaves.

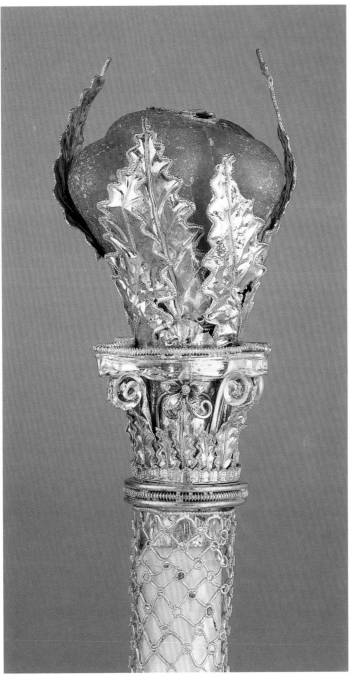

134

The fruit, perhaps a quince, was cast in one piece, ground to shape and then had a hole drilled vertically through it to take the end of the central core. The top of the hole was disguised by a small sheet of gold decorated with four ivy-like leaves.

BIBLIOGRAPHY: *BMCJ* 2070; A.B. Cook, *Zeus*, vol. II (Cambridge 1925), p. 763, n. 1, with figs 708–9; Wuilleumier *Tarente*, pl. 23, 4; *Taranto*, p. 321; Williams, pls 30 and 31, 1–2.

135

135 Gold rosette and lotus-palmette necklace with female head-pendants

Said to be from Taranto
350–330 BC
Length as strung 18.0 cm, height of head
    pendants 2.0 cm, droplets 2.5 cm; weight 30.5 g
British Museum GR 1872.6-4.667

Fourteen rosette and eight lotus-palmette units are preserved. The rosettes are three-tiered: the upper-level petals are flat, but those below are slightly convex. The lotus-palmettes consist of cut-out double palmettes with enclosing lotus leaves and a rosette in the centre. All these cut-out sheet-gold elements are bordered with spiral-beaded wire. At the backs of both the rosettes and the palmettes are double ribbed tubes for stringing.

Eight small pendant heads are attached to the lotus-palmette units. They are die-formed from sheet gold (two are from a much sharper mould than the rest). From the rosettes hang eight large seed-like pendants which alternate with female heads. The seed pendants have flat, sheet backs with a hole in the centre: the outer pendants are flatter than the rest. The fronts are decorated with three rows of feathers, below which are ribs with a row of dots down each valley. Seven female head pendants are preserved. They are all die-formed with added chased and filigree details and all have a flat sheet back with expansion hole. They wear spiral ear-rings, a necklace with a central pendant and a *stlengis* in their hair. The bottom of the neck is decorated with plain, beaded and rope wires. Two of the heads have added bull's horns and ears and therefore represent Io, the priestess of Hera who was changed into a heifer by the goddess.

The necklace was made up by Castellani to include eight spherical beads and two terminal beads, all with spiral filigree. These are totally out of place on a necklace such as this and are probably of eastern rather than western workmanship. Castellani also included two modern rosettes.

The combination of rosettes and lotus-palmettes recurs on a number of necklaces

from the North Pontic region (no. 94), but there is also an example from Homolion in northern Greece. Head pendants seem to have been popular in the west from the fifth century, on both necklaces and earrings.

BIBLIOGRAPHY: *BMCJ* 1952; Ruxer, pl. 35, 5; E. Coche de la Ferté, *Les bijoux antiques* (Paris 1956), pl. 20, 3; Miller, pl. 5b; Higgins *GRJ²*, pl. 28; R. Higgins in Barr-Sharrar and Borza, fig. 5; Deppert-Lippitz, pl. 11; *Seven Thousand Years of Jewellery*, p. 64, fig. 136; M. Pfrommer, *IstMitt* 36 (1986), pl. 21, 2; Williams pl. 31, 3–4 (attributed to the Crispiano workshop). All these publications predate the recent removal of alien and modern elements. On the necklace type see further Pfrommer, op. cit., pp. 59–76. Northern Greek example (Homolion J2): Miller, pl. 4. Head pendants on necklaces: (Naples, from Ruvo) Breglia, fig. 272; (Roccagloriosa) *L'oro dei Greci*, pl. 122, 2; on earrings: see no. 145 below, with comparanda; cf. also the pendants of the earrings from Crispiano, *Taranto*, no. 73.

136 Gold oval box-bezel ring

Said to be from Taranto
350–340 BC
Length of bezel 2.1 cm, height of box 0.6 cm,
    width of hoop 2.3 cm; weight 7.9 g
British Museum GR 1872.6-4.146

The sheet-gold bezel depicts, in low relief, a seated woman wearing a *chiton* and a cloak. Her right hand is down by her side, perhaps holding an object; her left hand is forward and slightly raised as if holding the sceptre, which is surmounted by a fruit enclosed within leaves. The bezel is bordered with wire ropes and a beaded rim. Around the sides of the box-shaped bezel is a band of spiral-beaded filigree wave pattern bordered by wire ropes. The underside of the bezel bears a filigree double palmette surrounding an expansion hole, itself ringed by plain wire.

The hoop is composed of a sheet-gold tube overlaid with aligned twisted wire ropes. The ends of the hoop are decorated with a band of ovolos and a series of plain and rope wires. Spreading over the edge of the box is a cut-out sheet palmette with filigree leaves.

This is the finest of a series of Western Greek box-bezel rings, produced most

136

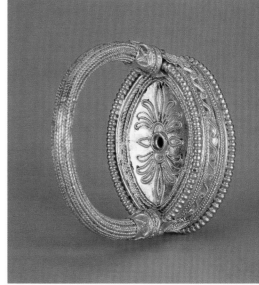

136

probably in Taranto. The seated woman may represent a priestess: the similarity between the sceptre that she holds and the actual example said to have been found with the ring (no. 134) is quite remarkable.

BIBLIOGRAPHY: *BMCR* 218; Richter *EGGE*, no. 279 with fig. k on p. 75; Williams, pl. 32, 2–3 (attributed to the Crispiano workshop). On box-bezel rings see Williams, pp. 87–9, and no. 1 in the present catalogue.

The Santa Eufemia Treasure *(nos 137–41)*

After a night of heavy rain, 7/8 April 1865, some gold objects were washed clean at the bottom of a two-metre-deep trench dug in an olive grove at the foot of a hill known as Elemosina, near Santa Eufemia in Calabria. Qualaro, the village idiot of Santa Eufemia, seems to have been the first to spot these glittering things as he was out collecting brushwood. He took them back to two of his fellow villagers, Antonio Zarra and Francesco Montessanti. They persuaded him to take them to the trench, where they found still more treasures, some in a medium-sized pot, as well as fragments of human bones and pottery. These spoils were then taken to the Estate Keeper employed by Pasquale Francica, the landowner. He knew the value of the gold, but not of the objects themselves, and after a further visit to the site, when still more gold was found, he crushed many of the objects and sold them to the local goldsmith. About two months later Francica himself learnt of the find and sought to retrieve as much of it as he could. Sadly, he recovered only a small part of the whole; the rest had been melted down. His heir's

137 Gold diadem

From Santa Eufemia
330–300 BC
Unbent length 15.0 cm, height in centre 4.2 cm,
    strap height 1.5 cm; weight 45.8 g
British Museum GR 1896.6-16.1

This sheet-gold diadem consists of a long band to which has been soldered a central pediment. The strap is decorated with three groups of three grooves and three rows of punched circles. The loop terminals have spiral ends. Each wing of the pediment and the section of strap below it are decorated with symmetrical floral tendrils in plain and spiral-beaded wire, with trumpet-shaped flowers and small rosettes. The trumpet flowers have sheet-gold infills and the tendrils at either corner of the pediment end in a corkscrew curl (Fig. 7). In the apex of the pediment is an

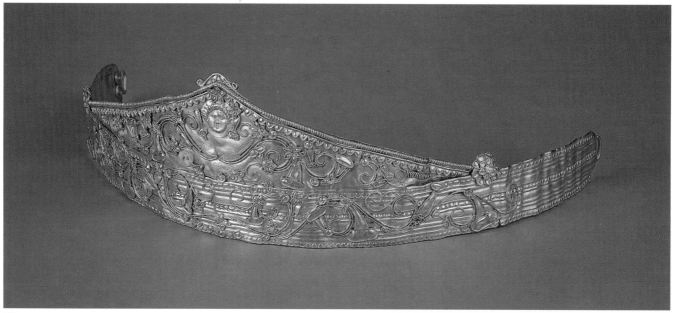

137

brief judgement on the affair speaks volumes: 'In tal modo la ignoranza di un villano fece finire nel crogiuolo dell'orefice, opere d'arte greca della più fine fattura.'

    Most of the Treasure was bought for the British Museum in 1896. A further piece, the gold scarab ring, was acquired in 1985.

BIBLIOGRAPHY: Francica, *passim*; B. van den Dreissche, *ArchCl* 42 (1973), pp. 552ff.; Williams, pp. 80–87.

138

embossed frontal head, perhaps Helios or a gorgoneion. The *sima* of the pediment is decorated with a row of darts, surmounted by beaded and plain wires. The central *akroterion* contains a three-leaved flower; the corner *akroteria* take the form of two-tier rosettes.

The thickness of the sheet gold and the sturdiness of the object, together with traces of apparently ancient repairs to a break in the strap at the left corner of the pediment, indicate that this diadem was actually worn.

BIBLIOGRAPHY: Francica, pl. 2; *BMCJ* 2113; Becatti, p. 349; R. Higgins in Barr-Sharrar and Borza, fig. 11; *Seven Thousand Years of Jewellery*, no. 153; *Taranto*, p. 113; Williams, pl. 33 (attributed to the Santa Eufemia Master); *LIMC* v, *sv* Helios, no. 164; Ogden *AJ*, p. 57, fig. 42.

138 Gold oval box pendant and chain with lion-head terminals

From Santa Eufemia

330–300 BC

Length of box 3.1 cm, width 2.7 cm, thickness 0.7 cm; length of chain 38.7 cm; weight of box 10.4 g; weight of chain 13.3 g

British Museum GR 1896.6-16.4 and 3

On one side of the oval box the thin sheet gold is embossed with a rather heavy and effeminate Eros, his arms raised above his head towards a filigree disc. Below his feet is an applied sheet-gold acanthus motif from which rise, on either side of him, long tendrils of spiral-beaded wire terminating in fine corkscrew curls. The inner border is of beaded, plain and rope filigree, and the outer border of beaded wire.

The other side of the box is decorated with four palmettes, each with a central acanthus leaf applied in sheet gold, separated by trumpet-shaped flowers. Some tendrils end in groups of granules, and granules also decorate the ends of the trumpet flowers and the palmettes. The border is the same as on the other side of the box. Around the edge of the box is a running spiral band, and at either end is a small attachment hole encircled by wire.

The doubled two-fold loop-in-loop chain terminates in small sheet-gold lion-heads with simple sheet-gold collars decorated with plain and beaded wires. The chains are attached to the terminals by means of wire ties, and each lion-head has a ring on its mouth for attachment to the pendant.

This ornament is a translation into gold of the large gemstone worn on a chain

or cord around the neck. Contemporary examples from South Italy include both cylindrical and scaraboid gems.

BIBLIOGRAPHY: Francica, pl. 3; *BMCJ* 2119 (box) and 2118 (chain); Williams, pl. 35, 1–4 (attributed to the Santa Eufemia Master); Ogden *AJ*, p. 57, fig. 41 (box). Gems: Boardman *GGFR*, colour pl. opp. p. 202, no. 3 (cylindrical); *Taranto*, p. 310 (cylindrical) and nos 271 (cylindrical) and 272 (scaraboid).

138

139

139 Pendant in the form of the heads of two African women set back to back

From Santa Eufemia
330–300 BC
Height 2.6 cm; weight 2.4 g
British Museum GR 1896.6-16.5

The pendant is made in two die-formed halves. The heads have typical African features and the ears share a gold wire earring. In the top of the pendant is a small suspension loop of plain wire. The base is closed with a sheet of gold, now mostly missing. The bottom of the neck is decorated with spiral-beaded and plain wires.

The size and two-sidedness of this piece suggest that it was not a pendant from a necklace but rather from an earring, like the Crispiano earrings with pendants in the form of a woman's head. Pendants in the form of African heads seem to have been popular in Italy: other examples come from Bari and Ruvo.

BIBLIOGRAPHY: Francica, pl. 3; *BMCJ* 2117; Williams, pl. 34, 4–5. Crispiano earrings: *Taranto*, no. 73. Bari head: E.M. de Juliis in *Archaeologia in Puglia* (Bari 1983), p. 46, fig. 79. Ruvo head: *BMCJ* 2272 (Etruscan).

140 Hollow gold scarab ring

From Santa Eufemia; formerly Tyszkiewicz, Guilhou and Harari collections
330–300 BC
Length 2.3 cm, width 1.8 cm, thickness 0.8 cm; weight 3.2 g
British Museum GR 1985.2-15.1

The scarab is of sheet gold and the upper die-made part is fairly rudimentary, although the wing cases, central spine, legs, head, eyes and pincers are all discernible. Across the back is a dotted band and there are a number of vertical strips, perhaps intended to imitate some sort of ties from the back of the scarab to the bezel. The hoop is missing.

The worn base shows, within a border of rope filigree, a figure of Eros playing the pipes. Behind him, on the ground, is a cockerel. Both the Eros and the cock stand on a small flower from which extend two long scrolling tendrils in spiral-beaded wire, ending in a tightly coiled corkscrew tendril. Traces of blue enamel remain in some of the buds among the scrollwork.

A number of gold scarab rings with designs in relief and incuse can be identified as products of South Italy. The filigree corkscrew curls suggest that this ring may be another work by the same jeweller as the oval box pendant from Santa Eufemia (no. 138) and the Avola box-bezel ring (no. 143).

BIBLIOGRAPHY: Francica, pl. 3; W. Froehner, *Collection d'antiquités du comte Michel Tyszkiewicz* (Hôtel Drouot, 8–10 June 1898), no. 209; S. de Ricci, *Catalogue of a Collection of Ancient Rings formed by the late E. Guilhou* (1912), no. 53 with pl. 2; Sotheby's, 9 November 1937, lot 67; J. Boardman and D. Scarisbrick, *The Ralph Harari Collection of Finger Rings* (1977), no. 20 and plate; D. Williams, *British Museum Society Bulletin* 55 (1987), p. 26; Williams, pl. 39, 1 and 3 (attributed to the Santa Eufemia Master). On other western scarab rings see Williams, pp. 89–90.

140

140

141

141 Two sections of a gold belt

From Santa Eufemia
330–300 BC
Length 18.2 (*BMCJ* 2125) and 16.0 cm (*BMCJ*
    2126), height 5.8 cm; weight 57.7 and 58.6 g
British Museum GR 1896.6-16.2

These two sections of broad corrugated
gold sheet are presumably the ends of a
belt. The sheet gold, of fairly substantial
thickness, has been shaped using a bronze
die to produce five corrugated bands.
Each end retains its attachment loop of
tapered gold wires with spiral ends. The
Santa Eufemia Treasure contained a
further four fragments, representing two
more such belts.

Although cord ties seem more the
fashion on the representations of women
on South Italian vases, belts are also
found; however, most of these appear to
be decorated with roundels or vertical
lines. They may or may not have been
made from precious metal. There is a thin
silver belt in the British Museum which
may be South Italian, and what seem to
be two particularly elaborate gold belts in
the Stathatos collection which are said to
come from northern Greece. The belt
from a tomb on the Dardanelles (no. 61)
is much more fragile and is completely
undecorated.

BIBLIOGRAPHY: Francica, pl. 1 a–b; *BMCJ*
2125–6; Williams, pl. 37, 1. Silver belt: *BMCJ*
2833. Northern Greek belts: *Stathatos*, nos 265–6.

The Avola Hoard *(nos 142–3)*

This hoard was found in November 1914 during the construction of a water cistern in the contrada Mammanelli, some 4 kilometres from Avola in Sicily. Inside a coarse vase were found about 300 gold coins and some jewellery, including a pair of bracelets and a ring. The material was divided into two large lots, although some isolated pieces, presumably the jewellery, slipped into the hands of a third person. It seems that the first lot, which was out of Sicily and in America by 1916, consisted of 190 coins, while the second, consisting of 128 coins, remained in Sicily until 1922. The coins included Syracusan staters with Herakles and the lion on one side and a running horse on the other, as well as Persian Darics.

BIBLIOGRAPHY: P. Orsi, *Atti e Memorie dell'Istituto Italiano di Numismatica* 3 (1917), pp. 7ff.; M. Thompson, O. Mørkholm and C.M. Kraay, *An Inventory of Greek Coin Hoards* (New York 1973), no. 2122; Williams, pp. 78–80.

142

142 Pair of gold bracelets

From Avola
330–300 BC
Maximum diameter 5.5 cm, width of band
 1.3 cm; weight 17.0 and 17.0 g
British Museum GR 1923.4-21.1–2

Both bracelets, which are mirror images of each other, take the form of gold bands terminating at each end in two snake-heads. One of these snake-heads extends forwards and slightly to one side; the other doubles back on itself. The snakes have chased or punched details, including dotted scales, and the bands are of substantial sheet gold with punched or struck bands of circles and a bead and reel pattern. The bands and snakes are formed from the same piece of gold. The junction between bands and heads is concealed by an applied double row of spirals in spiral-beaded wire between rope filigree borders and an applied sheet-gold acanthus leaf rising from a lyre-form spiral complex executed in thick plain wire.

The combination of snake-heads and strap-like bands is unusual, but best paralleled in Egypt in the mid-Ptolemaic period. The decoration of the bands recalls the strap of the Santa Eufemia diadem (no. 137). The fact that a ring attributable to the Santa Eufemia Master (no. 143) also formed part of this hoard suggests that these bracelets may also be of Tarentine workmanship.

BIBLIOGRAPHY: Williams, pl. 32, 1 and 4. For the Ptolemaic parallels see Ogden, forthcoming.

143

144 Gold boat-shaped earrings

About 350 BC
Width 2.2 cm, height 4.2 cm; weight 4.6 and
    4.7 g
New York 16.174.35 a and b; Rogers Fund, 1916

Each boat is made of sheet gold in two halves. On either side of a central vertical band of beaded and plain wires the whole surface of the earring is covered with plain wire circles surmounted by grains. The terminals are decorated with quatrefoil rosettes with plain wire borders, and a similar rosette conceals the suspension ring on the base of the boat which supports the seed-like pendant. Each pendant is formed in two halves from sheet gold and has a calyx made of two rows of feathers. A simple gold wire hoop is soldered into one terminal of each earring and arches over to locate into the other terminal.

The decoration of these boats is closely paralleled on two pairs of earrings from Taranto and a pair once on the New York market. The boat shape is particularly well represented in Tarentine graves, the decoration ranging from the very simple to the very elaborate. A pair is worn by the woman on a fine South Italian ring (no. 157).

BIBLIOGRAPHY: Alexander, fig. 49. For similar earrings see *Taranto*, nos 60–61; Deppert-Lippitz, fig. 126 (New York market). For the type in general see *Taranto*, nos 56–68.

143 Gold box-bezel ring decorated with a maenad

From Avola
330–300 BC
Maximum dimension of bezel 2.0 cm, thickness of bezel 0.5 cm, width of hoop 2.4 cm; weight 6.0 g
British Museum GR 1923.4-21.3

The top of the bezel is formed from an embossed gold sheet showing a maenad dancing to the right, her left arm up over her head, drapery swirling above, and her right arm down, holding a *thyrsos*. To each side of her are filigree tendrils in spiral-beaded wire, ending in a corkscrew curl, and the scene is bordered with plain and rope wires with an outer rim of beaded wire. The vertical sides of the box bear spiral tendrils, also with corkscrew curls. The underside of the bezel is left plain apart from a central expansion hole. The hoop is formed of a sheet-gold tube overlaid with twisted wire ropes. The joint between hoop and bezel is decorated with a palmette with a superimposed rosette and a collar of ovolos.

The corkscrew curls and many other features of this ring suggest that it is by the same Tarentine jeweller as nos 137–8 and 140.

BIBLIOGRAPHY: Williams, pl. 34, 1–2 (attributed to the Santa Eufemia Master).

144

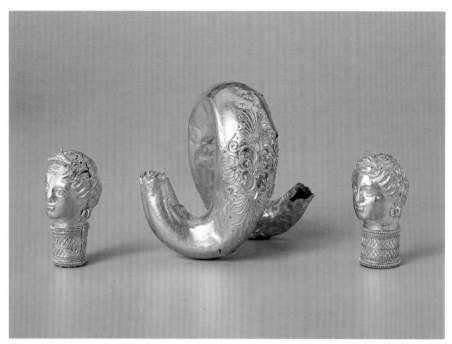

145

145 Gold spiral earring with female head terminals

Said to be from Taranto
350–320 BC
Height of heads 2.2 cm, height of spirals 3.5 cm; weight of spiral 7.4 g, weight of heads 1.6 and 1.5 g
British Museum GR 1872.6-4.826–7 and 1872.6-4.487

The heads are each formed from two sheet-gold halves, probably die-formed, with chased detailing, especially on the hair. The women each wear a pediment-shaped diadem and even have finely made spiral earrings, even though their ears are barely depicted. The necks are decorated with collars of plain and spiral-beaded wires, twisted ropes and two bands of serpentine filigree.

The tapering tubular spiral is decorated with an elaborate applied motif consisting of spiral-beaded filigree palmettes flanking spirals, perhaps intended as stylised lotus (?) flowers, on each side of a rosette with six concave petals. The spirals are formed from strips of gold on edge, not wires, and were probably enamelled. This type of 'cell-wall' or simple 'cloisonné'

enamelling is more common in Phoenician than in Greek work.

Castellani had the two heads made up as pins with ivory shanks, but they are clearly earring terminals. Although it is therefore not certain that the two heads belong with the spiral element, it seems very probable. Such earrings are particularly common in South Italy, and a variant has ram-heads as terminals. The type does not seem to have been popular on the Greek mainland in the Classical period, but on Cyprus it finds a close parallel in the series of earrings with griffin and lion-griffin head terminals (nos 165, 171–4).

The style of the heads and the spiral remind one of the jewellery from the tomb at Crispiano, now in Taranto, which in turn has connections with the ring and necklace from the Tomb of the Taranto Priestess (nos 135–6).

BIBLIOGRAPHY: *BMCJ* 2000 and 1652. Spiral associated with the Crispiano workshop: Williams, p. 91. For the type cf. *Taranto*, no. 103; (Naples) Siviero, no. 57, pl. 70; (Baltimore WAG, singleton) *Baltimore*, no. 254; (Geneva) G. Ortiz, *The George Ortiz Collection: Antiquities from Ur to Byzantium* (Bern 1993), no. 161. Ram-heads: (Naples) Siviero, pls 52–3.

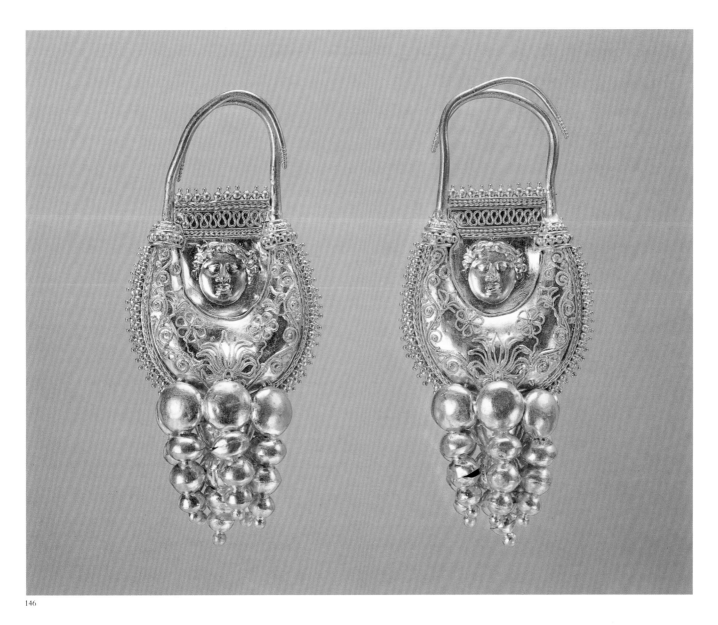

146

146 Pair of boat-shaped gold earrings with clusters of globes

Said to be from Taranto
340–320 BC
Height 6.5 cm, width 2.9 cm; weight 18.8 and
    18.9 g
British Museum GR 1872.6-4.516

The boats of these most unusual earrings are decorated in spiral-beaded filigree with a central palmette with rising spiral tendrils sprouting bell-shaped flowers, and a pair of floating rosettes. The lower borders are of rope and plain wire, with an outer fringe of three rows of two-tiered grains. Between the arms of the boat is a roughly semicircular panel embossed with a gorgon's head, surmounted by a rectangle decorated with a band of serpentine wire bordered above and below with plain and twisted rope wires and topped by a row of two-tiered grains. Below the boat are soldered five graduated rows of gold spheres (the top row rather flattened), each made in two halves from sheet gold.

The earrings have a pair of symmetrical tapered wire hooks, and the joints between boat and hooks are decorated with plain and beaded wire collars.

The clusters of spheres of sheet gold below the boats clearly imitate Late Etruscan earrings. The type is otherwise unparalleled. The earrings are probably the work of a Tarentine workshop.

BIBLIOGRAPHY: *BMCJ* 1657–8; Wuilleumier *Tarente*, p. 365f.; Higgins *GRJ*², p. 126.

147

147 Pair of gold disc and pyramid earrings

Said to be from Taranto

About 300 BC

Height 4.7 cm, diameter of disc 1.8 cm, height of pyramid 2.5 cm; weight 4.2 and 4.3 g

New York 26.209.1–2; purchase, funds from various donors, 1926

This type of earring is commonly seen in representations of women. It was a particular favourite in South Italy, and this pair is among the finest to survive.

Each disc consists of a pan-shaped sheet-gold disc with the edge bent back on itself. To this edge wall is attached an outer corrugated sheet surmounted by beaded wire and plain wire. The tondo of the disc is decorated with concentric bands of beaded, plain (large and small) and rope filigree, a frieze of spirals in spiral-beaded wire (double wires, grain over joints, circles in interstices) and a central lion-head of sheet gold in high relief. The lion-heads on both earrings were produced with the same die and both have separately applied tongues and eyes, with enamel set within spiral-beaded borders. The hooks soldered to the reverse of the discs have stylised snake-head terminals.

Below each disc is an enamelled rosette, and below that an inverted three-sided pyramid pendant. The pendants each hang from a ring soldered to a tube which extends into the top of the pyramid but is not soldered in place. Each face of the pyramid is decorated, from the top downwards, with horizontal bands of beaded, plain and rope filigree, pointed tongues with spiral-beaded wire borders, and finally a large attenuated palmette in spiral-beaded wire with hearts filled with enamel and a circle filled with enamel on either side of the long central leaf. On each corner of the top of the pyramid is a quatrefoil filled with enamel, surmounted by a large grain and a small grain. There is also a single grain in the middle of each side of the top of the pyramid.

BIBLIOGRAPHY: Alexander, pl. 2; *Taranto*, no. 92.

148

148

148 Gold double lion-head earring

320–300 BC
Height 3.3 cm, width (front to back) 2.6 cm;
    weight 8.9 g
New York 20.236; Rogers Fund, 1920

The lion-heads are formed in sheet-gold halves (left and right) and are carefully detailed with blue enamel eyes. The loop in the mouth of the larger head was probably linked in some way to the perforation through the mouth of the smaller head. The larger head has an elaborate filigree collar with bands of beaded and plain wire, a frieze of ivy leaves and spirals with a central trumpet-flower motif in typical South Italian style, and a band of ovolos. The smaller head has a simpler collar with a tongue design. The hoop is a tapering tube of sheet gold overlaid with coils of twelve fine wire ropes.

Representations on terracottas and bronze mirrors suggest that at least some of these double-headed earrings were worn by pushing the smaller head through the perforation in the earlobe from behind (Fig. 31). The larger head would thus be inverted below the ear. The apparent link between the lions' mouths on the present example may suggest that it was worn in a less ungainly way.

BIBLIOGRAPHY: Alexander, fig. 70.

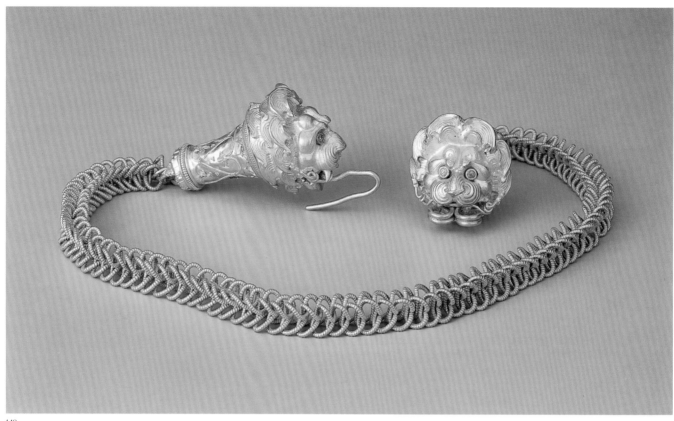

149

149 Gold chain necklace with lion-head terminals

Said to be from Capua
About 300 BC
Length 40.5 cm; weight 90.6 g
British Museum GR 1872.6-4.662

The magnificent lion-heads are made of sheet gold in two halves and the seams can just be traced over the foreheads and under the muzzles. The details are finely chased and blue enamel remains in the eye sockets. There is a double hook and eye fastening (one hook now missing) combined with what might be intended for a snake held in the teeth. The lions' manes have triple tiers of ruffs with chased details. After a band of beaded, plain and wire rope filigree, the heads join sheet-gold conical collars elaborately decorated with a double chain of small palmettes and small, three-lobed leaves in spiral-beaded filigree. The chain is a massive but simple open loop-in-loop type with beaded wire links with precise butt joints.

This type of necklet, with large lion-heads and rather stark loop-in-loop chains, is characteristically Tarentine. The present example is perhaps the finest to have survived. It was said to have been found with a pair of ear pendants.

BIBLIOGRAPHY: *BMCJ* 1968. For the chain cf. also necklace with lion-heads from Sedes, tomb 3: *AEphem* 1937, p. 879, figs 9–10, and Pfrommer, pl. 1, 2. Ear pendants: *BMCJ* 1769–70 (heads partly restored).

150

150   Gold disc brooch

330–300 BC
Diameter 3.4 cm; weight 4.2 g
British Museum GR 1872.6-4.742

The sheet-gold disc is shield-like in form
and the rim is bordered with spiral-
beaded, rope and plain wire filigree. In the
centre of the boss is a two-tier rosette set
on top of an eight-pointed star. Around
this is a frieze of palmettes attached to running spirals from which spring four corkscrew curls. Towards the rim is a row
of separately made and attached embossed
domes and a row of filigree ivy leaves.

On the back are two small gold straps,
one set at right angles to the rim, the other
following it. They were probably for
attachment to a textile, recalling the
attachment loops on the back of the
rosettes from the Great Bliznitza (no.
130). The twin to this disc, formerly in
the Stevens collection, is now in Naples.

BIBLIOGRAPHY: *BMCJ* 2062; Williams, pl. 39,
2 (attributed to the Santa Eufemia Master). Naples
disc: Siviero, no. 52, pl. 68b.

151   Gold fibula

330–300 BC
Length 4.8 cm; weight 11.5 g
British Museum GR 1824.4-34.35b; from the R.
   Payne Knight collection

This fibula or brooch takes the form of
an arched bow of biconical form with a
trapezoidal catch-plate and spherical terminal. It is made from heavy-gauge gold

sheet and, unusually for such thickness of
gold, is decorated with applied spiral-
beaded and rope filigree. The bow of the
fibula has a filigree palmette and wave pattern on each side of the central rib. The
catch-plate also bears a palmette and the
spherical terminal has acanthus leaves and
a running spiral with half-palmettes. The
end of the terminal is a seven-petalled
rosette.

The difficulty of soldering fine filigree
to relatively thick gold sheet has resulted
in a rather fused surface. A similar use of
filigree on a substantial thickness of gold
can be seen on the ring from Eretria (no.
3). This type of fibula recurs in bronze at
Lecce.

BIBLIOGRAPHY: *BMCJ* 1410. Lecce fibulae:
E.M. De Juliis, *Archeologia in Puglia* (Bari 1983),
Lecce, p. 31, fig. 38.

151

152

152 Gold ribbed bracelet with copper alloy core and terminals in the form of lion-heads

Said to be from Taranto
About 300 BC
Width 6.7 cm, height 7.5 cm; weight 47.5 g
New York 24.97.121; Fletcher Fund, 1924

This bracelet consists of a flat, fluted hoop of sheet gold to which is attached, at either end, a hollow sheet-gold lion-head terminal. Soldered seams can be seen under the muzzles but cannot be traced across the foreheads, perhaps suggesting that they were each formed from a single piece of sheet gold, rather than in two halves. The details are delicately chased and the eyes bear traces of enamel. To the neck of each lion-head is soldered a sheet-gold collar decorated with bands of beaded, plain and rope filigree and filigree palmettes (one full and two halves, inverted). The collars terminate in applied sheet-gold tongues.

The hoop, which has seven corrugations on the outer surface and is smooth on the inner, is formed of sheet gold over a copper alloy core. In section it is rec-tangular with rounded corners, and it is attached to the terminals by split pins with domed heads. The lion-heads are linked by gold wires with snake-heads, but these are soldered together and were never intended to be unfastened.

A number of such bracelets are known, several of which come from South Italy or have been associated with that region.

BIBLIOGRAPHY: Alexander, fig. 82. For similar bracelets see *Taranto*, nos 168–9; Hoffmann and Davidson, no. 63.

153

154

155

153 Gold ring engraved with a scene of a ewe being milked

From Tharros, 'tomb 12'
470–450 BC
Length of bezel 1.9 cm, height 1.9 cm; weight
    3.5 g
British Museum GR 1856.12-23.941

This pale gold ring has a pointed oval bezel with a scene of a ewe being milked. A boy sits at the back of a ewe, milking it, while a bearded man helps to hold the animal. There is a flower and a branch of a tree in the field. The border consists of a band decorated with diagonal hatching.

The main parts of the design are perhaps chased, but the details are added in shallow-groove engraving with deeper cuts for the sheep's fleece (Fig. 13). The ring is hammered from one piece of gold and at the back of the tapered hoop a faint, pale line indicates the position of the central solder seam (Fig. 27).

The pastoral nature of the scene is unusual in Greek art and may show Phoenician influence. At the other end of the Greek world, in the North Pontic kurgans of the Scythians, a number of such bucolic scenes have been found, most notably on the famous pectoral from the Tolstaya Mogila barrow.

BIBLIOGRAPHY: BMCR 44; Boardman GGFR, p. 215, pl. 660 (shape I, Penelope Group); R.D.

Barnett and C. Mendleson, *Tharros: A Catalogue of Material in the British Museum from Phoenician and Other Tombs at Tharros, Sardinia* (London 1987), p. 173, no. 12/18, pl. 97. Tolstaya Mogila pectoral: *Scythian Art*, pp. 118–21.

154 Gold ring with a frog between snake-heads

400–350 BC
Length of frog 1.7 cm, present height of hoop
    1.5 cm; weight 3.1 g
British Museum GR 1872.6-4.52

The hoop consists of three plain twisted wires with beaded wires laid along the channels. There is a corrugated sheet collar at either end, from which emerge two snake-heads. Between each pair of snake-heads is a rosette with spiral-beaded wire borders. The bezel of this unusual ring takes the form of a frog, made from a die-formed gold sheet with a plain back sheet. The frog's back legs grasp the pair of snake-heads behind it.

The ring is very probably the product of a Sicilian workshop. A virtual replica comes from a tomb at Megara Hyblaea, while a similar ring from Roccagloriosa has a Herakles knot instead of the frog. One might also compare a ring said to be

from Sicily on which a lion is set at right angles to the hoop: this piece is now in a Swiss private collection.

BIBLIOGRAPHY: BMCR 220; Richter EGGE, no. 472. Megara Hyblaea ring: L'oro dei Greci, pl. 117. Roccagloriosa: L'oro dei Greci, pl. 122, 5; Swiss private colection: Hoffmann and Davidson, no. 100.

155 Gold ring with Aphrodite and Eros in intaglio

Said to be from Syracuse
400–370 BC
Height of bezel 1.6 cm; height of hoop 2.0 cm;
    weight 7.7 g
British Museum GR 1872.6-4.72

The oval bezel of this elegant signet ring shows Aphrodite, wearing *chiton* and *himation*, a bracelet and a double droplet earring. She stretches one hand over the head of the naked Eros who kneels at her feet, adjusting her sandal. Above the Eros hovers a dove. The ground line is a groove with a tremolo line.

The design is engraved, perhaps with some chasing. It is of high quality and the figure of Aphrodite has a majestic calm. Stylistically, the engraving recalls that on a ring in Paris with a seated Penelope.

BIBLIOGRAPHY: BMCR 56; Boardman GGFR, pl. 716 (Iunx Group, shape VI). Paris Penelope: Boardman GGFR, pl. 687.

156

156 Gold ring with Nike driving a four-horse chariot

Said to be from Magna Graecia
400–350 BC
Diameter of bezel 2.5 cm, width of hoop 2.3 cm; weight 34.6 g
British Museum GR 1842.7-28.134; from the Thomas Burgon collection

This massive, man-sized gold signet ring has a large convex bezel of near-circular shape on which is a masterly depiction of the goddess Nike driving a four-horse chariot. Her reins are in her right hand, goad out in her left, as the chariot wheels round. There is a fine horizontal ground line.

The design is worked in a combination of chasing and shallow-groove engraving with some narrow v-shaped cuts. The hoop is rounded outside, bevelled inside, and hoop and bezel are probably hammered from a single piece of gold. There are a small number of platinum-group metal inclusions.

The motif of a Nike driving a chariot is common in many media, including coins, gems, vases and metalware.

BIBLIOGRAPHY: Furtwängler *AG*, pl. 9, 46; *BMCR* 42; Higgins *GRJ*, pl. 24D; Richter *EGGE*, no. 336; Boardman *GGFR*, col. pl. opp. p. 216, no. 2, and pl. 786 (shape XI); J. Cherry et al., *The Ring: From Antiquity to the Twentieth Century* (London 1981), no. 50; Ogden *JAW*, pl. 12 (upper left); *LIMC* VI, sv Nike, no. 179, pl. 577.

157 Gold ring engraved with the head of a woman

400–350 BC
Height of bezel 1.8 cm, height of hoop 2.0 cm; weight 9.1 g
British Museum GR 1884.4-9.1

The pointed oval bezel of this ring bears the beautiful head of a woman. She wears a head-scarf, a necklace with a single pendant (possibly an acorn) and a boat-shaped earring with a central vertical rib and two pendants. The faceted hoop is made in one piece with the bezel. The ring has a small number of platinum-group metal inclusions.

The earrings worn by the woman are of typical South Italian design. The head-scarf may be compared with representations on Campanian red-figured vases.

BIBLIOGRAPHY: *BMCR* 53; Richter *EGGE*, no. 320; Boardman *GGFR*, p. 222, pl. 714 (Iunx Group, shape VI). For the earrings cf. the pair from the via Umbria in Taranto, *Taranto*, no. 68; and a pair once on the Los Angeles market, Deppert-Lippitz, fig. 126, and *NFA Treasures from an Ancient Jewelbox* (Los Angeles 1991), no. 5.

158 Gold ring engraved with figures of Aphrodite and Eros

About 350 BC
Height of bezel 2.1 cm; height of hoop 2.0 cm; weight 16.0 g
British Museum GR 1865.7-12.59

This massive, elegant ring has a flat oval bezel and a hoop of rounded diamond-shaped cross-section. The design on the bezel, which is mainly, if not entirely engraved, shows a naked Aphrodite leaning against a small, fluted pillar on the top of which are her clothes. She wears a simple necklace, bracelets and anklets. A bird rests on the back of her outstretched hand. On the right a tiny Eros reaches up with a wreath. There is a plain ground line. The ring appears to have been hammered from a single piece of gold and there are occasional platinum-group metal inclusions.

The ease and grace of Aphrodite's pose compares well with that of a draped Aphrodite on a ring of the same shape in Taranto.

BIBLIOGRAPHY: *BMCR* 58; Richter *EGGE*, no. 251; Boardman *GGFR*, p. 224, pl. 736 (shape VIII, Salting Group). Taranto ring: *Taranto*, no. 207.

159 Glass ring with gold foil

350–300 BC
Height of bezel 2.4 cm, width of bezel 1.8 cm,
    width of hoop 2.7 cm
New York 17.194.2537; gift of J. Pierpont
    Morgan (formerly in the Gréau collection)

This ring is formed of pale, transparent green glass and contains within the bezel a thin gold foil representation of a dancing Nike. The technical procedure involved placing a gold foil cut-out in a depression in the bezel, covering it with a layer of similarly coloured glass, then grinding the whole ring and polishing it to shape.

The use of gold foils within glass became a favourite decorative motif in Hellenistic art and found uses from simple beads to superbly fashioned vessels. Four examples of this type of ring are known. Nos 159 and 160 and a third, now in the Louvre, lack provenances but are probably from South Italy. The fourth was found in the Kurjip barrow in the Kuban.

BIBLIOGRAPHY: W. Froehner, *Collection Julien Gréau . . . appartenant à M. John Pierpont Morgan* (Paris 1903), no. 1000, pl. 175, 10. Louvre: Hoffmann and Davidson, no. 106. Kurjip: *Scythian Art*, pl. 244.

160 Glass ring with a gold foil showing Aphrodite and an Eros

350–300 BC
Height of bezel *c.* 1.9 cm
British Museum GR 1872.6-4.291

The technique of this transparent glass ring matches that of no. 159. Here, however, the gold foil shows a seated Aphrodite, wearing a *chiton* and a *chlamys*, seeing to the hair of the small naked Eros that stands by her side. Much of the glass hoop of this ring is lost.

This type of ring must have been quite a novelty when it was first created, the gold seeming to float in the clear glass.

BIBLIOGRAPHY: Unpublished.

157

158

159

160

5 Cyprus, Egypt and the Eastern Mediterranean

Cyprus's location in the eastern Mediterranean has always meant that it had as much, if not more, in common with the Near East and Egypt as with Greece. Mycenaean contact was particularly strong in the fourteenth and thirteenth centuries BC, and around 1100 BC there were massive migrations to Cyprus following the final collapse of the Mycenaean world. The settlements of these Greek refugees eventually grew into the capital cities of the ancient kingdoms of Cyprus: Kourion, Paphos, Marion, Soloi, Lapithos and Salamis. Alongside these largely Greek-speaking cities there were thriving indigenous Cypriot communities, notably the city of Amathus, and, from early in the ninth century, the Phoenician colony of Kition.

Between the end of the eighth century and almost the middle of the seventh the Assyrians were in control of Cyprus. For the next hundred years the island enjoyed a glorious period of independence, during which her own culture flourished, but it was not to last. Egypt's rise in power began to affect Cyprus in the middle of the sixth century and, finally, in 526/5 BC the Cypriot kings submitted to the Great King of Persia.

With the exception of Amathus, all the kingdoms of Cyprus joined the East Greek cities in the Ionian Revolt of 499 BC. The Persians, however, were swift and eventually successful in their response. During the Classical period Cyprus remained under Achaemenid control, but in 411 BC Evagoras I seized the throne of Salamis and set about trying to extend his rule over the whole of the island. This he very nearly achieved and for some thirty years he maintained his independence until eventually he was defeated by a Persian expedition. Cypriot disaffection with Persian rule, however, was not to be quenched, and in 351 BC the cities joined in another revolt, this time along with Egypt and Phoenicia. Failure once again ensued, and it was not until Alexander the Great's defeat of the Persians at the battle of Issus in 333 BC that Persian domination was finally ended.

Bronze Age Cypriot jewellery is very abundant and quite distinctive. It reveals a mixture of Minoan, Mycenaean, Syrian and Egyptian traits, thereby reflecting the island's geographical and historical position as an interface between Greece and the Oriental world. Little material is preserved from the ninth and eighth centuries BC, but in the seventh century there seems to have been considerable contact between East Greek jewellers and those on Cyprus; indeed, Cypriot influence has been suggested for the Rhodian relief plaques, while one of the finest necklaces of the period, from the sanctuary of Aphrodite at Arsos, combines a Cypriot form with Egyptian motifs (a bee flanked by uraeus snakes with the crowns of Upper and Lower Egypt) and a generally East Greek style of granulation.

From the sixth, fifth and fourth centuries come various jewellery forms that are clearly eastern in origin, since they are largely absent in Greece but are also found in Syria and elsewhere in the east. Examples include the stone-set rings (no. 167) and the penannular, almost crescent-shaped earrings (nos 162 and 175), which have very close parallels in Syria and must ultimately relate to a well-known Achaemenid Persian earring type.

The origin and relationships of some fifth-century Cypriot forms, such as the large griffin-head spirals (nos 171–4), are harder to determine. The form of the heads recalls those found in gold on some of the earlier Rhodian goldwork and on archaic copper alloy griffin-head cauldrons, but there is a chronological difficulty in linking the Cypriot spirals with these. Since parallels from further east are also difficult to find, one might do better to consider that animal-headed and human-headed spirals are also known from South Italy (no. 145).

It is noticeable that the more intricate and flamboyant Classical and Hellenistic gold ornaments, such as strap necklets with festoons of pendants, or disc and pendant earrings, are largely absent, although some clearly imitative pieces are found (no. 177). The local forms tend to a sober, but often rather massive style.

Cyprus has yielded an immense number of burials containing jewellery dating from Mycenaean to Roman times. A notorious early explorer was General Louis di Palma Cesnola, who admitted to digging up an incredible 15,000 tombs. A large proportion of the collection amassed by Cesnola was eventually purchased by the Metropolitan Museum of Art in New York and, as the selection included in this catalogue shows, provides a good representative idea of Cypriot goldwork of the Classical period. However, the provenances given to the objects by Cesnola probably owe more to his imagination than to reality and his description of huge treasure vaults probably has little basis in fact.

Cesnola excavated on numerous Cypriot sites, including Kourion (nos 168, 172–5, 177–80, 183–4, 187–90). A British Museum expedition to Cyprus excavated at Amathus (1894), Kourion (1895) and Enkomi (1896). These excavations were also rewarded with a large quantity of gold objects, now divided between the Nicosia Museum and the British Museum: a selection of the British material is presented here. A further British expedition, this time by the Cyprus Exploration Fund, also found fifth- and fourth-century gold in burials at Marion (nos 170, 181–2, 185).

The interest in Greek contacts with Egypt in the Bronze Age, first from Crete and later from the Greek mainland, has recently been fuelled by exciting finds at Tel el-D'aba of Minoan-style frescoes, as well as a few pieces of Minoan pottery and even a Minoan gold pendant. This contact, however, barely continued into the early centuries of the first millennium. The magnificent Egyptian jewellery of the ninth century BC lacks the granulation and filigree work that we find in contemporary Greek work, while Iron Age Greek gold jewellery shows no direct technical or stylistic influence from Egypt. The occasional Egyptian or Egyptian-style object found in early Iron Age contexts in Greece may be evidence for some direct contact, but trade via Phoenician or Cypriot middlemen is also likely.

The Egyptian pharaoh Psammetichus I (664–610 BC) renewed more extensive contact with Greece, employing Greek mercenaries and encouraging Greek trade. From this period we begin to have more documentary evidence for Greeks in Egypt, including Greek names scratched on the legs of the colossal rock-cut statues on the façade of the temple at Abu Simbel in the far south of the country. The evidence would suggest that East Greeks were particularly involved in the trade with Egypt. The city of Naukratis, on the Canopic branch of the Nile, was established as a trading centre for the Greeks in about 630 BC and included temples to Greek deities, especially Aphrodite, Hera, Apollo and Zeus. This rich trading settlement (*emporion*) counted among its inhabitants not only merchants but also poets, artists, statesmen and historians, as well as rich *hetairai*, such as Rhodopis and Archedike. These ladies of easy virtue were surely decked out in the latest Greek fashions. Sadly, little of such finery has been found.

The Persians captured Egypt in 525 BC and so it is not surprising that some Achaemenid Persian gold and silverwork survives from Egypt. Traditional Egyptian goldwork, however, is surprisingly rare at this period, apart from the well-known priestly signet rings and some flimsy funerary ornaments.

Greek trade began to flourish again after about 500 BC, but even so minimal Greek jewellery of the fifth and early fourth century BC has been found in Egypt. The few examples include gold signet rings and animal-headed bracelets related to those from Cyprus. There is little evidence for any intermingling of Greek and Egyptian forms.

Following the arrival of Alexander the Great in Egypt in 332 BC, the jewellery industry of Egypt became almost totally Hellenised. In view of the scarcity of any local secular goldsmithing tradition in the preceding period, we can probably assume that in the Ptolemaic period most of the goldsmiths manufacturing for the general market were Greek and that the wearers of gold jewellery were also mainly Greek.

The most important group of Ptolemaic jewellery is from Tuch el-Karamus in the Egyptian Delta and comprises a number of hoards found between 1905 and 1906. Unfortunately, the exact origin and composition of these finds will probably never be known with certainty, but the main group of jewellery was discovered in Room 1 of the 'treasury' of the ruined temple in 1905. This included a number of bracelets, in particular a magnificent Herakles-knot bracelet. The uniformity of the weight standards of several of these objects suggests that they were the output of a single area. With the exception of the Herakles-knot bracelet, with its elaborate filigree, they share a massive, rather stark style that relates more to Cypriot ornament than contemporary work from South Italy or Greece.

Common jewellery forms in Egypt in the late fourth to early third century include lion- and griffin-head earrings and some fine gold rings (no. 195). The intricacy of the Tuch el-Karamus Herakles-knot bracelet is matched by a handful of other late fourth- to early third-century ornaments from Egypt, including the Herakles-knot centrepiece from a diadem or necklet, now in Cleveland, and a few disc ear studs. We might thus suspect the presence of Greek goldsmiths in Egypt from very soon after Alexander's invasion. However, the more exuberant early Hellenistic styles with abundant filigree, such as disc and pendant earrings and elaborate straps, are largely absent from their repertoire – a feature shared with Cyprus, Syria and the rest of the former Persian empire in general.

FIGURE 59 Painted wooden panel from Saqqara, Egypt, showing a woman, probably a goddess, seated on a throne. She wears a hairnet, earrings, a necklace and an armband. The necklace and armband are yellow and so probably of gold; the earring is brown and may be non-metallic. The style is Greek of the later fifth century BC (British Museum GR 1975.7–28.1).

As in other parts of the eastern Mediterranean, the later Hellenistic period in Egypt was to see an enthusiastic appreciation for the flimsier, stone-set goldwork epitomising the later Hellenistic 'Baroque'. The remarkable hair ornament (no. 197) is a superb example of this and is a fitting object to round off this catalogue.

Along the eastern seaboard of the Mediterranean, as in Egypt, it is not easy to find a representative selection of gold jewellery which can be defined as Greek prior to Alexander's conquests of the former Persian empire. The trading town of Al Mina on the Syrian coast, established by Greeks, probably Euboeans, in the mid-eighth century, rewarded its excavators with a pale gold necklet of around 400 BC and of unusual style, but, in general, there is little pre-Hellenistic Greek, or Greek-influenced, jewellery in evidence. Perhaps the main exceptions are gold signet rings of Classical Greek form which have turned up as far afield as Pakistan or Beirut (no. 192).

From the mid- to the late fourth century there is the important Pasargadae hoard, found in a pavilion in the so-called Royal Garden at Pasargadae, an ancient city near Persepolis, to the east of the Persian Gulf. This hoard of over 1,100 separate objects included numerous necklaces and necklet components, three pairs of elaborate penannular earrings of a fifth- to fourth-century type known in Persia, Anatolia and up into the Caucasus, and a pair of ibex-headed bracelets. Animal-head bracelets date back in the Near East to the eighth century BC, if not earlier, and it is probable that the concept was introduced to Classical lands from here. The oriental gold examples, however, like the related torques, tend to be solid, or at least lacking numerous separate components and filigree. The Pasargadae bracelets had hoops of twisted wires and hollow sheet-gold heads, with filigree-decorated collars and separately made and inserted horns and ears. In their assembly, then, they are far more Greek than Achaemenid. The finer filigree work, however, is in plain wire, not beaded or spiral-beaded (although they have coarser beaded wire borders), and the hoops have the slightly incurved form which is characteristically Achaemenid Persian. That they were imported from further west cannot be excluded, and an origin in Cyprus, the Syria/Levantine coast or Asia Minor is possible. On the other hand, some Greek or Greek-trained goldsmiths must have been working in Persia: certainly, Ionian craftsmen in other media worked for the Achaemenids and the Egyptian goldsmiths employed by Darius at Sardis are evidence of the Persians' admiration for foreign skills.

The rarity of beaded wires in purely Achaemenid goldwork is worth noting. This technique was well known around most of the Mediterranean from the seventh century BC onwards, but is almost entirely absent in Achaemenid goldwork and pre-Ptolemaic Egyptian jewellery.

It would be an over-simplification to say that we could distinguish Eastern from Greek on the basis of beaded wire, but it may prove a guide. Western Phoenician goldwork such as that from Carthage and Sardinia employs beaded wire, as does Iberian goldwork. North Pontic jewellery, and the fifth- and fourth-century goldwork from as far south as Vani, also employ beaded wire. When groups of objects with some plain wire filigree, some beaded, occur, as in a few earlier pieces from the North Pontic region and Cyprus, it may indicate a subtle but tangible trace of the meeting of two traditions.

Alexander occupied Syria in 333 BC and Mesopotamia two years later. After his death in 323 BC, his empire was divided among his military commanders. However, even in the century or so after Alexander's conquest of the former Persian empire, Greek jewellery forms are not common in this area: an example is the Herakles knot (no. 191), said to be from Syria, which is close, in its lack of set stones, repetitive spiral filigree and longitudinally attached diminutive figure, to the two examples from Egypt mentioned above. [J.O.]

BIBLIOGRAPHY: Cyprus: *SCE* IV, 2, pp. 161–9; Pierides, *passim*; *Amathonte* III, *passim*; Higgins *GRJ²*, pp. 85–7; Deppert-Lippitz, *passim*; Pfrommer, FK 189–200. Arsos necklace: Deppert-Lippitz, fig. 61 and colour pl. 7. L.P. di Cesnola, *Cyprus: Its Ancient Cities, Tombs, and Temples* (London 1877); *Excavations in Cyprus*; E. Goring, *A Mischievous Pastime* (Edinburgh 1988). Egypt: C. R. Clark, Ptolemaic jewelry, *BMetrMus* 30 (1935) pp. 161–4; Pfrommer, FK 1–6; Ogden, forthcoming. Syria and the East: C.L. Woolley, 'Excavations at Al Mina, Sueidia I–II', *JHS* 58 (1938), pp. 1–30 and 133–70; K.R. Maxwell Hyslop, *Western Asiatic Jewellery* (London 1971); J. el-Chehadeh, *Untersuchungen zum antiken Schmuck in Syrien* (diss. University of Berlin, Berlin 1972); D. Stronach, *Pasargadae* (Oxford 1978).

Kourion, Tomb 73 *(nos 161–4)*

This very large tomb was excavated on 5 March 1895. It consisted of three chambers, apparently of different dates, ranging from the fifth to the fourth century BC, and was full of earth, although seemingly intact. Only a selection of the jewellery discovered is presented here, but all these pieces came from the same part of the tomb – the earlier part, it would seem. The finds from the other part of the tomb included a fine bronze candelabrum, a silver cup and a silver tetradrachm of Alexander the Great.

BIBLIOGRAPHY: H.B. Walters, 'Notes at Curium' (manuscript in the Greek and Roman Department, British Museum); letter of H.B. Walters, 23 March 1895, also lists contents (British Museum, Central Archive P no. 1, 1341); *Excavations in Cyprus*, 82–3; Pfrommer, FK 190. The candelabrum is *BMCB* 193, see V.A. Tatton-Brown in *Cyprus Colloquium*, p. 133. The coin is now unidentifiable in the Department of Coins and Medals, British Museum.

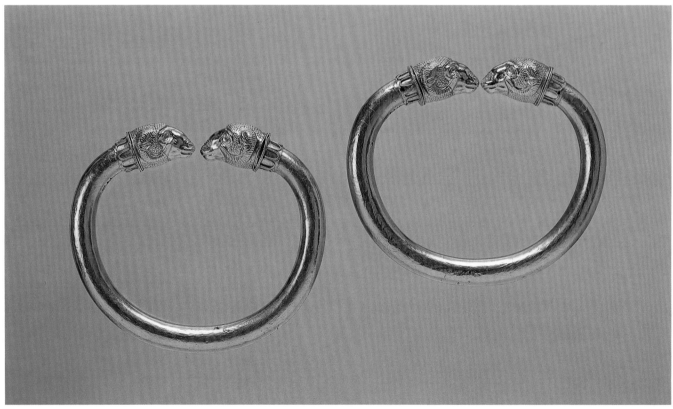

161

161   Pair of gold bracelets with
       copper alloy core and
       ram-head terminals

From Kourion, tomb 73
450–400 BC
Width 8.4 cm, height 7.2 cm; weight 108.1 and
    108.1 g
British Museum GR 1896.2-1.141–2

The heads were made in two halves, probably die-formed, and the faint soldered seams can be seen running along the foreheads and under the muzzles. There is some chased detailing, and a ring-punch was used to delineate the fleece. The eyes are recessed and may have been enamelled, but now only retain traces of copper corrosion products.

The junctions between heads and collars are decorated with plain and beaded wires and the collars themselves have simple sheet-gold tongues bordered with plain wires. The heads and collars were attached to the hoops with copper alloy rivets, perhaps originally disguised under gold caps. The hoops themselves are of thin sheet gold burnished over a copper alloy core. Faint soldered seams can be traced along their inner contours.

A number of bracelets with ram-head terminals are known from Cyprus: another pair from Kourion and now in Nicosia, a pair with gilded silver hoops from Marion, now in London, and an example in Berlin without a precise find-spot. They also occur in northern Greece (nos 25 and 32) and in the North Pontic region, in both silver and gold.

BIBLIOGRAPHY: *Excavations in Cyprus*, pl. 13, 11–12, and p. 82; *BMCJ* 1985–6; Higgins *GRJ*[2], pl. 30a; Deppert-Lippitz, fig. 110; Pfrommer, TA 143; D. Hunt (ed.), *Footprints in Cyprus* (2nd edn, London 1990), p. 89. Nicosia: Pierides, pl. 24, 1–2. London: *BMCJ* 1987–8. Berlin: Greifenhagen II, pl. 75, 2. North Pontic: (Berlin) Greifenhagen I, pl. 19, 4–5; (Oxford, from Nymphaion) Vickers, pl. 18e.

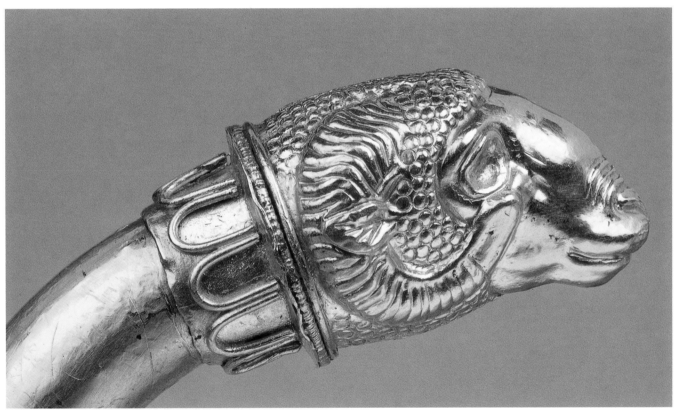

161

162

162 Pair of gold crescent-shaped
      earrings with filigree
      decoration

From Kourion, tomb 73
450–400 BC
Height 2.5 cm, width 2.2 cm; weight 2.6 and
    3.1 g
British Museum GR 1896.2-1.138–9

These earrings are composed of thick
sheet gold. The front faces are decorated
in plain wire filigree with four circumscribed palmettes resting on tight spirals
with a granule at the centre, and with
pointed buds between the palmettes (Fig.
19). The pitted gold surface suggests that
the design may have been enamelled,
although the thickness of the gold sheet
could also explain the fused surface. The
borders are of plain and beaded wires and
there is a fringe of gold grains along the
outer edge. The terminals have collars of
beaded and plain wire, and onto the back
of one terminal from each earring is soldered the ear-hook (one now a modern
replacement).

These earrings are matched by another
pair from Kourion (no. 175), which is
probably from the same workshop,
although the construction is slightly different.

BIBLIOGRAPHY: *Excavations in Cyprus*, pl. 13, 9,
and p. 82; *BMCJ* 2451–2; *SCE* IV, 2, p. 163,
fig. 34, 7.

163

163 Six gilded bronze spirals

From Kourion, tomb 73
450–400 BC
Width and height 1.6 cm; weight 9.5–9.7 g
British Museum GR 1896.2-1.143–8

These spirals are made of thin sheet gold burnished over a copper alloy core. The terminals are very simply decorated with triangles of chased lines and three lateral grooves. More examples of this type are preserved in New York.

The manner in which these spirals were worn is unclear. They may have decorated the hair or even the ears, being passed through holes in the ligament of the outer curve of the ear, a Cypriot fashion since the Bronze Age.

BIBLIOGRAPHY: *Excavations in Cyprus*, pl. 13, 1–6, and p. 82; *BMCJ* 1635–40. New York: Cesnola *Atlas* III, pl. 17, 10. On ear spirals see J.M. Hemelrijk, *BABesch* 38 (1963), pp. 28–51.

164

164 Gold ring decorated with filigree palmettes

From Kourion, tomb 73
420–400 BC
Length of bezel 1.1 cm, width of hoop 1.7 cm; weight 1.4 g
British Museum GR 1896.2-1.140

The pointed bezel is made from thin sheet gold and is decorated with two addorsed palmettes in plain wire filigree, set on spirals with a granule at the centre (Fig. 22). The border is of beaded wire. The tapered hoop is of plain wire and is soldered to each end of the bezel.

The simple decoration closely recalls the crescent-shaped earrings (nos 162 and 175): they are all probably products of the same workshop. The ring may also be compared with some simple rings of the later fifth century from Eretria (no. 3).

BIBLIOGRAPHY: *Excavations in Cyprus*, pl. 13, 14, and p. 82; *BMCR* 906; Higgins *GRJ*², p. 132.

Amathus, Tomb 256 *(nos 165–7)*

This undisturbed chamber-tomb was square in plan and contained three sarcophagi lined up side by side near the south wall. In the chamber were laid out a bronze strigil, two bronze spatulae, a bronze mirror and cover, three stone statuettes (a youth reclining and two standing females), a *lekythos* and a bottle of alabster, and eleven pieces of pottery, some Cypriot, others Athenian imports.

Sarcophagus II was plain, but it contained about eight skeletons. In addition to the jewellery shown here, there were, at the west end (the door end of the chamber) of the sarcophagus, two pairs of small silver spirals and 'seven spiral gold chain links (two were sticking to one of the spirals)'.

BIBLIOGRAPHY: *Excavations in Cyprus*, p. 125, with plan; Higgins *GRJ*, p. 218 (5th century BC); *Amathonte* III, pp. 68–71. Sarcophagus II: *BMCS* C 429. The vases in the chamber included British Museum GR 1894.11-1.687, a red-figured *askos*.

165

165 Two spiral earrings with copper alloy cores and terminals in the form of a crested griffin's head

From Amathus, tomb 256, sarcophagus II
425–400 BC
Height 3.0 cm, width 2.8 cm; weight 13.5 and
15.9 g
British Museum GR 1894.11-1.450–1

These gold-plated spiral earrings are not quite a pair but were probably worn as such. They have copper alloy cores.

Each griffin-head is made of sheet gold in left and right halves, with ears added separately and a hole pierced through between beak and tongue (Fig. 8). On one the chest of the griffin is decorated with a ruff of vertical lines, below which are six spirals of plain wire. In the centre is a small rosette with beaded wire petals enamelled alternately blue and green. The collar below the spirals is bordered above and below with a beaded wire. The frieze between is decorated with two rows of scales, the upper green, the lower blue, and a green band below. The other terminal has a cap decorated alternately with blue and green leaves, and a similar collar below. The griffin's head of the second earring has droplets filled with enamel instead of vertical lines on the ruff, a smaller rosette and two rows of ovolos (filled with enamel). The cap on the other terminal has a corrugated collar with smaller leaves on top (alternately green).

Another pair of similar earrings, a true pair, was also found with these pieces, but they are very damaged. They do, however, preserve the enamel in the eyes: a black pupil in a white eye. There are many parallels for the type (e.g no. 173).

BIBLIOGRAPHY: *Excavations in Cyprus*, pl. xiv, 2–3, and pp. 100–101 and 125; *BMCJ* 1646–7; Higgins *GRJ²*, pl. 25G (*BMCJ* 1646); *Amathonte* III, p. 70, fig. 98. Other British Museum pair: *BMCJ* 1644–5; *Excavations in Cyprus*, pl. xiv, 1 and 4, and pp. 100–101. Other parallels: *AA* 1904, p. 42 (13).

166

166 Necklace of double gold and glass tubes with a central acorn pendant

From Amathus, tomb 256, sarcophagus II
425–400 BC
Length as strung 21.0 cm, length of each unit
c. 0.8 cm
British Museum GR 1894.11-1.454–6

Each of the sixteen gold beads is formed from corrugated sheet gold rolled back on itself to form two tubes. The beads have sheet-gold end-plates and are supported by an internal filling of some sort of granular clay or plaster. In the centre of each is a rosette with narrow beaded wire borders, probably originally enamelled (three are now missing). The ten glass beads were cast, with some final hand-grinding. Four are of green glass, three of blue and three of reddish-brown: all have a central boss.

The central pendant consists of a finely shaped cornelian acorn with a gold cap decorated with triangles of granulation and ending in a dog-tooth setting. The construction, single suspension loop and

state of wear count against this pendant having originally been part of the necklace. It is almost certainly older and might well have been added in antiquity from an earlier ornament.

A very similar necklace, also from Amathus but without the central pendant, is in the Cyprus Museum. The example from Kourion (no. 178) is all of gold, as is a similar necklace from Nymphaion, now in Oxford.

BIBLIOGRAPHY: *Excavations in Cyprus*, pl. xiv, 16, and p. 101; *BMCJ* 1957; Ruxer, pl. 35, 1; *Amathonte* III, p. 70, fig. 98. Cyprus Museum J 103: Pierides, pl. 16, 2, p. 28; Nymphaion (Oxford 1885.502): Vickers, pl. 10a.

167 Gold ring set with a plain sard

From Amathus, tomb 256, sarcophagus II
425–400 BC
Length 1.1 cm, width of hoop 2.8 cm
British Museum GR 1894.11-1.457

The oval box-like bezel has a band of embossed dots and a plain, separately

167

formed, sheet-gold back. The top edge of the bezel is burnished over to grip the dark red sard. The hoop is made from a beaded wire soldered between two plain wires: the ends of the latter are bent round into decorative spirals at the shoulders.

BIBLIOGRAPHY: *Excavations in Cyprus*, pl. 14, 29, and pp. 102 and 125; *BMCR* 703; *Amathonte* III, p. 70, fig. 99.

168 Pediment-shaped gold diadem with palmettes in low relief

From Kourion (said to be from a 'tomb')
400–300 BC
Length 20.7 cm, height in centre 3.6 cm, general
  height c. 2.2 cm
New York 74.51.3535; the Cesnola Collection,
  purchased by subscription, 1874–6

Almost certainly a funerary ornament, the diadem consists of a thin gold sheet with traces of attachment holes at each end. The decoration consists of four palmettes resting on a pair of spirals and flanking a central double palmette on spirals addorsed vertically. The design was pro- duced by pressing the gold sheet into a copper alloy or stone die into which the palmette and scroll design had been carved. The same die was used for each of the palmettes on the diadem, but its position for the flanking palmettes was such that their bases could be excluded. As was usual, the gold sheet was trimmed after the designs had been impressed.

Many such diadems are preserved from Cyprus: they probably date from the fifth century BC into the Roman period.

BIBLIOGRAPHY: Cesnola *Atlas* III, pl. 12, 4; Myres, p. 397, no. 3535. Some other examples include *BMCJ* 1615 and 1617–25; Pierides, pl. 17.

168

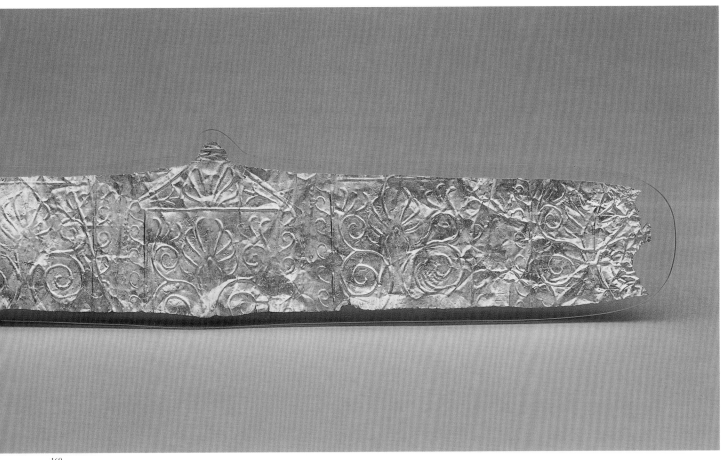

169

169 Sheet-gold diadem decorated with palmettes

Said to be from Cyprus
400–300 BC
Length 15.2 cm
British Museum GR 1881.7-25.5; bequeathed by
   W. Burges, 1881

The pattern consists of a repeated die-formed palmette and spiral motif. The palmette is set on two large spirals, from each of which springs a half-palmette. These palmette complexes, which are repeated five times, are separated by two vertical bands of waves. The central unit, however, is set lower so that there is room for all of the pediment on top, which is in turn filled with a palmette and a bud in either corner.

The diadem has been cut with a small pediment in the centre and rounded ends. There are remains of two holes pierced at either end. Many examples of this type of diadem are known (e.g. no. 168).

BIBLIOGRAPHY: *BMCJ* 1615. See further under no. 168.

Marion, Tomb 67 *(no. 170)*

This tomb was excavated in 1891 by J.A.R. Munro for the Cyprus Exploration Fund. On one of the two upright slabs that formed its door was painted in purple the Cypriot symbol *sa*. Outside the door were found the fragments of a terracotta reclining figure. The tomb contained a Cypriot long-necked amphora, a small bronze suspension ring, a bronze mirror case with a gorgoneion at the joint with the handle, and parts of a gold diadem.

As described in the publication, the diadem originally consisted of eight rosettes, eight stars, 'twenty-five little hemispherical gold buttons' and the myrtle flower centrepiece with two Erotes holding cockerels on top. The British Museum received the central element and two each of the eight stars and eight rosettes; other pieces are in Oxford.

BIBLIOGRAPHY: J.A.R. Munro, *JHS* 12 (1891), p. 323. Oxford (Ashmolean): 1891.446–7.

170 Fragments of a gold head-band with a myrtle flower, two rosettes and two stars

From Marion, tomb 67
350–300 BC
Height of central element 7.2 cm, diameter of
    rosettes 1.2 cm, width of stars 1.2 cm; weight
    of central element 2.4 g, weight of rosette
    0.3 g, weight of star 0.2 g
British Museum GR 1891.8-6.88–92

The central element consists of a myrtle flower with six leaves. Over a central tubular support are located two rings with radiating stamens terminating in granules and a third ending in small sheet discs bordered with beaded wire and containing traces of enamel. These elements are held in place by a sheet-gold bee mounted on a tube which is a tight push-fit into the lower tube.

Above the flower is a flanking pair of Erotes, each made from die-formed thin sheet gold over a thicker flat backing sheet. They are shown naked, seated and holding a cockerel in their laps: it is presumably the start of a cock fight. They are soldered together where their knees touch and are slotted and soldered into the flower-head beneath them.

Behind the myrtle flower are three attachment loops. From the lower one hangs a finely made doubled loop-in-loop chain, attached at its lower end to an eight-petalled rosette by means of an unsoldered ring. This rosette has petals bordered with fine beaded, not spiral-beaded, wire and each petal retains traces of enamel (once white?) at its outer extremity and red cinnabar near its centre.

The two other attachment loops on the back of the myrtle flower were presumably for attachment to the head-band. The other elements of the head-band all had the same loops on the back.

171

172

Among the other elements of the head-band were rosettes and stars. The eight-petalled rosettes are bordered with beaded wire and have a central small rosette with a granule in the middle. The stars are six-pointed (beaded wire contours) and also have a small six-petalled rosette in the centre.

This group forms a most unusual head ornament. The workmanship and method of construction suggest that it was of Cypriot origin, rather than an import from mainland Greece.

BIBLIOGRAPHY: J.A.R. Munro, *JHS* 12 (1891), p. 323 with pl. 15; *BMCJ* 2053–7. Part: V. Tatton-Brown, *Ancient Cyprus* (London 1987), p. 45, fig. 50.

171 Gold earring with a copper alloy core and lion-head terminals

450–400 BC
Height 2.0 cm; weight 15.5 g
British Museum GR 1917.6-1.1643; bequeathed by
    Sir A.W. Franks, 1897

The lion-heads are made in left and right halves. The mouths are open, the ears small and rounded, and the mane chased with strokes. The lower border is formed from a D-section band with lateral notches, a simple form of imitation beaded wire. The gold of the spirals is burnished over a copper alloy core.

A similar pair from Cyprus was recently on the antiquities market.

BIBLIOGRAPHY: *BMCJ* 1643. Market pair: Deppert-Lippitz, fig. 101.

172 Gold spiral earring with copper alloy core and a lion-head terminal (one of a pair)

From Kourion (said to be from a 'Vault')
450–400 BC
Height 1.9 cm, width 2.0 cm; weight 8.0 and
    9.1 g
New York 74.51.3368; the Cesnola Collection,
    purchased by subscription, 1874–6

The lion-head is made in two halves (left and right) from sheet gold. Details such as the mane are simply chased, and the mouth is left plain with neither tongue nor teeth. The ears are very simplified and appear almost human. The collar is decorated only with a beaded wire at the lower end. The terminal takes the form of a pointed sheet-gold cap decorated with beaded wire tongues and a single large grain at the apex; there is a corrugated sheet collar. The spiral (one and a half turns) is of sheet gold over a copper alloy core.

This is the simplest of the Cypriot series of lion-head earrings. There is a comparable pair in the Louvre, but the use of wire to outline the mane suggests a close connection with the more complex earrings (nos 173–4).

BIBLIOGRAPHY: Cesnola *Atlas* III, pl. 17, 14–15; Myres, p. 388, nos 3367–8; Alexander, fig. 42. Louvre pair (ex Cesnola): A. Caubet, A. Hermary and V. Karageorghis, *Art antique de Chypre au Musée du Louvre* (Paris 1992), no. 201.

173

173 Two pairs of gold spiral earrings with lion-griffin terminals

From Kourion (said to be from a 'Vault')
400–350 BC
3370 and 3373: height 3.71 and 3.49 cm, width 2.0 cm; weight 16.1 and 17.3 g
3371 and 3372: height 3.32 and 3.27 cm, width 2.0 cm; weight 14.9 and 14.8 g
New York 74.51.3370–3; the Cesnola Collection, purchased by subscription, 1874–6

Each lion-griffin head is made in left and right halves: the seams along the crests bear large and small grains. The horns, of thick beaded wire, provide points of attachment for a six-petalled rosette. The lower jaw has simple stippled chasing and the prominent mane around the neck is decorated with filigree flames in spiral-beaded wire. The open mouths have separately made and inserted tongues; the eyes and rosettes retain traces of enamel. Large two-tier rosettes at the base of the necks conceal the junctions between the griffin terminals and the spirals. The spirals are constructed from sheet gold over a copper alloy rod. After one and a half coils, the spirals terminate in sheet-gold caps, each with a corrugated collar. The caps are decorated with tongues in spiral-beaded wire and topped by large and small grains within a plain wire circle.

These two pairs of gold spiral earrings are very similar and are almost certainly by the same hand. A series of such earrings includes two pairs in London (no. 165) and a pair divided between Berlin and the Louvre.

BIBLIOGRAPHY: Cesnola *Atlas* III, pl. 17, 12–13; Myres, p. 388, nos 3370–3; Alexander, fig. 38 (one). Parallels: *BMCJ* 1644–5 and 1646–7; (Berlin) Greifenhagen II, pl. 38, 4–5; (Louvre AM 564 bis) A. Caubet, A. Hermary and V. Karageorghis, *Art antique de Chypre au Musée du Louvre* (Paris 1992), no. 197.

174

174 Pair of gold spiral earrings with double lion-griffin head terminals

From Kourion (said to be from a 'Vault')
400–350 BC
Height 3.5 cm, width 1.7 cm, box 1.7 by 0.7 cm; weight 14.1 and 14.6 g
New York 74.51.3374–5; the Cesnola Collection, purchased by subscription, 1874–6

Each griffin-head is made in left and right halves from thin sheet gold. The foreheads are each embellished with a large grain topped by a small one: the thick seam on the crest is covered with a row of large and small grains. The long sheet-gold ears, beaded wire horns, teeth, and the grooved tongues were all separately made and soldered in place. The eyes were probably enamelled. There are rows of short chased lines on the necks. The front of each wing is of thin sheet gold formed in a die and soldered onto a flat sheet-gold backing. At the back, the wings are supported by a horizontal tubular strut. The ridged collars around the necks are decorated with beaded wire waves. The tubular 'necks' of the griffins have circular end-plates decorated with circles of fine beaded wire, probably originally filled with enamel. The forelegs of the griffins were separately made and soldered into place.

The lion-griffin heads rise from a box-like construction of sheet gold and are attached to the tubular spiral by a corru-gated tube. Between the heads is attached a sheet palmette; in the centre of one is a circle and in the other a rosette. There is also a rosette on the front corners of one box. Below each box is a large multi-level rosette. The form of these rosettes differs slightly: one has additional ivy leaves.

Although there are minor differences, these, the most elaborate of the Cypriot lion, griffin and lion-griffin spiral earrings, were clearly made in the same workshop and were probably worn as a pair.

BIBLIOGRAPHY: Cesnola *Atlas* III, pl. 17, 16–17; Myres, p. 389, nos 3374–5; Alexander, fig. 39; Becatti, no. 379; *EAA* V, fig. 881.

175

175 Pair of gold crescent-shaped earrings

From Kourion (said to be from a 'Vault')
450–400 BC
Width 2.2 cm, height 2.9–3.0 cm; weight 4.6 and
    4.3 g
New York 74.51.3601–2; the Cesnola
    Collection, purchased by subscription, 1874–6

Each earring is of box-like construction with crescent-shaped front and back. The outer side-plate extends to form the hook of each earring. On both the front and the back of each earring, within a border of beaded wire, is a pattern of spectacle spirals in plain wire, with individual grains within and between spirals. The outer edge of each earring is decorated with a row of large grains surmounted by smaller ones.

Crescent-shaped earrings have a long history in the Near East, stretching back to the early Bronze Age. Close parallels of the later sixth century in silver come from North Syria. The type is also well known on Cyprus itself. The pair in the British Museum (no. 162) is particularly close, although the construction differs, and was most probably produced in the same workshop.

BIBLIOGRAPHY: Cesnola *Atlas* III, pl. 20, 21–2; Myres, p. 397, nos 3601–2; Alexander, fig. 48; Becatti, pl. 75, no. 296. For North Syrian parallels see K.R. Maxwell-Hyslop, *Western Asiatic Jewellery* (London 1971), pl. 256 with pp. 268–9.

176 Pair of gold earrings with rosette, bird, and pyramid

Said to be from Cyprus
330–300 BC
Height 5.1 cm, diameter of rosette 1.6 cm; weight
 12.0 and 11.8 g
British Museum GR 1906.4-11.2

The rosette is in five tiers with a central granule. The petals are all bordered with spiral-beaded wire and those in the upper three layers are concave, perhaps to hold enamel. The tiers of the rosette are separated by small rings of wire. The arched ear-hook is soldered to the back of the rosette and then extends down to form a loop, to which the pendant is attached.

Immediately below the rosette hangs a bird made of sheet gold in two halves, possibly die-formed. Each bird has a loop on its base which is attached by means of a split pin to the inverted pyramid (Fig. 28). On the front of the split pin is a rosette, the petals of which have spiral-beaded borders.

The upper edges of the pyramid pendants are decorated with small pyramids of four granules. Below these are a band of sheet gold and a beaded wire over a row of sheet-gold darts, followed by three rows of hollow sheet-gold spheres of decreasing size, decorated with vertical beaded wires. The lowest, cone-shaped section is made of sheet gold covered by a coil of beaded wire and terminating in two granules separated by a wire ring.

176

This type of earring, combining disc or rosette and inverted pyramid, appears to be otherwise unparalleled in Cyprus. A very similar pair, but without the birds, was bought in Smyrna. Indeed, the possibility must be considered that these earrings were in fact imported to Cyprus, perhaps from an East Greek workshop.

BIBLIOGRAPHY: *BMCJ* 1666–7. Smyrna pair: *BMCJ* 1668–9, bought by Franks from Lawson in 1893.

177

177 Pair of gold disc earrings with female head and cone pendants

From Kourion (said to be from a 'Vault')
350–300 BC
Height 10.5 cm, diameter of disc 1.8 cm, height of cone 2.0 cm; weight 6.4 g and 5.8 g
New York 74.51.3605–6; the Cesnola Collection, purchased by subscription, 1874–6

These finely made earrings consist of a decorated disc below which hangs a pendant in the form of an inverted cone. Each disc has a border of a beaded wire on a plain wire, within which are concentric rings of beaded, plain and twisted wires, and a frieze of spirals in doubled spiral-beaded wires with omega infills and a central rosette. This rosette is in two tiers, set on a tube, with a large central grain.

Four loops on the back of each disc support four short and two longer doubled loop-in-loop chains. The outer pairs of long chains (one missing on one earring) terminate in plain gold seeds surmounted by rosettes, and the two outer, shorter chains terminate in flat-backed plain seeds. The inner pair of chains on each earring is attached to a female head of sheet gold, below which is suspended the cone. The domed top of the cone is decorated with ivy leaves and tongues of spiral-beaded wire. The junction between dome and cone is covered with a beaded wire. Below is a band of running spirals in spiral-beaded wire and a series of palmettes with alternating in-turned and out-turned leaves, again in spiral-beaded wire. The point of the cone has a tongue surround and a collar of wire, and terminates in a large grain surmounted by a smaller one.

These earrings are probably a local combination of two types of disc and pendant earring – the disc and pyramid, and

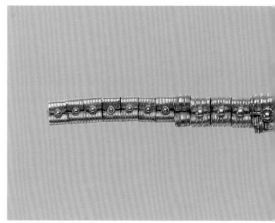

178

the disc and cone – types which are to be found in East Greece and South Italy. A Cypriot workshop also produced a pair of earrings, now in Berlin, which is a close imitation of the Kyme earrings (nos 49–50).

BIBLIOGRAPHY: Cesnola *Atlas* III, pl. 20, 16–17; Hadaczek, fig. 55; Myres, p. 397, nos 3605–6; Alexander, fig. 59; Becatti, no. 390; *EAA* V, fig. 883. Berlin earrings: Greifenhagen II, pl. 40, 2.

178 Gold necklace with corrugated double tubes

From Kourion (said to be from a 'Vault')
450–400 BC
Length as strung *c.* 14.5 cm; weight as strung 13.65 g
New York 74.51.3392; the Cesnola Collection, purchased by subscription, 1874–6

Five types of corrugated double tubes are strung together in this necklace. They differ in their size and applied decoration as follows:

(a) Seventeen large (length 0.6 cm), each with a six-petalled rosette of plain wire with a central grain;

(b) Three large (length 0.64 cm), each with a line of beaded wire along its centre, perpendicular to the corrugations, and a large grain within a beaded wire ring;

(c) Four large (width 0.78 cm), each with a central sheet-gold dome topped by a grain and surrounded by a beaded wire;

(d) Seven small (width 0.4 cm), each with a small central grain surrounded by a plain wire;

(e) Three small (width 0.4 cm), each with just a single central grain.

There is one additional small, damaged bead of corrugated sheet gold bent into an s-like double tube.

Each bead is made from a single piece of corrugated sheet gold, probably made by pressing the sheet onto a ribbed metal die. Damaged beads reveal that the corrugations are sharper on the interior than on the exterior of the beads. The three larger types all have end-plates, the smaller beads do not.

Two other examples of this type of necklace, from Amathus, contain glass beads (see no. 166). A third example, of gold only and from Nymphaion, is now in Oxford. It combines elements of two sizes, like this set. The original form and dimensions of the necklace or necklaces from which the Metropolitan beads come, however, must remain a matter for conjecture.

BIBLIOGRAPHY: Cesnola *Atlas* III, pl. 9, 4; Myres, p. 390, no. 3392. For another example from Amathus, see Pierides, pl. 16 (lower). Nymphaion, grave 3 (Oxford 1885.502): Vickers, pl. 10a.

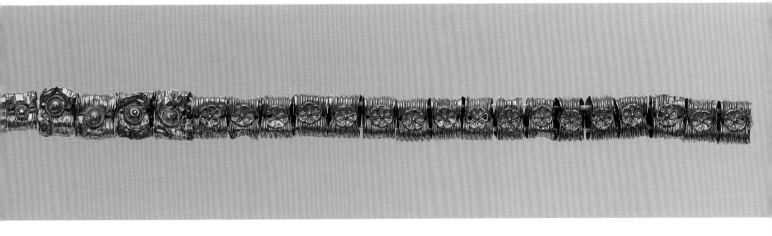

179

179 Gold necklace with seed-like pendants

From Kourion (said to be from a 'Vault')
450–400 BC
Length as strung 57.2 cm, height of seed-like
    pendants 2.7 cm; weight 64.6 g
New York 74.51.3397a (part); the Cesnola
    Collection, purchased by subscription, 1874–6

The necklace now consists of nineteen seed-like pendants strung with seven different varieties of gold beads. The pendants are a good example of the labour-saving methods sometimes used by craftsmen. On the finer necklaces of this type they may be made from a large number of sheet, wire and grain components soldered together, but here each pendant, from the suspension bead at its top to the 'grains' on its base, is made from just two pieces of thin sheet gold, a back and a front. These parts were made by pressing sheet gold into a die.

The gold beads now threaded with the pendants are of sheet gold, some filled with a pinkish clay, and bear various fluted or linear designs. All have applied wire collars.

The seed-like pendants may be compared with two pendants from Marion and a necklace recently on the market.

BIBLIOGRAPHY: Cesnola *Atlas* III, pl. 3, 8; Myres, p. 391, no. 3397 (part); Alexander, fig. 2 (detail). Marion: Pierides, pl. 22, 3. Market: Deppert-Lippitz, fig. 88 and colour pl. 8.

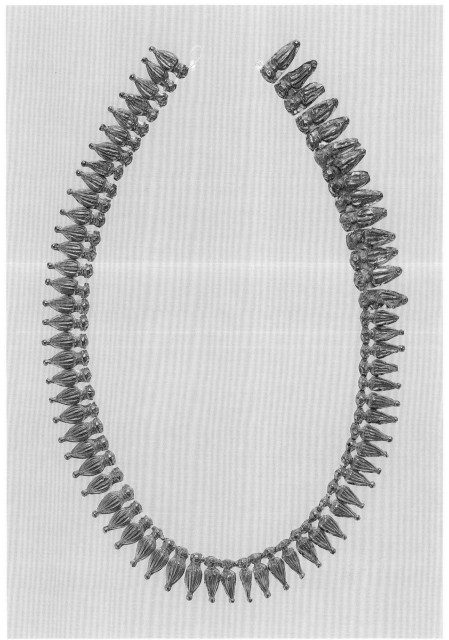

180

180 Gold necklace with pendants in the form of flattened, ribbed seeds

From Kourion (said to be from a 'Vault')
400–300 BC
Length as strung *c.* 50.0 cm, height of pendants
    1.3 cm; weight 6.1 g
New York 74.51.3394; the Cesnola Collection,
    purchased by subscription, 1874–6

Each of the sixty-nine seed-like pendants was made of thin sheet gold, like those of the necklet (no. 179), with die-formed fronts but flat backs and complete with suspension beads. The backs have small expansion holes to permit the escape of hot air during the soldering process.

Such a simple light-weight, mass-produced necklace may have been made especially for funerary or votive use. It is now extremely difficult to date.

BIBLIOGRAPHY: Cesnola *Atlas* III, pl. 10, 3; Myres, p. 391, no. 3394.

Marion, Tomb 10 *(nos 181–2)*

This tomb was excavated in 1890 by E.A. Gardner, H.A. Tubbs and J.A.R. Munro on behalf of the Cyprus Exploration Fund. It contained the remains of a man and a woman, arranged on either side of the door. The offerings included pottery (a lamp, an Athenian *lekythos* with a maenad, and a black-glaze *pyxis*) and a considerable amount of jewellery. There was a gilt-bronze ring with a dark green scarab, a pair of bronze silver-plated bracelets with gold rams' heads (cf. no. 161), three gold pendants (two of which are shown here), several gilt-bronze spirals ending in lions' heads (cf. no. 171), and a pair of bronze armlets with traces of silver plating ending in snakes' heads.

BIBLIOGRAPHY: J.A.R. Munro, *JHS* 11 (1890), pp. 1–82, esp. p. 54. The bracelets are *BMCJ* 1987–8; the third gold pendant is *BMCJ* 1237.

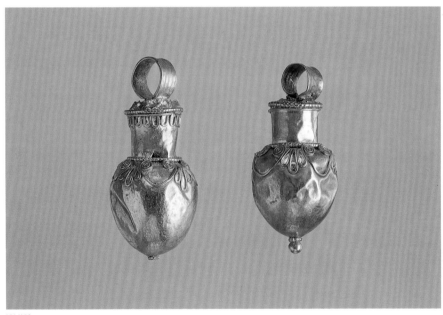

181/182

181 Amphora-shaped pendant

From Marion, tomb 10
450–400 BC
Height 2.1 cm; weight 0.9 g
British Museum GR 1890.7-31.11

The corrugated sheet-gold suspension loop, which shows signs of wear, is attached to the top of the cap of the pendant and held in place by burnishing over the top edge of the collar, not by solder-ing. The collar is a plain cylinder of gold sheet with beaded wire filigree at top and bottom. The top half of the bulbous, amphora-shaped body has a filigree frieze of linked palmettes with spirals in plain wire: there are traces of enamel in the central leaf of each palmette. The base of the pendant is decorated with a ring of beaded wire and a small granule.

This pendant was found with two others, one of which is almost a pair (no. 182), but the third, in the form of a pomegranate, was an heirloom. They may both have been strung on a necklace, or they could be pendants from earrings.

BIBLIOGRAPHY: J.A.R. Munro, *JHS* 11 (1890), p. 54, no. 8c; *BMCJ* 2031.

182 Amphora-shaped pendant

From Marion, tomb 10
450–400 BC
Height 2.3 cm; weight 0.9 g
British Museum GR 1890.7-31.12

This pendant is very similar to no. 181, but the collar has a row of ovolos at the top in plain wire filigree. The granule is now missing from the base of the pendant.

These two pendants are clearly from the same hand. The workmanship, particularly the plain wire filigree, is similar to the earrings (no. 162) and ring (no. 164) from Kourion tomb 73, and all are probably from the same Cypriot workshop.

This type of pendant is well represented on Cyprus, with further examples from Marion. It is also to be found all over the Greek world (e.g. no. 2).

BIBLIOGRAPHY: J.A.R. Munro, *JHS* 11 (1890), p. 54, no. 8c, pl. 5, 5; *BMCJ* 2032. Marion, tomb 57: *SCE* II, pl. 563, 14.

183 Gold pendant in the form of a gorgoneion

From Kourion (said to be from a 'Vault')
About 450 BC
Height 2.9 cm, width 1.8 cm; weight 2.8 g
New York 74.51.3397b (part; formerly strung
   with no. 179); the Cesnola Collection,
   purchased by subscription, 1874–6

The face is of sheet gold, die-formed or
stamped. The hair curls consist of small
coils of plain wire, each with a central
grain. The teeth are rendered in granulation and there is one remaining earring,

183

a circle of plain wire which probably originally held enamel. The recesses of the
eyes are left rough, probably to aid the
adhesion of enamel. The pendant is
backed· with a flat sheet of gold and
is attached, by means of a vertical beaded
tube, to a suspension bead of sheet gold.
The repoussé rather than applied granulation on the suspension bead relates this
pendant to the Metropolitan's sphinx pendant (no. 184).

A very similar pendant, from Marion,
is now in Berlin.

BIBLIOGRAPHY: Cesnola *Atlas* III, pl. 3, 8;
Myres, p. 391, no. 3397 (part); Alexander, fig. 2;
Ruxer, pl. 31, 2; *SCE* IV, 2, p. 165, fig. 35, 50;
Oliver, p. 272, fig. 6. Berlin pendant:
Greifenhagen II, pl. 5, 3 and fig. 16.

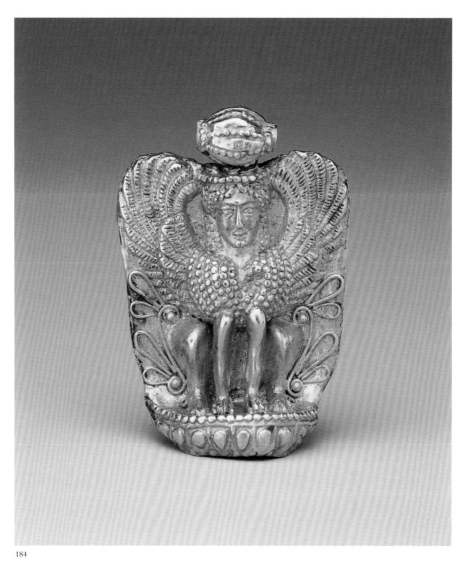

184

184 Gold sphinx pendant

From Kourion (said to be from a 'Vault')
About 450 BC
Height 2.95 cm, width 2.0 cm; weight 6.1 g
New York 74.51.3382; the Cesnola Collection,
   purchased by subscription, 1874–6

The front of this pendant is made from
sheet gold with repoussé details. Even the
line of beading is formed in the sheet gold
rather than applied granulation or beaded
wire. The forelegs were made separately
and soldered in place. The back of the pendant is closed by a flat sheet of gold. The
suspension bead was separately made in
two halves, again with repoussé beading.

The sphinx sits frontally with raised
wings and wears a diadem. She is flanked
by linked partial palmettes in applied plain

wire, with individual granules at the
centres of the spirals. On the front of the
curved base there is an egg and dart frieze
below the beaded line.

The face is archaic or, rather, archais-
ing. A number of similar examples from
Cyprus are known, including one
formerly on the market that had plain and
beaded wire decoration. The type is also
found in Magna Graecia, as part of a necklace (here of sheet gold with spiral-beaded
filigree).

BIBLIOGRAPHY: Cesnola *Atlas* III, pl. 5, 3;
Myres, p. 389, no. 3382; Alexander, fig. 30; *SCE*
IV, 2, p. 165, fig. 35, 50; Becatti, no. 311. Market
example: Deppert-Lippitz, fig. 87; cf. also
Pierides, pl. 22, 9–11. South Italian necklace
(Naples 12643, from Cumae): Siviero, no. 47, pls
59–63.

185

186

185 Gold sphinx pendant

From Marion, tomb K 28
400–350 BC
Height 1.6 cm; weight 0.3 g
British Museum GR 1890.7-31.9

This small pendant is in the form of a sphinx, seated frontally on a beaded border with ovolos below. The front is made from a single die-formed piece of sheet gold, beading and ovolos included, and has a flat sheet-gold backing. An attachment loop is soldered, rather poorly, to the top, and from it rise two links of a figure-of-eight chain.

A number of such relief pendants with a sphinx have survived from Cyprus (e.g. no. 184), although none is quite the same.

BIBLIOGRAPHY: J.A.R. Munro, *JHS* 11 (1890), pl. 5, 7, and p. 55; *AA* 1891, p. 132; *BMCJ* 2077. Cf. Pierides, pl. 22, 9–10.

186 Gold ram's head pendant

Said to be from Cyprus
450–400 BC
Length 1.8 cm; weight 10.4 g
British Museum GR 1895.10-25.1

This pendant was formed from massive sheet gold with hand-chased details, including the use of a ring punch for the fleece. The joint with the end-plate is decorated with a beaded wire between two plain wires. The suspension hoop similarly consists of a beaded wire between two plain wires. This type of filigree is reminiscent of the hoop of the ring from Amathus tomb 256 (no. 167).

The pendant shows signs of slight wear, particularly on one side where it might have rubbed against other necklace components.

BIBLIOGRAPHY: *BMCJ* 2023.

187

187 Gold lion-head pendant

From Kourion (said to be from a 'Vault')
450–400 BC
Diameter 1.3 cm, height 1.76 cm; weight 1.9 g
New York 74.51.3328; the Cesnola Collection,
    purchased by subscription, 1874–6

The lion-head is finely modelled in two
halves, left and right, with a flat gold sheet
closing off the neck aperture. This back-
plate has a triangular 'trap-door', to allow
the escape of hot air during soldering, and
the joint between back-plate and head is
concealed by an edging of beaded wire.
The workmanship is superb, and the
details of head and mane finely chased.
Enamel is preserved in one eye; the long
teeth and tongue were separately made
and soldered into place. The head is
attached to a corrugated suspension tube
by means of a small corrugated spacer.

Two other lion-head pendants were
found with this one at Kourion. A third
comes from Marion and a fourth from
Amathus. Lion-head pendants are also
found elsewhere, including Greece (no.
8), East Greece (no. 39) and the North
Pontic area. They may have been strung
singly, even simply on a cord, or in
greater numbers on more complex
necklaces.

BIBLIOGRAPHY: Cesnola *Atlas* III, pl. 4, 32;
Myres, p. 387, no. 3328. Other examples:
(Kourion) Cesnola *Atlas* III, pl. 4, 31 and 36;
(Marion) Pierides, pl. 22, 12; (Amathus) *BMCJ*
2046 (cf. also *BMCJ* 2047).

188 Gold calf's head pendant

From Kourion (said to be from a 'Vault')
450–400 BC
Height 1.8 cm, width 0.9 cm; weight 1.0 g
New York 74.51.3332; the Cesnola Collection,
    purchased by subscription, 1874–6

The small vestigial horns identify this as
a calf's rather than a bull's head. It is hollow and made of thin sheet gold in left
and right halves. The ears were added separately. Like the lion-head pendant (no.
187), this has a back-plate with beaded
wire edging and a triangular 'trap-door',

but the workmanship is cruder and the
overall effect flimsier. The remains of a
white plaster filling are visible inside the
head. The pendant hangs from a light-
weight, slightly corrugated tube with
plain spacer.

Calf-heads seem to be rather rare: lion-,
bull- and ram-head pendants are found
much more commonly throughout the
Greek world.

BIBLIOGRAPHY: Cesnola *Atlas* III, pl. 4, 33;
Myres, p. 387, no. 3332; *SCE* IV, 2, p. 165,
fig. 35, 43.

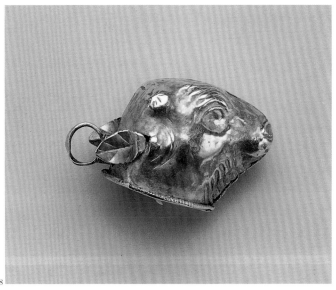

188

189

189 Pair of gold lion-head bracelets with copper alloy cores

From Kourion (said to be from the 'Treasure Vaults')

450–400 BC

Outer diameter 7.0 cm, length of heads 2.3 cm; weight 73.6 g and 76.2 g

New York 74.51.3560–1; the Cesnola Collection, purchased by subscription, 1874–6

The lion-heads are made of sheet gold in two halves (left and right), possibly modelled freehand with basic hand-worked details, such as the chased, low-relief lines of the mane, the short strokes on the nose, the stippled lower jaw and the tongue. The two upper and lower fangs in each mouth were separately made and soldered in place; the eyes were never inlaid. The heads are set into collars which have simple punched ovolo decoration, rather than applied filigree, and which narrow to simple corrugated sections slipped over the hoop. Each hoop consists of sheet gold burnished over a copper alloy core. This burnishing has obliterated all traces of a soldered seam line.

The style is rather crude and contrasts strongly with purely Greek workmanship. The bracelets were probably made on Cyprus, under Achaemenid and Greek influence. This is one of four similar pairs in the Metropolitan Museum. Other related bracelets from Cyprus include a pair in the British Museum from tomb 84 at Amathus.

BIBLIOGRAPHY: Cesnola *Atlas* III, pl. 1, 2; Myres, p. 393, nos 3560–1; *SCE* IV, 2, p. 167, fig. 36, 4; Pfrommer, p. 338, TA 80 (5th century BC; note that p. 96, fig. 16, no. 13 is not TA 80) and p. 102, n. 663. Amathus bracelets: *BMCJ* 1295–6.

190

190 Gold ring decorated with a female head

From Kourion, tomb 83
350–300 BC
Length of bezel 1.4 cm, height of hoop 1.8 cm;
    weight 5.4 g
British Museum GR 1896.2-1.189

The oval bezel is mainly chased, not engraved, and depicts a female head in profile. The woman wears a droplet earring, possibly a rosette and pyramid earring, and a necklace of spherical beads. Hoop and bezel are made from one piece of hammered gold, and a small crack at the back of the hoop may mark the original soldered seam. The ring has abundant small platinum-group metal inclusions.

The woman may have been intended to represent the goddess Aphrodite. The subject matches that of no. 157, but the treatment is very different.

BIBLIOGRAPHY: *Excavations in Cyprus*, pl. 13, 17 and p. 83; *BMCR* 67; Richter *EGGE*, no. 316.

191 Gold Herakles knot

Said to be from Syria
300–250 BC
Maximum length 3.6 cm, height of Eros 1.5 cm;
    weight 11.1 g
British Museum GR 1884.6-14.13

This Herakles knot is formed from hollow tubes bordered by beaded wire and decor-

ated with spirals of fine spiral-beaded wire. There are granules in the centre of each spiral and in the interstices. Thick spirals of partially spiral-beaded wire are inserted into the ends of the tubes. At the back of the knot is a central rib that probably had a hook at either end for attachment to the rest of the ornament.

In the centre of the Herakles knot is a small, wingless Eros, formed in the round from sheet gold. There is a row of dots across his chest and he holds a bow in his right hand. Traces on the back of the figure suggest the original presence of wings and, perhaps, the re-use of the

figure from a previous ornament, probably an earring.

Figures appear in the centre of a number of Herakles knots (e.g. no. 131), but they are usually orientated the other way. There seems to be a certain degree of curvature in this knot and it is possible that it came from a bracelet: the Tuch el-Karamus bracelet has a figure similarly orientated in the centre of its Herakles knot (see p. 225), as does a bracelet in Izmir.

BIBLIOGRAPHY: *BMCJ* 2001; Pfrommer, HK 150, pl. 5, 9. Tuch el-Karamus: Pfrommer, pl. 8, 1. Izmir: *Grèce d'Asie*, pl. 52 (left).

191

192

193

193

192 Gold ring with a seated woman holding a ritual basket

Said to be from Beirut
450–425 BC
Length of bezel 1.8 cm, height of hoop 1.6 cm; weight 4.0 g
British Museum GR 1917.5-1.45; bequeathed by Sir A.W. Franks, 1897

The flat, pointed oval bezel bears a representation of a woman wearing a *chiton* and a *himation*, a choker necklace with long pendants and a *sakkos*. Face upturned, she sits on a curved form, both hands raised; on her right palm she holds a ritual basket decorated with branches. In the field are seven crosses. The woman has been interpreted as the moon goddess, Selene, seated on a crescent moon and sur-

rounded by stars, but this is not certain and Boardman has suggested that she may, instead, be sitting on a swing.

The hoop, which tapers slightly towards the back, is soldered to the bezel.

BIBLIOGRAPHY: *BMCR* 45; Richter *EGGE*, no. 272; Boardman *GGFR*, pl. 665 (shape I, Waterton Group).

193 Gold ring with a sard engraved with a bird

Said to be from Beirut
400–350 BC
Length of bezel 2.0 cm, width of hoop 2.4 cm
British Museum, GR 1917.5-1.350; bequeathed by Sir A.W. Franks, 1897

The finely engraved red cornelian depicts a pigeon or a dove standing placidly to

the right on a short ground line. There is a simple hatched border. The gem is set in an oval box-like setting made from sheet gold. The sides bear a decorative frieze of plain wire and beaded wires flanking a plain wire running spiral. The back-plate of the setting bears a die-formed representation of a kneeling figure of Eros. The hoop is made from seven plain wires twisted together, and the joint between hoop and bezel is concealed by a short length of beaded wire.

Early fourth-century coins of Paphos on Cyprus have a similar bird. The relief on the back-plate is a most unusual feature.

BIBLIOGRAPHY: *BMCR* 350; *BMCG* 560; Richter *EGGE*, no. 454; Boardman *GGFR*, pl. 625; Higgins *GRJ*², p. 132 (top).

194 Gilded copper ring with Eros playing with a *iunx*

From Naukratis, cemetery area
About 300 BC
Length of bezel 1.8 cm, width of hoop 2.2 cm;
    weight 4.3 g
British Museum, GR 1888.6-1.1; presented by the
    Committee of the Egypt Exploration Fund,
    1888

The design on this ring shows Eros crouching to the left, holding a *iunx* between his hands. The *iunx* consists of a string with a wheel attached through the centre. When the string was pulled taut, the wheel span. It served as a magic love charm, intended to arouse desire. There is a simple, single ground line.

The copper ring was probably made by skilful hammering or, perhaps, by casting. The design was then chased into the bezel and mercury-gilded; finally, the flat surfaces were burnished. This is one of the earliest examples of mercury gilding.

BIBLIOGRAPHY: E.A. Gardner, *Naukratis*, vol. II (London 1888), p. 28, pl. 17. 7; *BMCR* 1258; Boardman *GGFR*, pl. 723 (shape VII; Nike Group); Ogden *JAW*, pl. 9 (left, upper left). For analysis of the bronze and the use of mercury gilding see P.T. Craddock, *JASc* 1977, pp. 109–10.

195 Gold ring engraved with a rat tied to a column

Said to be from Alexandria
300–250 BC
Length of bezel 2.4 cm; weight 13.0 g
British Museum GR 1854.5-19.147

The large circular bezel bears a chased and engraved depiction of a rat, with ears of corn in its mouth, tied to a column. The

194

195

196

column has a base and an Ionic capital. The ground line is double, with a beaded line above a plain line. The hoop, flat within, faceted without, is formed from the same piece of gold.

The significance of the scene – whether satirical, humorous or both – is now unknown. Egypt was a major exporter of grain, and indeed later became known as the 'Granary of Rome'. The design may be related to this export, or perhaps had a meaning only to its original owner.

A similar ground line is to be found on a ring with a circular bezel in Oxford.

BIBLIOGRAPHY: *BMCR* 89; Boardman *GGFR*, pl. 751. Oxford ring: Boardman *GGFR*, pl. 793.

196 Gold ring with a Herakles-knot bezel

Said to be from Alexandria
About 300 BC
Height of hoop 1.9 cm, length of bezel 1.3 cm;
    weight 4.1 g
British Museum GR 1917.5-1.913; bequeathed by
    Sir A.W. Franks, 1897

A double fluted, solid gold hoop rises to a Herakles-knot bezel. The junction with the bezel is disguised by collars, each consisting of a band of spiral-beaded wire and twisted wire 'ropes' and three angular sheet-gold tongues with spiral-beaded wire borders. The Herakles knot is constructed from sheet-gold tubes bordered with spiral-beaded wires; in the centre is a circular sheet with the die-formed head of a satyr.

BIBLIOGRAPHY: *BMCR* 913.

197

197 Gold openwork hairnet

Said to be from Egypt

200–150 BC

Diameter 9.0 cm, height *c.* 6.0 cm, diameter of
   disc 5.5 cm; weight 87.24 g

New York 1987.220; gift of Norbert Schimmel,
   1987

The centre of this remarkable hair ornament consists of a framed medallion.
From it radiate eight bands of single loop-
in-loop chain linked with gold spool beads
– a typical later Hellenistic form. The
chain bands are attached to a hollow fluted
sheet-gold hoop which helped to contain
the wearer's hair within the net. Finely
worked in repoussé, the medallion represents the head of a maenad wearing
spiral earrings, a wreath of vine leaves and
grapes, and a panther-skin over her right
shoulder. The medallion is held by wire
ties to the back-plate, which also forms
the backing for the two concentric bands
of spiral-beaded filigree work: a series of

palmettes in running filigree within a
heart-on-heart pattern.

The eight vertical chains are attached by
hinges to the periphery of the medallion's
back-plate and to the fluted D-section
hoop below. The hoop, in two hinged
sections, has sheet and filigree terminals
attached by simple wire pins with twisted
ends. The rather restrained decoration of
the terminals includes rosettes and a collar
of cut-out tongues. The hoop is closed by
means of a hinged fastener.

This magnificent piece once adorned
the coiffure of a well-to-do lady in Ptolemaic Egypt during the second century BC.
It may be the *kekryphalos*, a head ornament
described by Antipater of Sidon at this
period. The closest parallel for this ornament is part of a second-century BC group
of goldwork from Egypt now in the J.
Paul Getty Museum, Malibu. The Getty
example preserves a pendant tassel, which

may explain the function of a loop just
below the bust on the work in New York.
A hairnet of somewhat different construction, said to come from Taranto, has led
Heilmeyer to connect such objects with
head-cloths known as *tarantinidia*, but this
seems unlikely.

BIBLIOGRAPHY: *Search for Alexander, Supplement*
(Chicago 1981), no. S-15; *Search for Alexander,
Supplement* (Boston 1982), no. S-17; *Search for
Alexander, Supplement* (San Francisco 1982), no.
S-13; *Search for Alexander, Supplement* (New
Orleans 1982), no. S-4; *Search for Alexander,
Supplement* (Toronto 1983), no. S-53;
Deppert-Lippitz, pl. 30; B. Barr-Sharrar, *The
Hellenistic and Early Imperial Decorative Bust*
(Mainz 1987), p. 150; Pfrommer, p. 61, n. 451;
BMetrMus, Spring 1992, p. 50; Ogden,
forthcoming. On such hairnets see Hoffmann and
Davidson, no. 124, and E. Formigli and W.-D.
Heilmeyer, *Tarentiner Goldschmuck in Berlin* (Berlin
1990), pp. 66–80. For the Getty example see
Ogden, forthcoming.

Bibliography

The abbreviations for periodicals are those used by the German Archaeological Institute.

ABC
Antiquités du Bosphore Cimmérien, vols I and II (St Petersburg 1854)

Alexander
C. Alexander, *Jewelry, the Art of the Goldsmith in Classical Times. The Metropolitan Museum of Art* (New York 1928)

Amathonte III
R. Laffineur, *Amathonte III, Testimonia 3: L'Orfèvrerie* (Paris 1986)

Artamonov
M.I. Artamonov, *Treasures from Scythian Tombs in the Hermitage Museum, Leningrad* (London 1969)

ARV²
J.D. Beazley, *Attic Red-Figure Vase-Painters* (2nd edn, Oxford 1963)

Ashik
A. Ashik, *Vosporskoye Tsarstvo*, vol. II (Odessa 1848)

AT
N.L. Grach (ed.), *Antichnaja Torevtika* (Leningrad 1986)

Baltimore
Jewelry Ancient to Modern (Baltimore 1979)

Barr-Sharrar and Borza
B. Barr-Sharrar and E.N. Borza (eds), *Macedonia and Greece in Late Hellenistic Times* (*Studies in the History of Art*, vol. 10, Washington 1982)

Becatti
G. Becatti, *Oreficerie antiche dalle Minoiche alle Barbariche* (Rome 1955)

Benaki
B. Segall, *Museum Benaki, Athens. Katalog der Goldschmiede-Arbeiten* (Athens 1938)

BMCB
H.B. Walters, *Catalogue of the Bronzes, Greek, Roman, and Etruscan, in the Department of Greek and Roman Antiquities, British Museum* (London 1899)

BMCG
H.B. Walters, *Catalogue of the Engraved Gems in the British Museum* (London 1926)

BMCJ
F.H. Marshall, *Catalogue of the Jewellery, Greek, Etruscan and Roman, in the Departments of Antiquities, British Museum* (London 1911)

BMCR
F.H. Marshall, *Catalogue of the Finger Rings, Greek, Etruscan and Roman, in the Departments of Antiquities, British Museum* (London 1907)

BMCS I, II
F.N. Pryce, *Catalogue of Sculpture in the Department of Greek and Roman Antiquities of the British Museum, I, ii: Cypriote and Etruscan* (London 1931)

BMCS III
A.H. Smith, *Catalogue of Sculpture in the Department of Greek and Roman Antiquities of the British Museum*, vol. III (London 1904)

BMCV
C.H. Smith, *Catalogue of the Greek and Etruscan Vases in the British Museum, III: Vases of the Finest Period* (London 1896)

Boardman *GGFR*
J. Boardman, *Greek Gems and Finger Rings* (London 1970)

Bouzek
J. Bouzek, *Studies of Greek Pottery in the Black Sea Area* (Prague 1990), pp. 123–8 (jewellery)

Breglia
L. Breglia, *Le oreficerie del Museo Nazionale di Napoli* (Rome 1941)

Brooklyn
P.F. Davidson and A. Oliver, *Ancient Greek and Roman Jewelry in the Brooklyn Museum* (New York 1984)

Cesnola *Atlas* III
L.P. di Cesnola, *A Descriptive Atlas of the Cesnola Collection of Antiquities in the Metropolitan Museum of Art*, vol. III (New York 1903)

Coarelli
F. Coarelli, *L'oreficeria nell'arte classica* (Milan 1966)

Corinth XII
G.R. Davidson, *Corinth. Results of Excavations conducted by The American School of Classical Studies at Athens, XII: The Minor Objects* (Princeton 1952)

CR
Comptes Rendus de la Commission Impériale Archéologique (St Petersburg 1859–   )

Cyprus Colloquium
V.A. Tatton-Brown (ed.), *Cyprus and the East Mediterranean in the Iron Age* (London 1989)

Deppert-Lippitz
B. Deppert-Lippitz, *Griechischer Goldschmuck* (Mainz 1985)

EAA
Enciclopedia dell'arte antica (Rome 1958, continuing)

Excavations in Cyprus
A.S. Murray *et al.*, *Excavations in Cyprus* (London 1900)

Francica
A Francica (ed.), *Oggetti d'arte greca nel secolo III avanti l'era volgare* (n.d.: 1884/5?)

Furtwängler *AG*
A. Furtwängler, *Die Antiken Gemmen* (Leipzig and Berlin 1900)

Gold der Steppe
R. Rolle *et al.* (eds), *Gold der Steppe: Archäologie der Ukraine* (Schleswig 1991)

Gorbunova and Saverkina
X. Gorbunova and I. Saverkina, *Greek and Roman Antiquities in the Hermitage* (Leningrad 1975)

Grèce d'Asie
H. Stierlin, *Grèce d'Asie* (Fribourg 1986)

Greifenhagen I
A. Greifenhagen, *Schmuckarbeiten in Edelmetall, I: Fundgruppen* (Berlin 1970)

Greifenhagen II
A. Greifenhagen, *Schmuckarbeiten in Edelmetall*, vol. II (Berlin 1975)

Hadaczek
K. Hadaczek, *Der Ohrschmuck der Griechen und Etrusker* (Vienna 1903)

Haller Catalogue
H. Bankel (ed.), *Haller von Hallerstein in Griechenland* (Berlin 1986)

Higgins *GRJ*
R. Higgins, *Greek and Roman Jewellery* (London 1961)

Higgins *GRJ²*
R. Higgins, *Greek and Roman Jewellery* (2nd edn, London 1980)

Hoffmann and Davidson
H. Hoffmann and P.F. Davidson, *Greek Gold. Jewelry from the Age of Alexander* (Mainz 1965)

Jacobsthal, *Greek Pins*
P. Jacobsthal, *Greek Pins* (Oxford 1956)

LIMC
Lexicon Iconographicum Mythologicae Classicae (Munich and Zurich 1981, continuing)

L'oro dei Greci
D. Musti *et al.*, *L'oro dei Greci* (Novarra 1992)

MacPherson
D. MacPherson, *Antiquities of Kertch and Researches in the Cimmerian Bosphorus* (London 1857)

Makedonia
J. Vokotopoulou *et al.*, *E Makedonia apo ta Mukenaika chronia os ton Mega Alexandro* (Thessaloniki 1988)

Maxwell-Hyslop
K.R. Maxwell-Hyslop, *Western Asiatic Jewellery, c. 3000–612 B.C.* (London 1971)

Manzewitsch
A. Manzewitsch, *Ein Grabfund aus Chersonnes* (Leningrad 1932)

Miller
S.G. Miller, *Two Groups of Thessalian Gold* (Berkeley 1979)

Minns
E.H. Minns, *Scythians and Greeks* (Cambridge 1913)

MMA Greece and Rome
J.R. Mertens *et al.*, *The Metropolitan Museum of Art: Greece and Rome* (New York 1987)

Myres
J.L. Myres, *Handbook of the Cesnola Collection of Antiquities from Cyprus* (New York 1914)

Nelidow
L. Pollak, *Klassisch-Antike Goldschmiedearbeiten im Besitza Sr. Excellenz A.J. von Nelidow* (Leipzig 1903)

Newton
C. Newton, 'Greek art in the Kimmerian Bosporos', *Portfolio* 58 and 60 (1879?), reprinted in *Essays on Art and Archaeology* (London 1880), pp. 373–99

Ogden *JAW*
J. Ogden, *Jewellery of the Ancient World* (London 1982)

Ogden *AJ*
J. Ogden, *Interpreting the Past: Ancient Jewellery* (London 1992)

Ogden, forthcoming
J. Ogden, *Gold Jewellery in Ptolemaic, Roman and Byzantine Egypt* (forthcoming)

Oliver
A. Oliver, 'Greek, Roman, and Etruscan jewelry', *BMetrMus* 24 (1966), pp. 269–84

OlF XIII
H. Philipp, *Bronzeschmuck aus Olympia* (*Olympische Forschungen*, vol. XIII, Berlin 1981)

Olynthus X
D.M. Robinson, *Excavations at Olynthus. Part X: Metal and Minor Miscellaneous Finds, An Original Contribution to Greek Life* (Baltimore 1941)

Or des Scythes
B. Piotrovsky *et al.*, *Or des Scythes* (Paris 1975)

Perachora
H. Payne *et al.*, *Perachora: The Sanctuaries of Hera Akraia and Limenia* (Oxford 1940)

Pfrommer
M. Pfrommer, *Untersuchungen zur Chronologie früh- und hochhellenistischen Goldschmucks* (Tübingen 1990)

Pierides
A. Pierides, *Jewellery in the Cyprus Museum* (Nicosia 1971)

Reinach
S. Reinach, *Antiquités du Bosphore Cimmérien (1854) rééditées avec un commentaire nouveau et un index général des Comptes Rendus* (Paris 1892)

Richter
G.M.A. Richter, *Catalogue of Engraved Gems: Greek, Etruscan and Roman* (Rome 1956)

Richter *EGGE*
G.M.A. Richter, *Engraved Gems of the Greeks and the Etruscans* (London 1968)

Richter *Handbook*
G.M.A. Richter, *The Metropolitan Museum of Art. Handbook of the Greek Collection* (Cambridge, Mass. 1953)

Robertson
M. Robertson, *The Art of Vase-Painting in Classical Athens* (Cambridge 1992)

Rolle
R. Rolle, *The World of the Scythians* (London 1989)

Rostovtzeff *AD*
M.I. Rostovtzeff, *Antichnaja Decorativnaja Zhivopis'na Juge Rossii* (St Petersburg 1913)

Rostovtzeff *SuB*
M.I. Rostovtzeff, *Skythien und der Bosporus* (Berlin 1931)

Ruxer
M.S. Ruxer, *Historja Naszyjnika Greckiego*, vol. I (Poznań 1938)

Sardis
C. Densmore Curtis, *Sardis, XIII: Jewellery and Goldwork, Part I, 1910–1914* (Rome 1925)

SCE II
The Swedish Cyprus Expedition, vol. II (Stockholm 1935)

SCE III
The Swedish Cyprus Expedition, vol. III (Stockholm 1937)

SCE IV, 2
The Swedish Cyprus Expedition, vol. IV, part 2 (Stockholm 1948)

Schefold *UKV*
K. Schefold, *Untersuchungen zu den Kertscher Vasen* (Berlin 1934)

Scythian Art
B. Piotrovsky, L. Galanina and N. Grach, *Scythian Art* (Leningrad 1987)

Search for Alexander
N. Yalouris *et al.*, *The Search for Alexander: An Exhibition* (Boston 1980)

Search for Alexander, NY Suppl.
D. von Bothmer, *Search for Alexander: Supplement to the Catalogue* (New York 1982)

Segall
B. Segall, *Zur griechischen Goldschmiedekunst des 4. Jahrhunderts v. Chr. Eine griechische Schmuckgruppe im Schmuckmuseum Pforzheim* (Wiesbaden 1966)

Seven Thousand Years of Jewellery
H. Tait (ed.), *Seven Thousand Years of Jewellery* (London 1986)

Silantyeva
L.F. Silantyeva, 'Nekropol' Nimfeia', in V.F. Gaidukevich (ed.), *Nekropoli Bosporskich Gorodov* (*MAR* 69, Moscow 1959)

Sindos
J. Vokotopoulou *et al.*, *Sindos Katalogos tis ekthesis* (Thessaloniki 1985)

Siviero
R. Siviero, *Gli ori e le ambre del Museo Nazionale di Napoli* (Naples 1954)

Sokolov
G. Sokolov, *Antique Art on the Northern Black Sea Coast* (Leningrad 1974)

Stackelberg *Gräber*
O. Magnus, Baron von Stackelberg, *Die Gräber der Hellenen* (Berlin 1837)

Stathatos
P. Amandry, *Collection Hélène Stathatos. Les bijoux antiques* (Strasbourg 1953)

Stathatos III
P. Amandry, *Collection Hélène Stathatos, III: Objets antiques et byzantins* (Strasbourg 1963)

T&K
I.I. Tolstoy and N.P. Kondakov, *Russkia Drevnosti v Pamjatnikakh Iskusstva*, vols I and II (St Petersburg 1889). Translated into French as N. Kondakof, J. Tolstoi and S. Reinach, *Antiquités de la Russie Méridionale* (Paris 1891)

Taranto
E.M. De Juliis, *Gli ori di Taranto* (Milan 1984)

Thesauroi
K. Romiopoulou (ed.), *Thesauroi tis Archaias Makedonias* (Thessaloniki 1979)

Thracian Art
I. Venedikov and T. Gerasimov, *Thracian Art Treasures* (Sofia and London 1975)

Ukraine
Orfèvrerie ancienne de la collection du Musée des trésors historiques d'Ukraine (Moscow 1975)

Valavanis
P. Valavanis, *Panathenaikoi Amphoreis apo ten Erteria* (Athens 1991)

Vergina
M. Andronicos, *Vergina: The Royal Tombs and the Ancient City* (Athens 1984)

Vickers
M. Vickers, *Scythian Treasures in Oxford* (Oxford 1979)

Williams
D. Williams, 'Three groups of fourth-century South Italian Jewellery in the British Museum', *RM* 95 (1988)

Wuilleumier *Tarente*
P. Wuilleumier, *Tarente des origines à la conquête romaine* (Paris 1939)

Zürich
Aus den Schatzkammern Eurasiens: Meisterwerke antiker Kunst. Kunsthaus Zürich (Zurich 1993)